ON

"Knowledge is usually passed down through the ages in your reality, through books and historic writings, yet each individual contains within himself or herself a vast repository: direct knowledge of the past, in your terms, through unconscious comprehension.

"The unknown reality: Much of that reality is unknown simply because your beliefs close you off from your own knowledge. The reaches of your own consciousness are not limited. Because you accept the idea of a straight-line movement of time, you cannot see before or after what you think of as your birth or death, yet your greater consciousness is quite aware of such experience. *Ideally* it is possible not only to remember "past" lives, but to plan future ones now."

—From Session 708

A SETH BOOK

The "Unknown" Reality

Volume 2, Part I

□

Jane Roberts

Notes and Introduction by
Robert F. Butts

BANTAM BOOKS
TORONTO · NEW YORK · LONDON · SYDNEY · AUCKLAND

THE "UNKNOWN" REALITY, VOLUME 2, PART I

*A Bantam Book / published by arrangement with
Prentice Hall Press*

PRINTING HISTORY

The "Unknown" Reality, Volume 2 *was published in one volume by
Prentice Hall in 1986*

Bantam edition / April 1989

ISBN 0-553-27850-9

Published simultaneously in the United States and Canada

Bantam Books are published by Bantam Books, a division of Bantam
Doubleday Dell Publishing Group, Inc. Its trademark, consisting of the
words "Bantam Books" and the portrayal of a rooster, is Registered in
U.S. Patent and Trademark Office and in other countries. Marca
Registrada. Bantam Books, 666 Fifth Avenue, New York, New York
10103.

PRINTED IN THE UNITED STATES OF AMERICA

O   0 9 8 7 6 5 4 3 2 1

To Rob

Reader: This is Part I of a two volume edition. Please see THE "UNKNOWN" REALITY—VOLUME 2, Part II, for the second section.

Contents

"Nature, without nature's source,
would not last a moment."

Seth
September 19, 1977

With Winged

With winged brains
We swoop and swirl
Inside the blue bell
Of the outer world.

Birds of curved dimensions
Have their neighborhood
Limited by ceiling's
Weight of bone and blood.

But time and space are one to us.
The infinite skull
Opens skies all curled within,
Miniature world on world.

(*A note by R.F.B.: Jane was 32 years old when she wrote this poem in April 1961. It clearly foreshadows certain ideas in the Seth material, which she was to begin delivering 19 months later.* With Winged *also makes interesting reading along with the verse from her much earlier poem,* Summer Is Winter; *see page 1 of Volume 1 of* "Unknown" Reality.)

Introductory Notes
by Robert F. Butts

The two volumes making up *The "Unknown" Reality: A Seth Book,* were dictated by my wife, Jane Roberts, in cooperation with Seth, the nonphysical "energy personality essence" for whom she speaks when she's in trance. I wrote in the Introductory Notes for Volume 1 that Jane began delivering *"Unknown" Reality* (as we soon came to call it) in the 679th session for February 4, 1974, and finished it with the 744th session for April 23, 1975. She produced the two books in an accumulated trance time of about 90 hours—an accomplishment that I think quite remarkable.

Let me quickly recap a few more facts about the production of this work. Seth himself always referred to *"Unknown" Reality* as one unit until we reached the last session. He divided the manuscript into six sections of varying lengths. There are no chapters *per se*. As Seth explained in the 743rd session: "This book had no chapters [in order] to further disrupt your accepted notions of what a book should be. There are different kinds of organization present, however, and in any given section of the book, several levels of consciousness are appealed to at once."

Seth also presented the entire work in such a way that the events of our daily lives were intimately connected with his material, serving as personal examples of how his theories actually work in everyday experience. He hadn't been delivering *"Unknown" Reality* for long, then, before I realized that I'd have to devise a system of presentation that would handle his material, my own notes (which I could see were going to be considerably longer than they are in Seth's other books, *Seth Speaks* and *The Nature of Personal Reality*), excerpts from Jane's ESP classes, appendixes, and anything else that might be included.

As Seth continued dictation I was fired by *his* purpose to make the unknown elements of human life at least partially visible—an audacious goal, I thought—and I tried to do my own part in recording all such disclosures as they appeared in our lives and were reflected in the experiences of our friends and students.

The accumulated material further added to the length of the work, which was considerable. Finally we chose to divide *"Unknown" Reality* into two volumes. This meant that our readers could have access to part of the manuscript while I was preparing the rest. Seth agreed with our decision.

It isn't necessary to repeat many more of the Introductory Notes for Volume 1 here, although I'll ask the reader to review them in connection with the material presented below. But the most important thing about those notes, I think, is Jane's own account of her subjective relationship with Seth.

Seth's Preface is in Volume 1, of course, and it too should be studied again; to me, such acts of referral between the two volumes help the reader mentally unite them.

After I touch upon the contents of Volume 1, I'll have the freedom to move into some other topics that occurred to Jane and me as I put Volume 2 together—subjects regarding the Seth phenomenon itself, for example. I also want to present a few passages from both regular and private (or "deleted") sessions that were held before, during, or after Seth-Jane's actual production of *"Unknown" Reality* in its entirety. At least some of Jane's other books will be mentioned occasionally.

Seth often advances his ideas by weaving together several themes into a complex pattern in any given session, or throughout a body of material. This process can also result in a similar approach on my part when I discuss his dictation, so I'll initiate a summary of Volume 1 by using four sources presented by Seth himself: a key passage from his Preface; the headings he gave for the three sections that comprise Volume 1, along with a few elaborations of my own; a brief description of the appendixes which I assembled over a period of time; and a passage from the 762nd session, in which, eight months after he'd finished *"Unknown" Reality,* Seth speaks further about his purposes in producing it.

First, though, I'll explain that in sessions Seth refers to Jane by her male entity name, Ruburt—and that he does so (as I quote him in Appendix 18) simply because "the given entity identifies itself more with the so-called male characteristics than with the female." He also addresses me by my entity name, which is Joseph.

Now these quotations are from Seth's Preface (for Volume 1):

"Jane Roberts's experience to some extent hints at the multidimensional nature of the human psyche and gives clues as to the abilities that lie within each individual. These are part of your racial heritage. They give notice of psychic bridges connecting the known and 'unknown' realities in which you dwell.

"In my other books I used many accepted ideas as a springboard to lead readers into other levels of understanding. Here, I wish to make it clear that *["Unknown" Reality]* will initiate a journey in which it may <u>seem</u> that the familiar is left far behind. Yet when I am finished, I hope you will discover that the known reality is even more precious, more 'real,' because you will find it illuminated both within and without by the rich fabric of an 'unknown' reality now seen emerging from the most intimate portions of daily life. . . . Your concepts of personhood are now limiting you personally and *en masse,* and yet your religions, metaphysics, histories, and even your sciences are hinged upon your ideas of who and what you are. Your psychologies do not explain your own reality to you. They cannot contain your experience. Your religions do not explain your greater reality, and your sciences leave you just as ignorant about the nature of the universe in which you dwell.

"These institutions and disciplines are composed of individuals, each restrained by limiting ideas about their own private reality; and so it is with private reality that we will begin and always return. Period. The ideas in this book are meant to expand the <u>private reality</u> of each reader. They may appear esoteric or complicated, yet they are not beyond the reach of any person who is determined to understand the nature of the unknown elements of the self, and its greater world."

Where do the events of our lives begin or end? Where do we fit into them, individually and as members of the species? These questions, with Seth's explanations, are the heart of Volume 1. Because *"Unknown" Reality* is organized along intuitive rather than consecutive lines, though, it's difficult to provide a brief résumé. Jane probably described Volume 1 as simply as possible, however, when she said: "Volume 1 provides the general background and information upon which the exercises and methods in Volume 2 depend.'' I quoted that statement in Volume 1's Epilogue, and now, after finishing my own work on the entire manuscript, I realize how truly apropos it is.

The first volume, like this one, defies easy description, then, since it leaps over many definitions we usually take for granted; and with its lack of chapter divisions it even confounds our ideas of what a book is. Yet it certainly contains a most intriguing, multi-dimensional view of the nature of probabilities, a view in which our ideas of a ''simple, single event'' must vanish; at least we can never again look at any event as being concrete, finished, or absolute. Seth stresses the importance of probabilities as they exist in relationship to a thought, an ordinary physical event, or the mass event of *Homo sapiens* as a species, and emphasizes the existence of probable realities as the understructure of free will.

His headings for the three sections of Volume 1 do give some indications of its contents.

Section 1: ''You and the 'Unknown' Reality''—Nine sessions describing how probabilities merge with the events of our private lives.

Section 2: ''Parallel Man, Alternate Man, and Probable Man: the Reflection of These in the Present, Private Psyche. Your Multidimensional Reality in the Now of Your Being''—Eight sessions dealing with the vast unknown origin of our species in a psychological past that by contrast makes evolutionary time look like yesterday.

Section 3: ''The Private Probable Man, the Private Probable Woman, the Species in Probabilities, and Blueprints for Realities'' —Nine sessions devoted to the importance of dreams in the creation of ''concrete'' events from probable ones. This section also includes discussions on the True Dream-Art Scientist, the True Mental Physicist, and the Complete Physician, as well as material on subatomic particles and the spin of electrons in relationship to perceived reality.

Volume 1 of *''Unknown'' Reality* concludes with 11 appendixes compiled from Seth sessions related to the book's subject matter. These are supplemented by notes regarding the relationship involving Seth, Jane, and myself, and by other pertinent material that throws light upon the larger framework in which these sessions take place. I also provided a certain number of cross references, directing the reader to connected passages in Seth's and/or Jane's other books.

To me, some of the most important material in Volume 1 is Jane's information on her sensing of other neurological pulses as they're connected with probable events, and how she picked up those pulses by bypassing her direct, or ordinary neurological impact. See her work in appendixes 4 and 5. Seth also discussed such neurological changeovers in Session 685, among others. I think this kind of material offers a rich source for future scientific investigation.

This present book, Volume 2, goes on from there as Seth creates an intriguing thematic framework, and then invites us to "play along," to join in and to discover the unknown reality for ourselves through a series of exercises geared to illuminate the inner structures upon which our exterior ones depend.

In the 762nd session for December 15, 1975, mentioned earlier, Seth explained how *"Unknown"* Reality fit into the larger body of his material:

"In *Seth Speaks* I tried to describe certain extensions of your own reality in terms that my readers could understand. In *The Nature of Personal Reality,* I tried to extend the boundaries of individual existence as it is usually experienced . . . to give the reader hints that would increase practical, spiritual and physical enjoyment and fulfillment in daily life. Those books were dictated by me in a more or less straight narrative style. In *'Unknown' Reality* I went further, showing how the experiences of the psyche splash outward into the daylight, so to speak. I hope that [in those two books] through my dictation and through Ruburt's and Joseph's experiences, the reader can see the greater dimensions that touch ordinary living, and sense the psyche's greater magic. *'Unknown' Reality* required much more work on Joseph's part, and that additional effort in itself was a demonstration that the psyche's events are very difficult to pin down in time. Seemingly its action goes out in all directions. . . . As Joseph did his notes, it became apparent that some events . . . seemed to have no beginning or end."

Later in these notes I plan to return to Seth's point about the psyche's events and time. In any case, I finished preparing Volume 1 for publication in January 1977, and it appeared in print later that year. We were delighted that the public could take advantage of part of the material while I made the second volume ready. The days and weeks I spent working on my notes for Volume 2 began to pile up into months, however, and I became more and more concerned.

It seemed that I should have finished my part of both books long ago, even though simultaneously I was working on several other projects with Jane, as well as painting a few hours a day. Finally, the disparity between the time Seth-Jane had spent producing Volume 1 alone (around 45 hours), and my own commitment in ordinary time, became so great in my mind as to be almost overwhelming.

I also felt that the chronology of presentation for both Seth's and Jane's books was being distorted: Because I was so slow in finishing my work on Volume 2 of *"Unknown" Reality,* Jane published her *Psychic Politics* first, for example, when the reverse order should have prevailed. After all, I told myself innumerable times, these were Seth's and Jane's books, not mine. I wasn't hesitant about recognizing my own role in helping Jane's psychic abilities show themselves in a consistent way (as, say, in intuitively devising the session format for the presentation of the Seth material). But the recognition didn't make me feel any better.

Jane insisted that the notes were important, as a constant reminder to the reader that psychic or inner events happen in the context of daily life. Sometimes I thought she was simply being kind in so reassuring me. Seth too agreed that the notes, appendixes, and other additions were pertinent. He also stressed that our plan to divide the work was intuitively correct, and based on legitimate inner knowledge. This cheered me considerably, of course. (However, the decision to publish in two volumes, made when *"Unknown" Reality* was almost finished, caused me to rewrite most of my original notes for it with that new presentation in mind.)

The whole adventure has certainly been a learning experience, one demanding a kind of forbearance that neither Jane nor I could have really anticipated. If the waiting until I finished with Volume 2 has been difficult for me, it's been doubly so for Jane, since by nature she's much more spontaneous and quick than I am. Yet the wait itself was creative. As I show below, putting this Volume 2 together has represented a process of discovery for me—just as I hope studying it will for the reader.

It seemed that each time I searched through all of those unpublished sessions (covering well over a decade) for just the right supplementary material, I found something new. More often than not, this made me redo my own notes in unanticipated ways—always a creative challenge that was most enjoyable, and yet, paradoxically, one that at times was very frustrating. Such episodes often caused me to take much longer to produce finished work. I learned a patience that I hadn't suspected was possible for me. For this patience, employed in conjuring up thoughts and images through words, was objectively and subjectively quite different in quality from that which I was so used to using in producing painted images. I could feel my mind and abilities, using either words *or* pictures, stretch as a result.

Seth himself helped me out more than once—and others can find his material here useful in many situations. From the 751st session for June 30, 1975, which was held a couple of months after he'd finished his part of the long project:

"Now: You need not worry about *'Unknown' Reality*. You have already done the books in another probable reality, and completed them very well.

"The model for them and your notes already exists within your mind. Scan any paragraph of your notes, then turn your mind gently a half notch aside. As you do so you will be able to sense your own completed version, and any word that does not fit will be instantly sensed, while another will at once slip to mind.

"Your final paragraphs are already there in the probability, now, that you have chosen. That probability belongs with the present you have now—yet you chose it from an infinite number of other realities. The books arose from probabilities, both yours and mine as well as Ruburt's.

"In some we did not meet. Even those, however, contain the probability that we will, since here we do."

I used that information of Seth's many times while working with *"Unknown" Reality*. Even so, I learned that on such a long-term project it's easy to lose that acute sense of what one really wants to do and show—but I also learned how to constantly renew my focus. This presented me with what seemed like an endless series of challenges, yet I discovered again and again that I enjoyed them: Each time I sat down to work, whether on the most routine short note or the most complicated appendix, I searched for that particular, personal sense of intense concentration on the matter at hand. And each time I achieved it

I experienced once more that complete inner and outer, mental and physical involvement in which time was often significantly negated. These were actual, felt episodes during which I rose above those frustrations mentioned earlier. (I've often wondered how much one's ordinary bodily aging processes are either slowed or superseded during such periods of great focus.)

Now, Jane and I also see much more clearly how our respective characteristics contribute to our joint work. Without Jane's psychic ability and spontaneity there would be no Seth sessions or books, as I tell her often. Then she tells me that without my persistence and diligence, the Seth material might not have been recorded or correlated, or might exist in different form entirely. I wonder.

Questions, questions, questions—why do Jane and I have so many of them? First, the very nature of her abilities leads to hosts of them, in ways that would have been entirely unexpected earlier in our lives. A second group stems from what Seth *says*, and what we've come to believe about what he tells us. A third set arises from the reactions of others to the first two, through the letters and calls we receive and the questions of people knocking on our doors. In spite of all this, we've found that any one group of questions amplifies or adds to those related to the other two categories—i.e., like energy regenerating itself, the questions automatically proliferate. Many times I've had the idea that a good analogy here is furnished by Seth's concept of the "moment point." As he told us in the 681st session for Volume 1 of *"Unknown" Reality:*

"In your terms—the phrase is necessary—the moment point, the present, is the point of interaction between all existences and reality. All probabilities flow through it, though one of your moment points may be experienced <u>as centuries, or as a breath</u>, in other probable realities of which you are a part." Thus, just as a moment point can be explored indefinitely, so each newly arising question results in an ever-widening pool of inquiry.

In my notes introducing Volume 1, I wrote about placing the basic "artistic ideas" embodied in the Seth material at our conscious, aesthetic, and practical service in daily life. That's really what Seth's work is all about, in my opinion. Such an endeavor essentially involves the pursuit of an ideal, and represents our attempts to give physical and mental shape to the great inner, creative commotion of the universe that each person intuitively feels. Of course Jane and I want Seth's ideas and our own to touch responsive reflexes within others; then each individual can use the material in his or her own expression of that useful ideal, letting it serve to stimulate inner perceptions.

In Jane's case, at least, the role of the "medium" (or of the investigator or initiator) is extremely challenging. It's also arduous: In our Western societies it's much more comforting to grapple with chemistry, say, or farming or salesmanship, or with any of numerous other "practical" jobs or disciplines, than it is to confront the inner senses.

What Jane has to offer results from the study of consciousness itself, as it's expressed through her own experience and abilities. By choice, she has no buffers between herself and the exterior world—no assured status, for example. She doesn't enjoy the protection a scientist does, who probes into a particular subject in depth, then makes a learned report on it from an "objective" position that's safely outside the field of study. At the same time, I know that Jane feels a responsibility to "publish her results," and make them available to others. She's tough in ways that science, for instance, doesn't understand at all.

Still, her work has met with a great deal of understanding from many people, if hardly from everyone who's heard of it. It's interesting to ask how even extensive accepted credentials would help her respond to the extremes of feeling with which she and Seth are sometimes greeted; the outright rejection or the sheer adulation—or the threats she receives on occasion from those who say they'll commit suicide if Seth doesn't come through with a session for them immediately.

In important ways, Jane's work *is* outside of society's accepted frameworks—scientific, "occult," philosophical, or whatever. Not that we dwell upon that comparative isolation much, but we are aware of it. And I know that Jane sometimes misses the kind of camaraderie enjoyed by professionals who fit more comfortably into accepted structures. Actually, though, we consider many of our correspondents as friends, even though we never meet most of them, and despite the fact that Jane can only reply to their cheering communications with Seth's dictated letter (as well as our own), or with notes scribbled quickly on postcards. We've become quite aware of *that* kind of support, for which we're very grateful. Many such people are somewhat like us—refusing to accept any kind of dogma.

But some others, according to Seth, are uneasy with Jane's mental independence. In a personal session given for us in 1977, he said: "Some [people] do not want my authority questioned. (*Humorously:*) They think that if they had their own Supersoul, they would have far better sense than Ruburt; and they would use me as if I were a magic genie. They are afraid that Ruburt might question me out of existence. . . ." He went on to say that such individuals didn't understand that Jane's questioning nature fired the sessions' onset to begin with, and is somewhat responsible for the production of his work and books, as well as her own.

And in one form or another, Jane carries all of those books with her from reality to reality. During an ESP class, Seth called them her "beloved paraphernalia," or symbols, then continued:

"They are more than symbols, however. They are means of recognition that stand for something else, a reality; signs that stand for words, spoken before the birth of words; words imprinted in molecules; words that were inprinted in other ways before the birth of molecules; and yet (*to class members*) words that echo within your own individual psyches. In one way or another these words, like pebbles, are left along the beach of your [collective] reality.

"Some will pick them up and say, 'What lovely stones,' and gaze upon them and see what they mean, and others will kick them aside. But in one way or another . . . those words continue to be spoken, whether through these lips, or through the sound of leaves, or through the invisible music of your own cells. So do they exist. And that is the meaning behind the books and the symbols."

Certainly Seth is saying that Jane's books (and his) represent her acknowledgment of and search for an ideal. So do my own efforts in life. (See Seth's material on "ideals set in the heart of man" in sessions 696-97 for Volume 1 of *"Unknown" Reality*.) Apropos of such concepts, I'll close these introductory notes by quoting from a personal session Seth gave for Jane and me, in which he reiterates the importance of the individual and the pursuit of the ideal. Seth initiated the following passages by talking to me about "the safe universe" that each person can create, and live within. Although his words were directed to me, they have a broad general application:

"In your mind you creatively envision the ideal—the sanity of some future culture that, you hope, our work and [that of] others will bring about. If not tomorrow, then sometime.

"When you thoroughly understand what is meant by the entire safe-universe concept, then the physical, cultural climate is seen as a medium through which the ideal can be expressed. The ideal is meaningless if it is not physically manifest to one degree or another. The ideal <u>seeks</u> expression. In so doing, it often <u>seems</u> to change or alter in ways that are not understood. Yet those <u>distortions</u> may be the very openings that allow others to perceive.

"In a way, with [this] book and with your art, your purpose is the expression of the ideal, and that <u>expression</u> must be physically materialized, obviously. Your joy, your challenge, should be in the manifestation of the ideal as you see it, whether or not you can in your terms count the consequences or the impediments— whether or not the expression comes to fulfillment in your terms—and even if it seems to fall on the ground on which it will not grow.

"As an artist alone your purpose is expression, which involves disclosures, the difference between the ideal and the actual. Be reckless in the expression of the ideal, and it will never betray you. Treat it with kid gloves and you are in the middle of a battle."

To be truly reckless in the sense of Seth's definition—how daring! I'd say that attaining such a state represents quite an achievement. For most of us, including myself, it means shedding many encrusted and limiting personal beliefs. I do get glimpses of that condition of inner and outer freedom; just enough to understand some of the many practical benefits that can flow from it. I can't think of a better goal.

I hope these Introductory Notes have prepared the reader to take up *"Unknown" Reality* in the middle, more or less, with the 705th session. But as I wrote in introducing Volume 1, whatever comments I make along the way will explain Jane's trance performances from my view, as best I can offer them— her behavior while she's "under," the varied, powerful or muted use of her voice as she speaks for Seth, her stamina and humor in sessions, the speed or slowness of her delivery. But above all I try to help the reader appreciate the uncanny feeling of energy and/or intelligence—of *personality*—in the sessions, as exemplified by and through Seth; conscious energy, then, taking a guise that's at least somewhat comprehensible to us, in our terms of reality, so that we can understand what's happening.

As in Volume 1, notes are presented at session break times as always, but I've indicated the points of origin of what would ordinarily be footnotes by using consecutive (superscription) numbers within the text of each session. Then, I've grouped the actual notes at the end of the individual sessions for quick consultation. All such reference numbers are printed in the same small type throughout both volumes. Footnotes will be found "in place" only when they're used to call attention to a specific appendix in the same book. For the most part, then, these approaches keep the body of each session free of interruptions between break designations.

The appendix idea worked out well in *The Seth Material* and in *Seth Speaks*, and in both volumes of *"Unknown" Reality* each excerpt or session in an appendix, with whatever notes *it* might carry, is usually fairly complete in itself. These pieces can be read at any time, but I'd rather the reader went over each one when it's first mentioned in a footnote; just as he or she ought to check out all other reference material in order throughout both volumes. I think it especially informative to compare Jane's *Psychic Politics* with Volume 2 of *"Unknown" Reality,* for she produced large sections of both works concurrently; there are many interesting exchanges of viewpoint between the two.

Section 4

□

**EXPLORATIONS.
A STUDY OF THE PSYCHE
AS IT IS RELATED TO PRIVATE LIFE
AND THE EXPERIENCE OF THE SPECIES.
PROBABLE REALITIES AS A COURSE
OF PERSONAL EXPERIENCE.
PERSONAL EXPERIENCE AS IT IS RELATED TO
"PAST" AND "FUTURE" CIVILIZATIONS OF MAN**

Session 705

□

June 24, 1974
9:09 P.M. Monday

(The 704th session was held a week ago. In it Seth gave the heading for Section 4, just before finishing his evening's work with a few minutes of personal information for Jane and me. He's remarked more than once that he'll close a session by dictating the heading for the next chapter, or whatever, "so that Ruburt [Jane] knows what I am doing. It gives him confidence." But I'd say his procedure also helps satisfy Jane's spontaneous impatience about learning what's coming next in the material.

(In this case, though, too much time passed between sessions. The regularly scheduled session for last Wednesday night wasn't held while we made ready for several approaching events, and as the days went by Jane [and I] simply forgot about what was coming up in "Unknown" Reality. I read her the heading for Section 4 now, while we waited for Seth to come through. "I haven't the vaguest idea, even, of what all that means," she said. Usually a certain kind of serene existence makes the best kind of day-by-day framework for these sessions and our other creative work, even while those days may contain within them points of unusual interest or excitement [such as Jane's weekly ESP class]. But given that right kind of equanimity, time—our ordinary time—slides by; then, looking back periodically, we discover that we've accomplished at least something of what we wanted to do.

(One of the events we've been preparing for is the visit tomorrow of Tam Mossman, Jane's editor at Prentice-Hall, Inc. He plans to attend ESP class tomorrow night, then stay over

15

Wednesday to read and discuss the two works Jane has in progress, Adventures in Consciousness: An Introduction to Aspect Psychology, *and* "Unknown" Reality. *Tam will also look at my first rough sketches for Jane's book of poetry,* Dialogues of the Soul and Mortal Self in Time.[1] *Then on Wednesday night he'll witness the scheduled 706th session. If Seth comes through with material for* "Unknown" Reality, *Tam will be the first "outsider" to sit in on a session for this work. Almost always Jane dictates book material without witnesses other than myself, and uses the framework of ESP class for emotional interactions involving herself, Seth, and others. That rather formal division in her trance activities suits us well; we enjoy doing most of our work by ourselves, no matter what kind it may be.*

(The atmosphere in our second-story living room was very pleasant and prosaic this evening. We had lights on in the approaching dusk. From the busy intersection just west of our apartment house the sounds of traffic rose up through the open windows. Jane smoked a cigarette and sipped a beer as she waited for the session to start; she was in the process of turning her consciousness inward, actually, on her way to meet Seth in a nonphysical journey that had nothing to do with our ordinary concepts of space or distance.

(When that meeting took place, Jane was in trance; off came her glasses; once again she'd met Seth on the psychological bridge the two of them had established when these sessions began, over a decade ago. Seth has explained such a connective as "a psychological extension, a projection of characteristic on both of our parts, and this I use for our communications . . . it is like a road that must be kept clear of debris."[2]

(As is usually the case in our private sessions, Jane's Seth voice was only a little deeper than her own regular one. Her Seth accent, however, was quite unique. I often think it bears traces of a European heritage—but one that's impossible to pinpoint by country. Her eyes in trance were much darker, and seemingly without highlights.)

Good evening.

("Good evening, Seth.")

Dictation: Let us begin this section with a brief discussion concerning "evolution."

For now think of it as you usually do, in a time context. It has been fashionable in the past to believe that each species was oriented selfishly toward its own survival. Period. Each was seen in competition with all other species. In that framework cooperation was simply a by-product of a primary drive toward survival. One species might use another, for instance. Species were thought to change, and "mutants" form, because of a previous alteration in the environment, to which any given species had to adjust or disappear. The motivating power was always projected <u>outside</u>* (underlined).

All of this presented a quite erroneous picture. Physically speaking, earth itself has its own kind of gestalt consciousness. If you <u>must</u>, then think of that earth consciousness as grading (*spelled*) upward in great <u>slopes</u> of awareness from relatively "inert" particles of dust and stone through the mineral, vegetable, and animal kingdoms. Even then, remember that those kingdoms are not so separate after all. Each one is highly related to each of the others. Nothing happens in one such kingdom that does not affect the others. A great, gracious cooperation exists between those seemingly separate systems, however. If you will remember that even atoms and molecules have consciousness, then it will be easier for you to understand that there is indeed a certain kind of awareness that unites these kingdoms.

In your terms, consciousness of self did not develop because of any exterior circumstances in which your species <u>won out</u>, so to speak, In fact, that consciousness of self in any person is dependent upon the constant, miraculous cooperations that exist between the mineral, vegetable, and animal worlds.[3] The inner intent always forms any exterior alteration. This applies on any scale you use. Consciousness forms the environment. <u>The environment itself is conscious</u> (*forcefully*). Atoms and molecules themselves operate in their own fields of probabilities. In their own ways, they "yearn" toward all probable developments. When they form living creatures they become a physical basis for species alteration. The body's adaptability is not simply an <u>adjusting</u> mechanism or quality. The cells have inner capabilities that you have not discovered. They contain within themselves memory of all the "previous" forms they have been a part of.

I would like to make an aside here: In certain terms, you cannot destroy life by a nuclear disaster. You would of course destroy life as you know it, and in your terms bring to an end, if

---

the conditions were right (or wrong), life forms with which you are familiar. In greater terms, however, mutant life would emerge—mutant only by your standards—but life quite natural to itself.

(9:38.) To return to our main subject of the moment: The fact is that the so-called process of evolution is highly dependent on the cooperative tendencies inherent in all properties of life and in all species. There is no transmigration of souls, in which the entire personality of a person "comes back" as an animal. Yet in the physical framework there is a constant intermixing, so that the cells of a man or a woman may become the cells of a plant or an animal,[4] and of course vice versa. The cells that have been a part of a human brain know this in their way. Those cells that now compose your own bodies have combined and discombined many times to form other portions of the natural environment.

This inner and yet physical transmigration of consciousness has always been extremely important, and represents a natural method of communication, uniting all species and all physical life. Inside all physical organisms, therefore, there is a thrust for development and change, even as there is also a pattern of stability within which such alterations can take place.

Give us a moment . . . Historically, of course, you follow a one-line pattern of thought, so you see a picture in which fish left the oceans and became reptiles; from these mammals eventually appeared, and apes and men. That is, I admit, a simple statement, but it is the way most people think evolution occurred. The terms of "progression" are tricky. You never imagine the situation being reversed, for example. Few of you ever imagine a conscious reptilian man. It seems to you that the direction you took is the only direction that could have been taken.

Give us a moment . . . You identify a highly evolved self-consciousness with your own species development, and with your own kind of perceptive mechanisms. You apply these as rules or conditions whenever you examine any other kind of life. In your system of probabilities there are no reptilian men or women, yet in other probabilities they do indeed exist. I mention this only to show you that the evolutionary system you recognize is but one such system. *(Intently:)* The physical basis rests latently within your own cellular structure, however. You think that evolution is finished. Its impetus, however, comes from within the nature of consciousness itself. It always had. In some quarters it is fashionable these days to say that man's consciousness is <u>now</u> an element in a <u>new kind</u> of evolution—but that "new consciousness" has always been inherent. You are only now beginning to recognize its existence. Every consciousness is aware of itself as itself.[5] Each consciousness, then, is self-aware. It may not be self-aware in the same way that you are. It may not reflect upon its own condition. On the other hand, it may have no need to.

(10:02.) Give us a moment . . . So-called future developments of your species are now dependent upon your ideas and beliefs. This applies genetically in personal terms. For instance, if you believe that you can live to a <u>healthy and happy</u> old age, well into your nineties, then even in Western civilization you will do so. Your emotional intent and your belief will direct the functioning of your cells and (*emphatically*) <u>bring out in them those properties</u> and inherent abilities that will ensure such a condition. There are groups of people in isolated places who hold such beliefs, and in all such cases the body responds. The same applies to the race—or the species, to be more exact. There is an inexhaustible creativity within the cells themselves, that you are not using as a species because your beliefs lag so far behind your innate biological spirituality and wisdom. Your ideas <u>are</u> beginning to change. But unless you alter your framework you will continue to emphasize medical and technological manipulation. Period. In isolated cases this will show you some of the results <u>possible</u> on a physical basis alone. However, such techniques will not work in mass terms, or allow you, say, to prolong effective, productive life unless you change your beliefs in other areas also, and learn the inner dynamics of the psyche.

(The telephone started to ring. I jumped. Once again, I'd forgotten to turn off the bell before the session began. As Seth, Jane stared up at me.)

Take your break.

(10:14. The call was from out of town. A young man had finished reading The Seth Material *this evening. He had many questions—and was too impatient to finish the letter to Jane that he'd just started. His enthusiastic response was one we'd experienced many times before. I talked to him for a few minutes while Jane rested after coming out of trance, and suggested that he call her later in the week. Resume at 10:36.)*

Now: It is true, then, that the cells do operate on the one hand apart from time, and on the other with a firm basis <u>in</u> time, so that the body's integrity as a time-space organism results.

It is true that on a conscious level you do not as yet operate outside of time, but are bound by it. When you learn to free yourselves from those dimensions to some extent, you are not simply duplicating or "returning" to some vaster condition, but <u>adding a new element to that condition</u>. The kind of self-awareness you have *is* unique, but <u>all kinds</u> are unique. Each triumph you make as an individual is reflected in your species and in its cellular knowledge.

Give us a moment . . . In a way you are all your own mutants, creatively altering cellular formations. Period. When your fate seems dependent on heredity, for example, then the transmission of ideas and beliefs operates; these give signals to the chromosomes. They cause miniature self-images, so to speak, that are mirrored in the cells. In many cases these images can be altered, but not with the technology that you have.

(Long pause at 10:48.) Give us a moment . . . *(Over a one-minute pause. Then quietly:)* Basically, cellular comprehension stradles time. There is, then, a way of introducing "new" genetic information to a so-called damaged cell in the present.[6] This involves the manipulation of consciousness, basically, and not that of gadgets, as well as a time-reversal principle. First the undesirable information must be erased. It must be erased in the "past" in your terms. Some, but very few, psychic healers do this automatically without realizing what they are doing. The body on its own performs this service often, when it automatically rights certain conditions, <u>even though</u> they were genetically imprinted. The imprints become regressive. In your terms, they fade into a probable series of events that do not physically affect you.

End of dictation.

(Pause at 10:57. After delivering material on several other subjects, Seth said good night at 11:20 P.M.)

NOTES: Session 705

1. For those who are interested in publishing matters: Like counterpoint endeavors, Jane's *Dialogues* and *Adventures* have become interwound with her Seth books. She discussed her "own" works in her Introduc-

tion to *Personal Reality*. I mention them in various notes in that book, and selections of poetry from *Dialogues* itself are presented in chapters 10 and 11; in the latter chapter Seth used one of those excerpts in connection with his own material. Then in Volume 1 of *"Unknown"* *Reality*, Seth refers to *Adventures* on occasion, while I give information about it in Note 3 for his Preface, and Note 5 for Session 680, among others.

Jane finished *Dialogues* last year (in March 1973), and now (in June 1974) is halfway through the final draft of *Adventures*. I'm to finish illustrations for each of them by the end of this year, if possible, since Prentice-Hall will publish both books in 1975. Therefore, I have much work to do on the 40 pen-and-ink drawings for *Dialogues*, and on a series of diagrams for *Adventures*.

Throughout this volume, as in the first one, I'll be referring to Jane's other books. They're listed in the front matter.

2. The quotes are from *Seth Speaks:* see Chapter 1 at 9:35. In this present volume, perhaps in an appendix, I hope to add excerpts from some of Seth's unpublished observations on the psychological bridge linking Jane and himself. Right now, however, see Jane's essay on her relationship with Seth as given in the Introductory Notes for Volume 1 of *"Unknown"* *Reality*.

3. A note added five months later: Diagram 11 in Chapter 19 of Jane's *Adventures* is relevant to Seth's material here. It schematically shows the relationship of the individual birth-to-death cycle (including probable events), to the other, successively less differentiated kingdoms or realities that help make up the world. See Note 1.

4. Jane and I understand Seth's point when he tells us that "the cells of a man or woman may become the cells of a plant or an animal." However, for the reasons given in Note 3 for Session 687, in Volume 1, we'd rather think of the molecular *components* of cells as participating in the structures of a variety of forms. (And I can note a week later that at the end of Session 707, Seth makes his own comment about cells surviving changes of form.)

For additional material on cellular life and death as mediated by Seth's CU's, or units of consciousness, see the 688th session between 10:26 and 10:59: "When the cell dies physically, its inviolate nature is not betrayed. It is simply no longer physical."

5. Seth's statement here reminded me of my question about the consciousness of our species, as noted at the end of Session 699, in Volume 1.

6. Session 654, in Chapter 14 of *"Unknown"* *Reality*, contains information on the changing cellular memory, genetic codes, and neuronal patterns. Then, in Volume 1 of *"Unknown"* *Reality*, see the 690th session to 10:16 for material on biological precognition.

Session 707

□

July 1, 1974
9:21 P.M. Monday

(The 706th session was held as scheduled last Wednesday night, and our guest, Tam Mossman, did witness it—but since Seth didn't come through with any dictation for "Unknown" Reality during the session, it's hereby deleted.

(Earlier this evening I reminded Jane of the conversation about cells, versus their components, that we'd had because of Seth's material at 9:38 in Session 705. Some of tonight's book work refers to the questions growing out of our talk, I think, as does Seth's brief clarification near the end of the session.)

Now: Good evening.

("Good evening, Seth.")

Dictation . . . The cells of course are changing. The atoms and molecules within them are always in a state of flux. The CU's[1] that are within all matter have a memory bank that would far surpass any computer's. As cellular components, the atoms and molecules, therefore, carry memory of all the forms of which they have been part.

At deep levels the cells are always working with probabilities, and comparing probable actions and developments in the light of genetic information. The most intricate behavior is involved and calculations instantly made, for instance, before you can take one step or lift your finger. This does not involve <u>only</u> the predictive behavior of the physical organism alone, however. At these deeper levels the cellular activity includes making predictive judgments about the environment <u>outside</u> of the body. The body obviously does not operate alone, but in relationship with

22

everything about it. When you want to walk across the room, the body must not only operate using hindsight and a "prediction" as far as its <u>own</u> behavior is concerned, but it must take into consideration the predictive activity of all of the other elements in that room.

Give us a moment . . . At basic levels, of course, the motion of a muscle involves the motion of cells and of cellular components. Here I am saying that the atoms and molecules themselves, because of their characteristics, not only deal with probabilities within the body's cellular structure, but also help the body make predictive judgments about entities or objects outside of itself.

(Pause, then humorously:) You "know" that a chair is not going to chase you around the room, for instance—at least the odds are against it. You <u>know</u> this because you have a reasoning mind, but that particular kind of reasoning mind <u>knows</u> what it knows because at deep levels the cells are aware of the nature of probable action. The beliefs of the conscious mind, however, set your goals and purposes. "You" are the one who decides to walk across the floor, and then all of these inner calculations take place to help you achieve your goal. The conscious intent, therefore, activates the inner mechanisms and changes the behavior of the cells and their components.

In far greater terms, the goals set consciously by your species also set into operation the same kind of inner biological activity. The goals of the species do not exist apart from individual goals. As you go about your life, therefore, you are very effectively taking part in the "future" developments of your species. Period. Let us look for a moment at the private psyche.

(9:48.) The "private psyche" sounds like a fine term, but it is meaningless unless you apply it to <u>your</u> psyche. A small amount of self-examination should show you that in a very simple way you are always thinking about probabilities. You are always making choices between probable actions and alternate courses. A choice presupposes probable acts, each <u>possible</u>, each capable of actualization within your system of reality. Your private experience is far more filled with such decisions than you usually realize. There are tiny innocuous instances that come up daily: "Shall I go to the movies, or bowling?" "Shall I brush my teeth now or later?" "Should I write to my friend today or tomorrow?" There are also more pertinent questions having to do with

careers, ways of life, or other deeper involvements. <u>In your terms</u>, each decision your make alters the reality that you know to one degree or another.

PRACTICE ELEMENT 9

For an exercise, keep notes for a day or so of all the times you find yourself thinking of probable actions,[2] large or small. In your mind, try to follow "what might have happened" had you taken the course you did not take. Then imagine what might happen as a result of your chosen decisions. You are a member of the species. Any choice you make privately affects it biologically and physically.

You can literally <u>choose</u> between health and illness; between a concentration upon the mental more than the physical, or upon the physical more than the mental. Such private decisions affect the genetic heritage of the species. Your intent is all-important—for you can alter your own genetic messages[3] within certain limits. You can cause a cell, or a group of cells, to change their self-image, for example; and again, you do this often—as you healed yourselves of diseases because of your *intent* to become well. The intent will be conscious, though the means may not be. Period. In such a case, however, the self-healing qualities of the cells are reinforced, and the self-healing abilities of the species are also strengthened.

Take your break.

(10:05 to 10:32.)

Now: Your private psyche is intimately concerned with your earthly existence, and in your dream state you deal with probable actions, and often work out in that condition the solutions to problems or questions that arise having to do with probable sequences of events.[4]

On many occasions then you set yourself a problem—"Shall I do this or that?"—and form a dream in which you follow through the probable futures that would "result" from the courses available. While you are sleeping and dreaming, your chemical and hormonal activity faithfully follows the courses of the dreams. Even in your accepted reality, then, to that extent in such a dream you react to probable events as well as to the events chosen for waking physical experience. Your daily life is affected, because in such a dream you deal with probable predictabilities. You are hardly alone, however, so each individual alive also has his and her private dreams, and these help form the <u>accepted probability sequence</u> of the following day, and of "time to come." The personal decisions all add up to the global happenings of any given day.

Give us a moment . . . *(Long pause, eyes closed.)* There are <u>lands of the mind</u>.[5] That is, the mind has its own "civilizations," its own personal culture and geography, its own history and inclinations. But the mind is connected with the physical brain, and so hidden in its [the brain's] folds there is an archaeological memory. To some extent what you know <u>now</u> is dependent on what <u>will</u> be known, and what <u>has</u> been known, in your terms. The "past" races of men live to that extent within your Now, as do those who will seemingly come after. So, <u>ideally speaking</u>, the history of your species can be discovered quite clearly within the psyche; and true archaeological events are found not only by uncovering rocks and relics, but by bringing to light, so to speak, the memories that dwell within the psyche.

Now that is the end of dictation.

(10:45. Next, Seth came through with a page of information for Jane and me. In it were these lines; "I believe, incidentally, that I cleared up your question for you. Cells, as entities, do not drop off [the physical form] like apples. I was using, I suppose, a kind of shorthand I believed was clear in the context given."

(End at 11:01 P.M.)

NOTES: Session 707

1. See Note 3 for Appendix 1 in Volume 2 Part I.

2. In Volume 1 of *"Unknown" Reality,* Seth designed all but two of his eight exercises, or practice elements, to help the reader directly explore some of the aspects of probable realities—although even the exceptions (numbers 6 and 8) aren't far removed from probability concepts. His first practice element grew out of Jane's projection into a probable past in her hometown of Saratoga Springs, N.Y.

3. See the 705th session at 10:48.

4. In Volume 1, see Session 687 at 10:01: Seth discussed how the dreamer and his or her probable selves, having "the same psychic roots," can share in working out a given challenge in a probable reality.

I also suggest a rereading of the material on dreams and probable realities in chapters 14 and 15 of *The Seth Material.*

5 Jane herself first mentioned ''lands of the mind'' during break in the 703rd session, which was held some three weeks ago—but she'd picked up the phrase from Seth. See the notes at the close of that session, in Volume 1.

Session 708

□

September 30, 1974
8:58 P.M. Monday

(Jane and I hadn't realized it at first, but we were to take a long rest from work on ''Unknown'' Reality following the 707th session, for July 1. We were busy during the next 14 weeks, of course; there follow a few notes about some of our activities, grouped together by subject matter rather than chronology.

(We did have a few ''deleted'' sessions for ourselves. Jane also kept her ESP class going, and within that spontaneous format she often spoke for Seth, or sang in Sumari,[1] her trance language. The break in book dictation gave me time to begin attending class regularly, and I plan to continue doing so. And when I began sitting in on class, I discovered anew that its loose structure served as a catalyst for certain little psychic events that I find most enjoyable: Tuesday night is class night, and often such an experience takes place as I rest for half an hour late that afternoon. I record each episode [no matter when I have it]. Sometimes I make a drawing also, and use that to supplement my description of the event in class.

(Following the conference with her editor late in June, Jane has devoted herself to finishing her manuscript for Adventures, *while I've worked steadily on the diagrams for it, as well as on the drawings for* Dialogues. *I completed the detailed pencil guides for both sets of art this week. Next comes the finished work for publication, which I'll produce by placing a sheet of clear acetate over each guide, then rendering on that untouched surface the final version in ''line,'' or pen and ink. This is my own system; the acetate, riding above the penciled outlines,*

27

leaves me free to search for various spontaneous effects that are quite inhibited if I try to follow those preliminary images too literally. Then in late August, long before I had the 16 diagrams [plus two other pieces of art] done for Adventures, *I mailed to Prentice-Hall Jane's completed manuscript for that book.* Adventures *is scheduled for publication in mid-1975, but I'll continue referring to it in these notes.*

(In the meantime, on Saturday morning, July 27, Jane received her first copy of The Nature of Personal Reality: A Seth Book, *from her publisher. She was delighted. So was I. The book's physical appearance was most pleasing to us. As an artist, I'm very conscious of whether I think the "package" equals its contents, though since she is verbally oriented this is less important to Jane.*

(However, the emergence of Personal Reality *into the marketplace soon resulted in an increase in the number of letters and calls that we'd been receiving. Requests for personal appearances also mounted. We're no longer into that activity for a number of reasons; yet when the host for a Miami, Florida, radio show called Jane early this morning [September 30] about the possibility of a taped interview, she impulsively suggested to that rather startled individual that the tape be made then—and so for half an hour she exchanged with him a free, unrehearsed dialogue about her work for later airing.*

(Just as I had some small psychic adventures during our time off from "Unknown" Reality, Jane did too. One of hers that I'll mention here is related to published material. During the night following the arrival of that first consciousness, Jane received information of how "the ancients paralyzed the air." It could then be walked upon and manipulated in various other ways. She woke me up to tell me about the experience, and to remind her to write an account of it the next day. She couldn't identify its source, except to say that she hadn't been dreaming. At the breakfast table, I told her I thought the material was connected to the sessions in Personal Reality *on the interior sound, light, and electromagnetic values "around or from which" the physical image forms. Involved here also, I added, were certain ideas in her novel,* The Education of Oversoul Seven.[2]

(I haven't read "Unknown" Reality since I finished typing the last session for it over three months ago; Jane had reviewed all of Seth's material on the book last week, yet still had to remind

herself today of the contents of that [707th] session. While we went over it this afternoon I became aware of a familiar, though infrequent, sound; the honking of geese. It was the kind of transient commotion I could listen to indefinitely. The south-bound flight was soon out of sight in the rainy sky, and in another few moments it was out of hearing.

(I took the sign of migration as a good omen, though, for the circumstances of the flight were strongly reminiscent of those described at the beginning of the 687th session, in Volume 1 of "Unknown" Reality. It had been raining then, too, on that day last March—and as I wrote at the time, in some half-romantic fashion I've hooked up the flights of geese with Jane's and my work on the Seth books. I'm still surprised that I've done so, for whatever reasons; but we're ready to dig in for a winter's work.

(As we sat waiting for the session at 8:50 Jane felt a little nervous; she often does after a layoff from book dictation. But she laughed, as she has before in such cases: "I just want to get it—the beginning—over with." At 8:55, moving closer to that familiar dissociated state, approaching that psychological bridge which serves as a common meeting ground for Seth and herself, she announced that she felt "a rather generalized idea of what Seth will say on the book stuff." Less clear were some data about herself, but she thought Seth would cover all of that along with his material on "Unknown" Reality. "I guess we'll start out with the book. . . ."

(Jane's delivery as Seth was good. Indeed, it was often fast, with no sense of the three-month break that had ensued since the 707th session.)

Good evening.

("Good evening, Seth.")

Now, dictation: Consciousness operates with what you may call code *(spelled)* systems. These are beyond count. Consciousness differentiates itself, therefore, by operating within certain code systems that help direct particular kinds of focus, bringing in certain kinds of significances[3] while blocking out other data.

These other data, of course, might well be significant in <u>different</u> code systems. In their way, however, these systems are interrelated, so that at other levels there is communication between them—secondary data, you might say, that is supportive but not primarily concentrated upon.

These code systems involve molecular constructions and light values,[4] and in certain ways the light values are as precisely and effectively used as your alphabet is. For example, certain kinds of life obviously respond to spectrums with which you are not familiar—but beyond that there are electromagnetic ranges, or rather extensions of electromagnetic ranges, completely unknown to you, to which other life forms respond.

Again, all of these code systems[5] are interrelated. In the same way, the private psyche contains within it hints and glimpses of other alternate realities. These operate as secondary codes, so to speak, beneath the existence that you officially recognize. Such secondary systems can tell you much about the potentials of human reality, those that are latent but can at any time be "raised" to primary importance. Such secondary systems also point toward the probable developments possible for individuals or species.

All of the probabilities practically possible in human development are therefore present to some extent or another in each individual. Any biological or spiritual advancement that you might imagine will of course not come from any outside agency, but from within the heritage of consciousness made flesh. Generally, those alive in this century chose a particular kind of orientation. The species chose to specialize in certain kinds of physical manipulation, to devote its energies in certain directions. Those directions have brought forth a reality unique in its own fashion. Man has not driven himself down a blind alley, in other words. He has been studying the nature of his consciousness—using it as if it were apart from the rest of nature, and therefore seeing nature and the world in a particular light.[6] That light has finally made him feel isolated, alone, and to some extent relatively powerless *(intently)*.

(Rapidly:) He is learning how to use the light of his own consciousness, and discovering how far one particular method of using it can be counted upon. He is studying what he can do and not do with that particular focus. He is now discovering that he needs other lights also, in other words—that he has been relying upon only a small portion of an entire inner searchlight that can be used in many directions. Let us look at some of those other directions that are native to man's consciousness, still waiting to be used effectively.

I am speaking in your historical terms because before the historical system that you recognize, man had indeed experimented with these other directions, and with some success. This does not mean that man in the present has fallen from some higher spiritual achievement to his current state.

(Pause at 9:16.) There are cycles in which consciousness forms earthly experience, and maps out historical sequences. So there have been other species of mankind beside your own, each handling physical data in its own way. Some have taken other directions, therefore, than the one that you have chosen. Even those paths are latent or secondary, however, within your own private and mass experience. They reside within you, presenting you with alternate realities[7] that you may or may not choose privately or *en masse,* as you prefer.

Each system, of course, brings forth its own culture, "technology," art, and science. The physical body is basically equipped to maintain itself as a healthy long-living organism far beyond your present understanding, medically speaking. The cellular comprehension[8] provides all kinds of inner therapeutics that operate quite naturally. There is a physical give-and-take between the body and environment beyond that which you recognize; an inner dynamics here that escapes you, that unites the health of plants, animals, and men. In the most simple and mundane of examples, if you are living in a fairly well-balanced, healthy environment, your houseplants and your animals will also be well. You form your environment and you are a part of it. You react to it, often forgetting that relationship. Ideally, the body has the capacity to keep itself in excellent health—but beyond that, to maintain itself at the highest levels of physical achievement. The exploits of your greatest athletes give you a hint of the body's true capacity. In your system of beliefs, however, those athletes must train and focus all of their attention in that direction, often at the expense of other portions of their own experience. But their performances show you what the body is capable of.

The body is equipped, ideally again now, to rid itself of any diseases, and to maintain its stability into what you would call advanced old age, with only a gradual overall change. At its best, however, the change would bring about spiritual alterations. When you leave for a vacation, for example, you close down your house. In these ideal terms, death would involve a closing down of your [physical] house; it would not be crumbling about you.

(Pause at 9:34.) Now, certain individuals glimpse this great natural healing ability of the body, and use it. Doctors sometimes encounter it when a patient with a so-called incurable disease suddenly recovers. "Miraculous" healings are simply instances of nature unhampered. Complete physicians, as mentioned earlier,[9] would be persons who understood the true nature of the body and its own potentials—persons who would therefore transmit such ideas to others and encourage them to trust the validity of the body. Some of the body's abilities will seem impossible to you, for you have no evidence to support them. Many organs can completely replace themselves; diseased portions can be replaced by new tissue.

(Pause, in a slower delivery.) Many people, without knowing it, have developed cancer and rid themselves of it. Appendixes removed by operations have grown back. These powers of the body are biologically quite achievable in practical terms, but only by a complete change of focus and belief. Your insistence upon separating yourselves <u>from</u> nature automatically prevented you from trusting the biological aspects of the body, and your religious concepts further alienated you from the body's spirituality.

In your reality, your consciousness is usually identified with the body, on the other hand—that is, you think of your consciousness as being always within your flesh. Yet many individuals found themselves outside of the body, fully conscious and aware *(including Jane and me).*

(9:45. Jane left her trance state very easily, as she usually does. "Well," I asked her, "how do you feel now?"

("It's good to be back with the book sessions," she replied, smiling.

(We sat quietly. We could hear the automobiles swooshing across the new Walnut Street Bridge that lifted gracefully over the Chemung River, less than a quarter of a block from our apartment house; it had been raining earlier this evening and the traffic noise was softened. Incidentally, in a brief ceremony, the four-lane span had been opened to the public just this morning. Its old-fashioned predecessor had been destroyed by Tropical Storm Agnes in June 1972; see my notes for the 613th session in Chapter 1 of Personal Reality.

(Resume at a slower pace at 9:56.)

Under certain conditions, therefore, the body can maintain itself while the "main consciousness" is away from it. The body consciousness is quite able, then, to provide the overall equilibrium. At certain levels of the sleep state this does in fact happen. In sleepwalking the body is active, but the main consciousness is not "awake." It is not manipulating the body. The main consciousness is elsewhere. Under such conditions the body can perform tasks and often maneuver with an amazing sense of balance. This finesse, again, hints at physical abilities not ordinarily used. The main consciousness, because of its beliefs, often hampers such manipulability in normal waking life.

Let us look for a moment at the body consciousness.

It is equipped, as an animal is, to perform beautifully in its environment. You would call it mindless, since it would seem not to reason. For the purpose of this discussion alone, imagine a body with a fully operating body consciousness, not diseased for any reason or defective by birth, but one without the overriding ego-directed consciousness that you have. There have been species of such a nature. In your terms they would seem to be like sleepwalkers, yet their physical abilities surpassed yours. They were indeed as agile as animals—nor were they unconscious.[10] They simply dealt with a different kind of awareness.

In your terms they did not have [an overall] purpose, yet their purpose was simply to be. Their main points of consciousness were elsewhere, in another kind of reality, while their physical manifestations were separate. Their primary focuses of consciousness were scarcely aware of the bodies they had created. Yet even those bodies learned, in quotes now, "through experience," and began to "awaken," to become aware of themselves, to discover time, or to create it. Period.

(Pause.) The sleepwalkers, as we will call them, were not asleep to themselves, and would seem so only from your viewpoint. There were several such races of human beings. Their [overall] primary experience was outside of the body. The physical corporal existence was a secondary effect. To them the real was the dream life, which contained the highest stimuli, the most focused experience, the most maintained purpose, the most meaningful activity, and the most organized social and cultural behavior. Now this is the other side of your own experience, so to speak. Such races left the physical earth much as they found it. The main activity, then, involved consciousness apart from the body. In your terms, physical culture was rudimentary.

Now the physical organism as such is capable of that kind of reality system. It is not better or worse than your own. It is simply alternate behavior, biologically and spiritually possible. No complicated physical transportation systems were set up. In the physical state, in what you would call the waking state, these individuals slept. To you, comparatively speaking, their waking activities would seem dreamlike, and yet they behaved with great natural physical grace, allowing the body to function to capacity. They did not saddle it with negative beliefs of disease or limitation. Such bodies did not age to the extent, now, that yours do, and enjoyed the greatest ease and sense of belonging with the environment.

(10:24.) Consciousness connected with the flesh, then, has great leeway spiritually and biologically, and can focus itself in many ways with and through the flesh, beside your own particular orientation. There have been highly sophisticated, developed civilizations that would not be apparent to you because the main orientation was mental or psychic, while the physical race itself would seem to be highly underdeveloped.

In some of their own private dreams, many of my readers will have discovered a reality quite as vivid as the normal one, and sometimes more so. These experiences can give you some vague hint of the kind of existence I am speaking of.[11] There are also physical apparatuses connected with the hibernation abilities of some animals that can give further clues as to the possible relationships of consciousness to the body. Under certain conditions, for example, consciousness can leave the corporal mechanism while it remains intact—functioning, but at a maintenance level. When optimum conditions return, then the consciousness reactivates the body. Such behavior is possible not only with the animals. In systems different from your own, there are realities in which physical organisms are activated after what would seem to you to be centuries of inactivity[12]—again, when the conditions are right. To some extent your own life-and-death cycles are simply another aspect of the hibernation principle as you understand it. Your own consciousness leaves the body almost in the same way that messages leap the nerve ends.[13] The consciousness is not destroyed in the meantime.

Now in the case of an animal who hibernates, the body is in the same state. But in the greater hibernation of your own experience, the body as a whole becomes inoperable. The cells within you obviously die constantly. The body that you have now is not the one that you had 10 years ago; its physical composition has died completely many times since your birth, but, again, your consciousness bridges those gaps *(with gestures)*. They could be accepted instead, in which case it would seem to you that you were, say, a reincarnated self at age 7 *(intently)*, or 14 or 21. The particular sequence of your own awareness follows through, however. In basic terms the body dies often, and as surely as you think it dies but once in the death you recognize. On numerous occasions it physically breaks apart, but your consciousness rides beyond those "deaths." You do not perceive them. The stuff of your body literally falls into the earth many times, as you think it does only at the "end of your life."

Again, your own consciousness triumphantly rides above those deaths that you do not recognize as such. In your chosen three-dimensional existence, however, and in those terms, your consciousness finally recognizes a death. From the outside it is nearly impossible to pinpoint that intersection of consciousness and the seeming separation from the body. There is a time when you, as a consciousness, decide that death will happen, when in your terms you no longer bridge the gap of minute deaths not accepted.

(Pause at 10:43, during a strong delivery.) Here consciousness decides to leave the flesh, to accept an official[14] death. You have already chosen a context, however, and it seems that that context is inevitable. It appears, then, that the body will last so long and no longer. The fact remains that you have chosen the kind of consciousness that identifies with the flesh for a certain period of time. Other species of consciousness—of a different order entirely, and with a different rhythm of experience—would think of a life in your terms as a day, and have no trouble bridging that gap between apparent life, death, and new life.

Some individuals find themselves with memories of other lives, which are other days to the soul. Such persons then become aware of a greater consciousness reaching over those gaps, and realize that earthly experience can contain [among other things] a knowledge of existence in more than one body. Inherently then consciousness, affiliated with the flesh, can indeed carry such comprehensions. The mind of man as you know it shows at least the potential ability for handling a kind of memory with which you are usually not acquainted. This means that even biologically the species is equipped to deal with differ-

ent sequences of time, while still manipulating within one particular time scheme. This also implies a far greater psychological
richness—quite possible, again, within corporal reality—in which
many levels of relationships can be handled. Such inner knowledge is inherent in the cells, and in ordinary terms of evolution is
quite possible as a "future" development.

Knowledge is usually passed down through the ages in your
reality, through books and historic writings, yet each individual
contains within himself or herself a vast repository: direct
knowledge of the past, in your terms, through unconscious
comprehension.

The unknown reality: Much of that reality is unknown simply
because your beliefs close you off from your own knowledge.
The reaches of your own consciousness are not limited. Because
you accept the idea of a straight-line movement of time, you
cannot see before or after what you think of as your birth or
death,* yet your greater consciousness is quite aware of such
experience. <u>Ideally</u> it is possible not only to remember "past"
lives, but to plan future ones now. In greater terms, all such
lives happen at once. Your present neurological structure makes
this <u>seem</u> impossible, yet your inner consciousness is not so
impeded.

(Louder:) Take your break, or end the session as you prefer.

("We'll take the break."

*(11:00. Jane's trance had been excellent. She vaguely remem-
bered that Seth had talked about "sleepwalkers." I described
the material briefly, then added, "It would be a joke if that
information applied to our own ancestors, our cavemen, as we
think of them." Whereupon Jane said she thought it* did *at one
level, but she didn't elaborate.*

*(She wanted Seth to discuss a couple of her own questions,
now that he had "Unknown" Reality* underway *again, so I
suggested we ask for that material now. Jane hesitated. "I sense
stuff on both the book* and *me; I don't know what to do.
Wait—there's a practice element involved. . . ."*

(Resume at 11:25.)

Now:

PRACTICE ELEMENT 10

You can hold within your conscious attention far more data than you realize. You have hypnotized yourselves into believing that your awareness is highly limited.

Think back to yesterday. Try to remember what you did when you got up; what you wore. Attempt to follow the sequence of your activities from the time you awakened until you went to sleep. Then flesh in the details. Try to recall your feelings at all of those times. Most of you will be lucky to get this far. Those who do, go even further and try to recall the daydreams you might have had also. Try to remember what stray thoughts came into your mind.

At first, doing this will take all of your attention. You might do the exercise sitting quietly, or riding a bus or waiting for someone in an office. Some of you might be able to do the exercise while performing a more or less automatic series of actions—but do not try to carry it out while driving your car, for example.

As you become more expert at it, then purposely do something else at the same time—a physical activity, for instance. When most of you begin this exercise it will almost seem as if you were a sleepwalker yesterday. The precise, fine alignment of senses with physical activity will seem simply lost; yet as you progress the details will become clear, and you will find that you can at least hold within your mind certain aspects of yesterday's reality while maintaining your hold in today.

In larger terms there are other entire lives, which for you are forgotten essentially as yesterday is. These too, however, are a secondary series of activities, riding beneath your present primary concern. They are as unconsciously a part of your present, and as connected with it, as yesterday is.

Now: the second part of the exercise.

Imagine vividly what you will do tomorrow, and in detail plan a probable day that will rise naturally from your present experience, behavior, and purposes. Follow through as you did with the first part of the exercise. *(Pause.)* That day's reality is already anticipated by your cells. Your body has prepared for it, all of its functions precognitively projecting their own existences into it. Your "future" life exists in the same manner, and in your terms grows as much out of your present as tomorrow grows out of your today.

Doing the exercise will simply acquaint your normal consciousness with the sense of its own flexibility. You will be
exercising the invisible muscles of your consciousness as certainly as you might exercise your body with gymnastics.

To other portions of yourself you would seem to be a sleepwalker. Full creative participation in any moment, however,
awakens you to your own potentials, and therefore allows you to
experience a unity between your own consciousness and the
comprehension of your physical cells. Those cells are as spiritual
as your soul is.

(11:40.) Now give me a moment. A good one . . . This is not
dictation.

*(What followed were three and a half pages of material for
Jane and me. Here are a few condensed, more generalized
excerpts:)*

*To one extent or another in your society, you are taught to not
trust yourself. There are various schools and religions that try to
express the self's validity, but their distortions have smothered
the basic authenticity of the teachings.*

*In those terms, Ruburt started from scratch as a member of
your society who finally threw aside, as you did [Joseph], the
current frameworks of belief. For some time he was simply
between belief systems, discarding some entirely, accepting portions of others; but mainly he was a pioneer—and this while
carrying the largely unrealized, basic belief of society that you
cannot trust the self . . .*

*While that emotionally invisible belief is carried, then any-
thing the self does must be scrutinized, put to the test; in the
meantime beliefs that have sustained others are suspended. The
development of Ruburt's abilities would, therefore, lead him
away from comforting structures while he searched for others to
sustain him . . .*

*He has put to the test much of what he has learned. His own
personality has blossomed in all aspects, especially in terms of
relating with others and in personal creativity . . . He has been
testing out our information in the world that he knows. He felt
that it was necessary . . . For how could the self, taught that it
was bad, bring forth good?*

*There were frameworks that could have offered help, but he
saw that they were not intrinsically valid, and so did not depend
upon them. . . .*

(Seth said good night at 12:18 A.M. Jane's deliveries had been very energetic throughout the session.

(In his material above, concerning Jane's search for newer, larger frameworks of belief once she began to dispense with her old "comforting" ideas, Seth very lucidly dealt with certain aspects of the role she's chosen for this life. However, I want to emphasize here the emotional terms of Jane's search—and state that at times those qualities have been very difficult for her to contend with. To some degree I've been involved in many changes of belief also, but I'm a participator in the development of the Seth material, not its originator; the pressures and challenges weren't—aren't—as demanding. [With a humor born out of many a struggle, however, I note that it isn't easy to give up certain cherished old beliefs, even when they're demonstrably wrong; they may fit the personality all too well. . . .]

(In connection with these notes, and Seth's excerpts after 11:40, then, I recommend a review of the following in Volume 1:

(1. The material on Jane, religion, and mysticism in the Introductory Notes, the 679th session, and Appendix 1 for that session.

(2. Note 8 for the 679th session, on Jane's beliefs and physical symptoms.

(3. Appendix 10 [for Session 692], on Jane's efforts to make a "middle ground" between the extremes of society's reactions to her psychic abilities: rejection by the conventionally closed-minded at one end, and gullible acceptance at the other.

(And added the next day: Now see Appendix 14 for the little episode that developed on Jane's part as we retired for the evening.)

NOTES: Session 708

1. See chapters 7 and 8 in *Adventures*.

2. In *Personal Reality*, see sessions 623–25 in Chapter 5. In *Oversoul Seven*, see the material in Chapter 12, for example, wherein Jane described not only the airborne movement of objects—rocks—but an "extra tension" in the air itself, "as if a million vowels and syllables rose into the air, all glittering, all . . . alive; like animals of sound. . . ."

3. In Volume 1 of *"Unknown" Reality*, see the 681st session from 11:47, and the 682nd session from 10:21.

4. The sessions in Chapter 5 of *Personal Reality*, referred to in Note 2, contain information on the functions of the body's inner sound, light,

and electromagnetic values. Session 625 especially mentions those attributes on atomic and molecular levels.

5. See Appendix 4 (for Session 685) in Volume 1.

6. In Volume 1, all of the material in Session 686, including that for Practice Element 1, can apply here.

7. All in Volume 1: Seth refers to some varieties of ancient man in Session 689 (also see Note 4), and in Session 691 after 10:30. Then see Appendix 6 for Jane's material on parallel man, alternate man, and probable man.

In addition, the reader might review Seth's information on ancient civilizations, as presented in Chapter 15 of *Seth Speaks*.

8. See the 705th session after 10:36.

9. See sessions 703–4 in Volume 1.

10. This material immediately reminded me that before the session tonight Jane and I had discussed Seth's promise to answer the two questions I'd posed for him before sessions 698–99, in Volume 1. The question of interest here (I summarized them both in the notes following the 699th session) had to do with my inability to comprehend an "unconscious" species state. Not that I thought Seth was going out of his way to deal with such concepts tonight, but by the time he was through with his material on the sleepwalkers, I thought he'd considered at least one possible facet of my inquiry.

11. See Note 4 for Session 707.

The 699this session, in Volume 1, dealt in part with dream images and subjective dream "photographs." I used Note 1 for that session to insert one of my favorite Jane poems: *My Dreaming Self.* She wrote it in 1965, a year and a half or so after beginning the Seth material. Now I can add that at the time Jane actually wrote two poems on dreaming; I've been saving the second one for use in Volume 2.

In Midnight Thickets

In midnight thickets
Dreamers plunge
While the moon
Shines calmly on.
The town is sleeping.
Bodies lie
Neat and empty,
Side by side.

But every self
Sneaks out alone
In darkness with
No image on,

> And travels freely,
> All alert,
> Roads unlisted
> On a map.
>
> No man can find
> Where he has been,
> Or follow in flesh
> Where the self tread,
> Or keep the self in
> Though doors are closed,
> For the self moves through
> Wood and stone.
>
> No man can find
> The post or sign
> That led the self
> Through such strange land.
> The way is gone.
> The self returns
> To slip its smooth-skinned
> Image on.

12. And added two weeks or so later: I see connections between the "centuries of inactivity" that Seth describes in this (708th) session, and certain unique psychic abilities of Jane's—namely, those involving "massiveness" and "long sound." In Volume 1, see not only Session 681 between 10:22 and 11:47 for data on one of her massive experiences, but that sessions accompanying Appendix 3. Then in this section of Volume 2, see both Note 9 and Appendix 8 for the 712th session, concerning material on Jane's long-sound trances; during one of these it could theoretically take her a week—or a century—of our time to pronounce just one syllable of one word.

13. By "nerve ends" Seth means the synapses, which are the minute sites where neurons, or nerve cells, contact each other.

14. In Volume 1, see Note 2 for Session 695.

Session 709

□

October 2, 1974
9:21 P.M. Wednesday

(At 9:18 Jane said, "I feel him around." Then: "I have an idea of what he's going to talk about—but I haven't quite got it yet so I have to wait. . . ." Then, very quietly:)

Good evening.

("Good evening, Seth.")

Now: Dictation: Everything that is apparent three-dimensionally has an inside source, out of which its appearance springs. Some of this, again, is difficult to explain—not because Ruburt does not have the vocabulary, but because serial-word language automatically prepackages ideas into certain patterns, and to escape prepackaging can be a task. We will try our best, however.

The cell as you understand it is but the cell's three-dimensional face. The idea of tachyons[1] as currently understood is basically legitimate, though highly distorted. Before a cell as such makes its physical appearance there are "disturbances" in the spot in which the cell will later show itself. Those disturbances are the result of a slowing down of prior effects of faster-than-light activity, and represent the emergence into your space-time system of energy that can then be effectively used and formed into the cellular pattern.

The very slowing-down process itself helps "freeze" the activity into a form. At the death of a cell a reverse process occurs—the death is the escape of that energy from the cell form, its release, the release itself triggering certain stages of acceleration. There is what might be called a residue, or debris energy, "coating" the cell, that stays within this system. None

42

of this can be ascertained from within the system—that is, the initial faster-than-light activity or the deceleration afterward. Such faster-than-light behavior, then, helps form the basis for the physical universe. This characteristic is an attribute of the CU's, which have already slowed down to some extent when they form EE units.[2]

(Pause, one of many, at 9:37.) While operating through the body structures, consciousnesses such as your own focus largely upon the three-dimensional orientation. In out-of-body states, however, consciousness can travel faster than light—often, in fact, instantaneously.

This frequently happens in the dream state, although such a performance can be achieved in varying altered states of consciousness. At such times consciousness simply puts itself in a different relationship with time and space. The physical body cannot follow, however. It is by altering its own relationship with the physical universe that consciousness can best understand its own properties, and glimpse from another vantage point that physical universe, where it will be seen in a different light. Operating outside the body, consciousness can better perceive the properties of matter. It <u>cannot</u> (*intently*) experience matter, however, in the same fashion as it can when it is physically oriented.

From your ordinary point of view the traveling consciousness is off-focus, not locked into physical coordinates in the designated fashion. The so-called inner world can be at least theoretically explored, however, in just such a way. Consciousness "unlocks" itself for a while from its usual coordinates. When this happens the out-of-body traveler is not simply out of his or her corporal form. The person steps out of usual context. Even if an individual leaves the body and wanders about the room no more than a few feet away from where the body is located,[3] there are alterations, dash—the relationship of consciousness to the room is different. The relationship of the individual to time and space has altered. Time out of the body is "free time" by your standards. You do not age, for example, although this effect varies according to certain principles. I will mention these later.[4]

(9:48.) Such a traveling consciousness may journey within physical reality, colon: While not relating to that system in the usual manner, it may still be allied with it. From that viewpoint matter itself will seem to appear differently than it does ordinar-

ily. On the other hand, an out-of-body consciousness may also
enter other physically attuned realities: those operating "at different frequencies than your own." The basically independent
nature of consciousness allows for such disentanglement.[5] The
body consciousness maintains its own equilibrium, and acts somewhat like a maintenance station.

Any discussion of the unknown reality must necessarily involve certain usually dismissed hypotheses about the characteristics of consciousness itself. The world as you know it is the
result of a complicated set of "codes" *(as given at the beginning
of the last session)*, each locked in one to the other, each one in
those terms dependent upon the others. Your precise perceived
universe in all of its parts, then, results from coded patterns,
each one fitting perfectly into the next. Alter one of these and to
some extent you step out of that context (underlined). Any event
of any kind that does not directly, immaculately intersect with
your space-time continuum, does not happen, in your terms, but
falls away. It becomes probable in your system but seeks its own
"level," and becomes actualized as it falls into place in another
reality whose "coded sequence" fits its own. Period.

(Pause at 10:10.) When consciousness leaves the body, therefore, it alters some of the coordinates. There are various questions involving the nature of perception that then occur, and
these will be discussed somewhat later *(but see Note 4)*. Consciousness is equipped to focus its main energy, in your terms at
least, generally within the body, or to stray from it for varying
amounts of time. Theoretically, your human consciousness can
take many different roads while still maintaining its physical
base. In far-east historical times, different kinds of orientation
were experimented with *(as by the "sleepwalkers" described in
the last session, for instance)*. Your own present private experience can give hints and clues about such other cultures, for those
abilities reside within the natural framework, now, but are
underdeveloped.

To one extent or another, therefore, all of the potentials of the
species are now latent within each individual. Often these spring
to the surface through events that may seem bizarre. The "unknown" reality is unknown only because you have not looked
for its aspects in yourself. You have been taught to pay almost
exclusive attention to your exterior behavior. Privately, then,
much of your inner life escapes you. You often structure your

life according to that exterior pattern of events. These, while important, are the result of your own inner world of activity. That inner world is your only real connection with the exterior events, and the objective details make sense only because of the subjectivity that gave them birth.[6]

In the same way, when you look at the current state of the world, or at history, you often structure your perceptions so that only the topmost surfaces of events are seen. Using the same kind of reasoning, you are apt to judge the historic past of your species in very limited terms, and to overlook great clues in your history because they seem to make no sense.

(Long pause, eyes closed.) While you believe, for example, that technology <u>as you understand it</u> (underlined) alone means progress, and that progress <u>necessarily</u> requires overriding physical manipulation of the environment that must forever continue, you will judge past civilizations in that light. This will blind you to certain accomplishments and other orientations to such an extent that you will not be able to see evidence of achievement when it appears before your eyes.

(Well over a one-minute pause at 10:30, eyes closed.) Give us a moment . . . You have not worked with the power of thought or feeling, but only with its physical effects. Therefore, to you only physically materialized events are obvious. You do not accept your dreams as real, for example, but as a rule you consider them fantasies—imaginative happenings. Until very recently you generally believed that all information came to the body through the outer senses, and ignored all evidence to the contrary. It was impossible to imagine civilizations built upon data that were mentally received, consciously accepted, and creatively used.[7] Under such circumstances scientists could hardly look for precognition in cells.[8] They did not believe it existed to begin with.

The human body itself has limitless potentials, and great variations that allow for different kinds of orientation. Probable man represents alternate man from your viewpoint, alternate versions of the species. The same applies individually. In out-of-body states many people have encountered probable selves and probable realities. They have also journeyed into the past and the future as you think of them. The private psyche contains within itself the knowledge of its own probabilities, and it contains a mirror in which the experience of the species can at least be glimpsed.

You are used to a particular kind of orientation, accustomed to using your consciousness in one particular manner. In order to study the "unknown" reality, however, you must try to see what else your consciousness can do. This really means that you must learn to regain the true feeling of yourself.

There are two main ways of trying to find out about the nature of reality—an exterior method and an interior one. The methods can be used together, of course, and from your vantage point must be for the greatest efficiency. You are well acquainted with the exterior means, that involve studying the objective universe and collecting facts upon which certain deductions are made. In this book, therefore, we will be stressing interior ways of attaining, not necessarily facts, but knowledge and wisdom. Now, facts may or may not give you wisdom. They can, if they are slavishly followed, even lead you away from true knowledge. Wisdom shows you the insides of facts, so to speak, and the realities from which facts emerge.

Much of the remainder of *"Unknown" Reality*, then, will deal with an inside look at the nature of reality, and with some exercises that will allow you to see yourself and your world from another perspective. Later I intend to say far more about some civilizations that, in your terms, came before your own *(but see the last sentence in Note 4)*. Before you can understand their orientation, we will have to speak about various alternate kinds of consciousness and out-of-body experience. These will help you to understand how other kinds of cultures could operate in ways so alien to your own.

(Louder:) You may take a break or end the session as you prefer.

("We'll take the break.")

(10:55. Jane's delivery had become somewhat faster and very absorbed as it progressed. Just as they had before our three-month layoff from book work [after Session 707], her trances for "Unknown" Reality were proving to be more "difficult" to initiate than those for the previous Seth books.[9] She often had to wait for just the right moment to get back into dictation following a break, too; so tonight, after we'd shared an apple, she sat rather impatiently anticipating Seth's return. Resume, finally, at 11:25.)

Dictation: We will be discussing alternate methods of orientation that consciousness can take when allied with flesh, trying to give the reader some personal experience with such altered conditions, along with a brief history of some civilizations that utilized these unofficial orientations as their predominant method of focus.

To become familiar with the "unknown" reality you must to some extent grant that it exists, then, and be willing to step aside from your usual behavior. All of the methods given are quite natural, inherent in the body structure, and even biologically anticipated. Your consciousness could not leave your body and return to it again unless there were biological mechanisms that allowed for such a performance.

I have said *(as at 9:48)* that the body can indeed carry on, performing necessary maintenance activities while the main consciousness is detached from it. To some extent it can even perform simple chores. *(Pause.)* In sleep, in fact, it is not at all necessary that the main consciousness be alert in the body. Only in certain kinds of civilizations, for that matter, is such a close body-and-main-consciousness relationship necessary. There are other situations, therefore, in which consciousness ordinarily strays much further, returning to the body as a home station and basis of operation, relying upon it for certain kinds of perception only, but not depending upon it for the entire picture of reality. Physical life alone does not necessarily require the <u>kind</u> of identification of self with flesh that is your own.

This does not mean that an alienation results in those realities—simply a relationship in which the body and consciousness relate to other events. Only your beliefs, training, and neurological indoctrination prevent you from recognizing the true nature of your consciousness while you sleep. You close out those data. In that period, however, at an inner order of events, you are highly active and do much of the interior mental work that will later appear as physical experience.

(Slowly at 11:43:) While your consciousness is so engaged, your body consciousness performs many functions that are impossible for it during your waking hours. The greatest biological creativity takes place while you sleep, for example, and certain cellular functions[10] are accelerated. Some such disengagement of your main consciousness and the body is therefore obviously

necessary, or it would not occur. Sleeping is not a by-product of waking life.

In greater terms you are just as awake when you are asleep, but the focus of your awareness·is turned in other directions. As you know, you can live for years while in a coma, but you could not live for years without ever sleeping. Even in a coma there is mental activity, though it may be impossible to ascertain it from the outside. A certain kind of free conscious behavior is possible when you are not physically oriented as you are in the waking state, and that activity is necessary even for physical survival.

This also has to do with pulsations of energy in which consciousness as you know it, now, exercises itself, using native abilities that cannot be expressed through physical orientation alone.

Your own main consciousness has the ability to travel faster than light *(as noted at 9:37),* but those perceptions are too fast, and the neurologically structured patterns that you accept cannot capture them. For that matter, cellular comprehension and reaction are too fast for you to follow. The poised framework of physical existence requires a particular platform of experience that you accept as valid and real. At that level only is the universe that you know experienced. That platform or focus is the result of the finest cooperation. Your own free consciousness and your body consciousness form an alliance that makes this possible.

(With many pauses:) Give us a moment . . . Such a performance actually means that physical reality clicks off and on.[11] In your terms, it exists only in your waking hours. The inner work that makes it possible is largely done in the sleep state. The meeting of body consciousness and your main consciousness requires an intense focus, in which the greatest manipulations are necessary. Perceptions must be precise in physical terms. To some extent, however, that exquisite concentration means that certain limitations occur. Cellular comprehension is not tuned into by the normally conscious self, which is equally unaware of its own free-wheeling nature at "higher" levels. So a disengagement process must happen that allows each to regenerate. The consciousness then leaves the body. The body consciousness stays with it.

Give us a moment . . . We are about to end the session after a few remarks.

(Pause at 12:07. Seth's comments were for Jane, and took up another page of notes. End at 12:19 A.M.

(After the session we had something more to eat, then relaxed by playing with our cat, Willy. When we did get to bed Jane fell asleep at once. As I lay beside her in a most pleasant daze, I heard quite clearly in the cool night air the honking of geese as they flew south. Drowsily I remembered the flight I'd listened to in the rain the day before yesterday. . . .)

NOTES: Session 709

1. Tachyons, or meta-particles, are supposed faster-than-light particles that are thought to be possible within the context of Einstein's special theory of relativity. Physicists are still trying to experimentally discover them. As I interpret Seth here, then, tachyons or something much like them will be found.

In Volume 1 of *"Unknown" Reality,* see Note 4 for Session 682.

2. For material on CU and EE units in Volume 1, see sessions 682 (with notes 3 and 4), 683–84, and 688. The last two sessions also contain some of Seth's comments on cellular consciousness.

3. One of the most unique out-of-body experiences, or projections, I've had was much like that which Seth describes here. It took place in April 1971, and I wrote about it in Chapter 20 of *Seth Speaks.* See the notes for the 583rd session. My consciousness didn't travel more than 10 feet from my body that time, but the little journey, so vivid and pleasant, did much to reinforce the enlarged view of reality that I'd gradually begun to adopt after Jane started delivering the Seth material late in 1963. I've never forgotten the sense of freedom that that modest projection engendered within me—and during it, my temporal relationships *were* different.

In Note 12 for Appendix 1, Volume 2 Part I, I wrote about out-of-body travel and naïve realism.

4. A note added some eight months later: Once in a great while Seth refers to the slower rate of physical aging connected with the out-of-body state, and notes the "certain principles" involved, as he does here. Jane and I have always felt that he has some very interesting material on the subject, and that we'll get it someday. But it didn't come through before *"Unknown" Reality* was finished, in April 1975.

5. "Disentanglement" immediately reminded me of the inner senses—those qualities and abilities which the personality uses to apprehend its physical (or camouflage) world. Seth began describing the inner senses early in 1964. His "Disentanglement From Camouflage" happened to be number eight on a list of nine, although the order is unimportant. Jane devoted Chapter 19 of *The Seth Material* to the inner senses.

"With disentanglement," Seth stated in the 43rd session, "the inner self disengages itself from one particular camouflage before it either adopts another set smoothly or dispenses with camouflage entirely. This is accomplished through what you might call a changing of frequencies or vibrations . . . In some ways, your dream world gives you a closer experience with basic inner reality than does your waking world, where the inner senses are so shielded from your awareness."

A note: Just as he periodically reminds us of his material-to-come on physical aging and out-of-body states (see Note 4, above), Seth then adds that many of them are so far removed from reality as we understand it that our comprehension will be intellectual at best; in such cases we won't be able to identify with them emotionally. And then other groups of inner senses, Seth continues, are truly "Beyond verbalization."

6. Much of the material in Appendix 1 in Volume 2 Part I (including the notes), deals with connections between our inner and outer worlds.

7. In Volume 1, see the 689th session. In Volume 2, see the references in Note 7 for Session 708.

8. So far in the two volumes of *"Unknown" Reality*, Seth has discussed the freedom of cells from time, along with a number of their other attributes, in well over a dozen sessions. In Session 684 (in Volume 1) he said at 10:07: "Your body's condition at any time is not so much the result of its own comprehension of its 'past history' as it is of its own comprehension of future probabilities. The cells precognate."

9. Appendixes 4 and 5, in Volume 1, show the insights Jane herself has gained so far about the more complicated trances she experiences while delivering the sessions for *"Unknown" Reality*. As noted in Appendix 4, she waits for that "certain clear focus" she needs before taking up the challenges of "translating multidimensional experience into linear terms and thought patterns." And from Appendix 5: "It's as though my consciousness is trying to use a new kind of organization— for me, for it—and so there's a kind of unfamiliarity."

10. Perhaps I should have asked Seth to be more specific about those "certain cellular functions" that are accelerated in the sleep state, but I didn't; I was tiring. It's well known that parts of the brain are much more active when we sleep than when we're awake, for instance, but I doubt that Seth was referring to such phenomena here.

The brain itself never sleeps, of course, since it's endlessly involved in running the vastly complicated physiological functions of the body. Sleep for the conscious mind results when neural activity in the reticular activating system (the RAS), which screens the sensory information reaching consciousness, falls below a minimum level.

11. In Volume 1, see sessions 681 and 684.

Session 710

□

October 7, 1974
9:31 P.M. Monday

(We have two compositions, both of them by Jane, to add to this session. She produced the first very short one, given below, yesterday. Seth briefly mentions it in the excepted material at the end of tonight's session, with a promise to say more later.

(Those excerpts, in turn, came from his remarks about Jane's second composition, which she wrote late this afternoon after we'd finished reading certain material. Since this [second] piece is much longer, it's presented as Appendix 15. I suggested that it be read now, or at least before reaching the end of this session.

(From Jane's dream journal, then, for Sunday, October 6, 1974:

("I heard Seth's voice, very loud and powerful, as I lay asleep in bed last night [Saturday]. This was the first time I've had such an experience. The voice was coming from the area of the room next door or just beyond, but also from above; like out of the sky or something. It wasn't speaking through anyone—that is, it wasn't coming from inside my head or through me as it always has so far, even in the dream state. I tried to understand what was said. The words didn't seem to be directed at me, particularly, but just to be there. It seemed that Seth was really laying it on somebody. At first I thought he was angry, but then I realized I was interpreting the power of the voice that way. This wasn't part of a dream, but I awakened almost at once as I tried to make out the words. Subjectively, I wasn't aware of Seth's presence in any way. The sound was like a supervoice; maybe

51

*like Nature speaking, or something; not the way a person would
speak.'')*

Now, good evening.

(''Good evening, Seth.'')

Dictation *(quietly):* To explore the unknown reality you must
venture within your own psyche, travel inward through invisible
roads as you journey outward on physical ones.

Your material reality is formed through joint cooperation.
Period. Your own ideas, objectified, become a part of the physical environment. In this vast cooperative venture the thoughts
and feelings of each living being take root, so to speak, spring-
ing up as objectified data. I said *(in the 708th session)* that each
system of reality uses its own codified system. This effectively
provides a sort of framework. Generally speaking, then, you
agree to objectify certain inner data privately and *en masse* at
any given ''time.'' In those terms the airplane objectified the
inner idea of flying in ''your'' time, and not in A.D. 1500, for
example.

You may have heard people say of an idea: ''It's time has not
yet come.'' This simply means that there is not enough energy
connected with the idea to propel it outward into the world of
physical experience as an objective mass-experienced event.

In the dream state and in certain other levels of reality, ideas
and their symbols are immediately experienced. There is no time
lag, then, between a feeling and its ''exteriorized'' condition. It
is automatically experienced in whatever form is familiar and
natural to the one who holds it. The psyche is presented with its
own concepts, which are instantly reflected in dream situations
and other events that will be explained shortly. If you dream of
or yearn for a new house in physical life, for instance, it may
take some time before that ideal is realized, even though such a
strong intent will most certainly bring about its physical fulfillment. The same desire in the dreaming state, however, may lead
to the instant creation of such a house as far as your dream
experience is concerned. Again, there is no time lag there between desire and its materialization.

(Pause, one of many, at 9:49.) There are levels within dreams,
highly pertinent but mainly personal, in that they reflect your
own private intents and purposes. There are other levels, further
away in your terms, that involve mass behavior on a psychic
level, where together the inhabitants of the physical world plan

out future events. Here probabilities are recognized and utilized. Symbolism is used. There is such an interweaving of intent that this is difficult to explain. Private desires here are magnified as they are felt by others, or minimized accordingly, so that in the overall, large general plans are made having to do with the species at any given "time." Here again, these desires and intents must fit into the codified system as it exists.

(Pause, in a quiet but intent delivery.) At these levels you are still close to home. Beyond, there are layers of actuality in which your psyche is also highly involved, and these may or may not appear to have anything to do with the world that you know.

When you travel into such realms you usually do so from the dream state, still carrying your private symbols with you. Even here, these are automatically translated into experience. This is not your own codified system, however. You may journey <u>through</u> such a reality, perceiving it opaquely, layering it over with your own perceived symbols, and taking those for the "real" environment. In these terms the real environment will be that which was generally perceived by the natural inhabitants of the system.

To begin with, your own symbols rise from deep levels of the psyche, and in certain terms you <u>are</u> a part of any reality that you experience—but you may have difficulty in the interpretation of events.

If you are in a world not yours, with your consciousness drifting, you are in free gear, so to speak, your feelings and thoughts flowing into experience. You have to learn how to distinguish your psychological state from the reality in which you find yourself, if you want to maintain your alertness and explore that environment. Many of my readers find themselves in just such situations while they are sleeping. While still dreaming they seem to come suddenly awake in an environment that appears to make no sense. Demons may be chasing them. The world may seem topsy-turvy. The dead and the living may meet and speak.

(10:16.) Now: In almost all instances, demons in dreams represent the dreamer's belief in evil, <u>instantly materalized</u>. They are not the inhabitants of some nether world, then, or underground. We will be giving some instructions that will enable readers to experiment with the projection of consciousness at least to some extent. It is very important for you to realize that even in dreams you form your own reality. Your

state of mind, freed from its usual physical focus, creatively expresses itself in all of its power and brilliance. The state of mind itself serves as an intent, propelling you into realities of like conditions.

(Pause.) In your world you travel from one country to another, and you do not expect them to be all alike. Instead, you visit various parts of the world precisely because of the differences among them—so all out-of-body journeys do not lead to the same locale.

Instinctively you leave your body for varying amounts of time each night while you sleep, but those journeys are not "programmed." You plan your own tours, in other words. As many people with the same interests may decide to visit the same country together, on tour, so in the out-of-body condition you may travel alone or with companions. If you are alert you may even take snapshots—only as far as inner tours are concerned, the snapshots consist of clear pictures of the environment taken at the time, developed in the unconscious, and then presented to the waking mind.

There are techniques for using cameras,[1] and a camera left at home will do you little good abroad. So it is the conscious alert mind that must take these pictures if you hope to later make sense of your inner journeys. That conscious reasoning mind must <u>therefore</u> be taken along. There are many ways of doing this, methods not really difficult to follow. Certain techniques will help you pack your conscious mind for your journey as you would pack your camera. It will be there when you need it, to take the pictures that will be your conscious memories of your journey.

Do you want to rest your hand?

(10:22. "No," I said, although I'd been writing pretty steadily for the better part of an hour. Jane, in trance, held up a fresh bottle of beer. I opened it for her. Then:)

You must remember that the objective world <u>also</u> is a projection from the psyche.[2] Because you focus in it primarily, you understand its rules well enough to get along. A trip in the physical world merely represents the decision to walk or to choose a particular kind of vehicle—a car will not carry you across the ocean, so you take a ship or a plane. You are not astonished to see that the land suddenly gives way to water. You find that natural alteration quite normal. <u>You expect time to stay</u>

in its place, however. The land may change to water, for example, but today must not change into yesterday in the same fashion, or into tomorrow in the beginning of today's afternoon.

Walking down the avenue, you expect the trees to stay in their places, and not transform themselves into buildings. All of these assumptions are taken for granted in your physical journeys. You may find different customs and languages, yet even these will be accepted in the vast, overall, basic assumptions within whose boundaries physical life occurs. You are most certainly traveling through the private and mass psyche when you so much as walk down the street. The physical world seems objective and outside of yourself, however. The idea of such outsideness is one of the assumptions upon which you build that existence. Interior traveling is no more subjective, then, than a journey from New York to San Francisco. You are used to projecting all destinations outside of yourself. Period. The idea of varied inward destinations, involving motion through time and space, therefore appears strange.

Now take your break.

(10:36. Jane's delivery had remained quiet and steady. "Boy, he was going strong," she said. "He kept me under a good long time because of the noise [in the apartment] upstairs—and because of those phone calls, too, I'll bet. . . ." Here she referred to a number of out-of-state calls she'd taken after supper this evening; she'd found two of them in particular to be rather upsetting.

(Resume in the same manner at 10:58.)

Generally speaking, you have explored the physical planet enough so that you have a good idea of what to expect as you travel from country to country.

Before a trip, you can produce travel folders that outline the attractions and characteristics of a certain locale. You are not traveling blind, therefore, and while any given journey may be new to you, you are not really a pioneer: The land has been mapped and there are few basic suprises.

The inner lands have not been as well explored. To say the least, they lie in virgin territory as far as your conscious mind is concerned. Others have journeyed to some of these interior locales, but since they were indeed explorers they had to learn as they went along. Some, returning, provided guidebooks or travel folders, telling us what could be expected. You make your own reality. If you were from a foreign land and asked one person to give you a description of New York City, you might take his or her description for reality. The person might say: "New York City is a frightful place in which crime is rampant, gangs roam the streets, murders and rapes are the norm, and people are not only impolite but ready to attack you at a moment's notice. There are no trees. The air is polluted, and you can expect only violence." If you asked someone else, this individual might say instead: "New York City has the finest of museums, open-air concerts in some of the parks, fine sculpture, theater, and probably the greatest collection of books outside of the Vatican. It has a good overall climate, a great mixture of cultures. In it, millions of people go their way daily in freedom." Period. Both people would be speaking about the same locale. Their descriptions would vary because of their private beliefs, and would be colored by the individual focus from which each of them viewed that city.

One person might be able to give you the city's precise location in terms of latitude and longitude. The other might have no such knowledge, and say instead: "I take a plane at such-and-such a place, at such-and-such a time, giving New York City as my destination, and if I take the proper plane I always arrive there."

(Pause at 11:13.) Explorers traveling into <u>inner</u> reality, however, do not have the same kind of landmarks to begin with. Many have been so excited with their discoveries that they wrote guidebooks long before they even began to explore the inner landscape. They did not understand that they found what they <u>wanted</u> to find, or that the seemingly objective phenomena originated in the reflections of the psyche.

You may, for example, have read books numbering the "inner realms," and telling you what you can expect to encounter in each. Many of these speak of lords or gods of the realm, or of demons. In a strange way these books do provide a service, for at certain levels you will find your own ideas materialized; and if you <u>believe</u> in demons then in those terms you will encounter them. The authors, however, suppose that the devils have a reality <u>outside</u> of your belief in them, and such is not the case. The demons simply represent a state of your own mind that is seemingly out there, objectified. Therefore, whatever methods the authors used to triumph over these demons is often given as proof not only of the demons' reality, but of each method's effectiveness.

Now if you read such books you may often program your activity along those lines, in the same way that a visitor to New York City might program experience of the city in terms of what he or she had been told existed there.

That kind of structuring also does a disservice, however, for it prevents you from coming in contact with your own original concepts. There is no reason, for example, to encounter any demons or devils in any trance or out-of-body condition.[3] *(Pause.)* In such cases your own hallucinations blind you to the environment within which they are projected. When your conscious is not directly focused in physical reality, then, the great creativity of the psyche is given fuller play. All of its dimensions are faithfully and instantly produced as experience when you learn to take your "normally alert" conscious mind <u>with</u> you; and when you are free of such limiting ideas, then at those levels you can glimpse the inner powers of your own psyche, and watch the interplay of beliefs and symbols as they are manifested before your eyes. Until you learn to do this you will most certainly have difficulty, for you will not be able to tell the difference between your projections and what is happening in the inner environment.

Any exploration of inner reality must necessarily involve a journey through the psyche, and these effects can be thought of as atmospheric conditions, natural at a certain stage, through which you pass as you continue. Period.

(Louder at 11:31:) Now give us a moment. . . .

("I'm in between," Jane said after a pause, and in her "own" voice. "I don't know what's coming. I'm sort of half in trance and half out. . . ." She lit a cigarette.

("Do you want me to get you some more beer?"

("I don't think it'll last that long," she said. Seth returned—and stayed longer, probably, than she'd anticipated he would. His material was for Jane, and grew out of the paper she wrote this afternoon on Eastern religious thought [see Appendix 15]. The more personal parts of Seth's delivery aren't given here, yet enough remains to show Jane's main challenges some 11 years after she began speaking for him.

(The quotations also indicate how pervasive the regular Western view of "reality" is in our society, and what an undertaking it is to step outside of that framework, or just to enlarge upon it.

Jane is still in the process of that objective, intellectual—and yet very emotional—movement of her psyche [as I am], but she's made considerable progress. In each of her books she tries to more clearly communicate the details and developments of her journey. [I note also that neither one of us is trying to get rid of our Western orientation, or to desert it—but to understand it more fully.]

(Now Seth said in part, beginning at 11:33:)

Ruburt is working through the philosophical problems that were really only questions not completely asked. All of the writing he did today is important. He is preparing to go ahead in all directions.

There are too many levels here to discuss all at once . . . One such level reinforces a trust in himself. The trust is accepted, however, because he is finally ready to work through the <u>issues</u>. As given *[at various times over the years, mostly in personal material]*, they involve cultural training and religious indoctrinations.[4] He is challenging, finally, the old beliefs that say that the self's spontaneity is not to be trusted. He is challenging those ideas emotionally and philosophically, uniting physical action and inner mobility. In the past he was still afraid to touch those beliefs with any but the slightest of hands.

Give us a moment . . . What he wrote <u>is</u> pertinent. Before he could go fully ahead he had to accept the challenges of the past, and this meant he had to examine those old beliefs. He is only now really beginning to do so. . . .

They were not only his <u>private</u> religious beliefs, but those of his contemporaries generally—and *(loudly:)* <u>the foundations upon which your present civilization was made</u>. He had to find the courage to encounter those old beliefs boldly, and he is finally doing so. I will have more to say to him in the dream state this evening, and I will shortly explain his experience with my voice.

In a way, then, the session will continue at another level of communication. It will all be down in black and white for you before too long, however.

My heartiest wishes to you both, and a fond good evening.

("Thank you, Seth, and the same to you. Good night.")

(11:46 P.M. All Jane could say the next morning was that she had no conscious memory of any contact Seth might have made

with her in the dream state. Looking ahead a bit: In tomorrow night's session, though, Seth does explain her weekend sleep-state encounter with his voice.)

NOTES: Session 710

1. A note added six weeks later: Seth further "develops" his camera analogy (as dream photography, for instance), in Section 5. See sessions 719–20.

2. Is there really an objective world—"something out there"— for each of us to perceive? See my passage on naive realism in Appendix 1 in Volume 2 Part I, along with Seth's own material on the question in Note 13 for that appendix.

3. In Chapter 14 of *The Seth Material*, Jane and Seth gave a humorous-serious account of her out-of-body encounter with a demon, or "black thing," of her own creation.

4. See the notes (at 12:18 A.M.) concluding the 708th session.

Session 711

□

October 9, 1974
9:17 P.M. Wednesday

(ESP class had really jumped last night. The 32 people crowded into our living room enjoyed rich, active, loud, and even profane exchanges among themselves, with Jane, and with Seth. "Fuck you, Seth!" one girl screamed—which daunted that worthy not at all: Class members hardly agree with Seth or anyone else all of the time. As usual, Jane found herself learning along with her students. She also took time to sing very delicately in Sumari, in contrast to Seth's powerful deliveries. All was recorded, of course. Class lasted from 7 P.M. until after midnight, and by the time it was over everyone involved was, if not exhausted, certainly well exercised emotionally. We're to get a transcript of the evening's Seth material at next week's class.*)

Good evening *(whispering.*

("Good evening, Seth.")

Now: Dictation *(still whispering)*. Never as dramatic as our noisy class sessions.

Your world, again, is the result of a certain focus of consciousness, without which that world cannot be perceived. Period. The range of consciousness involved is obviously physically oriented, yet within it there are great varieties of consciousness, each experiencing that seemingly objective world from a private perspective. The physical environment is real in different terms to an animal, a fish, a man, or a rock, for example, and different

---

*See Appendix 5, Volume 2 Part I

portions of that environment are correspondingly <u>un</u>real [to each of those forms]. This is highly important.

If an inhabitant from another reality outside of your own physical system entirely were to visit it, and if "his" intelligence was roughly of the same degree as your own, he would still have to learn to focus his consciousness in the same way that you do, more or less, in order to perceive your world. He would have to alter his native focus and turn it in a direction that was foreign to him. In this way he could "pick up your station."[1] There would be distortions, because even though he managed such manipulations he might not have the same kind of native physical structure as your own, of course, through which to receive and interpret those data his altered consciousness perceived.

Your visitor would then be forced to translate that information as best he could through his own native structure, if it were to make any sense to his consciousness in its usual orientation. All realities are the result of certain unique focuses taken by consciousness, therefore. In those terms, there <u>is</u> no outside. The effects of objectivity are caused as the psyche projects its experience into inner dimensions that it has itself created.

(9:35.) Within, those frameworks are ever expanding, so that in your terms at least it seems that greater and greater distances are involved. Travel to any other land of physical reality must then involve alterations of consciousness.[2]

New paragraph. While all of your own thoughts and feelings are "somewhere" materialized, only some of them become physical in your terms. They are then accepted as physical reality. They provide the basis for the physical events, objects, and phenomena upon which you all agree. Therefore your world has a stability that you accept, a certain order and predictability[3] that works well enough for daily concerns. At that point you are tuned in precisely on your "home station." You ignore the ghost symbols or voices, the probable actions that also occur, but that are muffled in the clear tones of your accepted reality. When you begin to travel away from that home station, you become more aware of the other frequencies[4] that are you buried within it. You move through other frequencies, but to do this you must alter your own consciousness.*

The probable realities connected with your own system are

---

*See Appendix 6, Volume 2 Part I

like the suburbs, say, surrounding a main city. If for simplicity's sake you think of other realities as different cities, then after you leave your own you would pass through the suburbs, then into the country, then after a time into other suburbs until you reached another metropolis. Here each metropolis would represent a conglomeration of consciousnesses operating within an overall general frequency of clearest focus, a high point of psychic communication and exquisite focus in the given kind of reality. Unless you are tuned in to those particular frequencies, however, you could not pick up that reality. You might instead perceive the equivalent of jumbled sound or meaningless static *(as Jane has done)*, or jigsaw images *(as I have done)*. You might simply realize that some kind of activity was there, but without being able to pinpoint it.

Now all consciousness, including your own, is highly mobile. While you focus your attention primarily in your own world, certain portions of your consciousness are always straying. When you are sleeping, then, your consciousness often ventures into other realities, usually in a wandering fashion without tuning itself in to any precise frequencies. Beneath many seemingly chaotic dreams there are often valid experiences in which your consciousness "lights" in another reality, without being attuned to it with the necessary precision that would allow for clear perception. The information cannot be sifted or used effectively and is translated into dream images, <u>as</u> your consciousness returns toward your own home station. Therefore, it has been difficult to achieve any kind of clear picture of such other realities.

(Pause at 9:59.) Certain particular focuses then bring in different worlds, but unless your consciousness is tuned in with exquisite precision you will not be able to perceive clearly. You will instead pick up at best the ghost images, probabilities, and private date that are not officially recognized as part of the main reality's official structure of events.

New paragraph. <u>Basically</u>, however, consciousness is freewheeling. Such realities therefore always exist—in your own psyche—outside of your "home station," and some portion of your own consciousness is always involved in them. Period. There are bleed-throughs, so to speak, in the form of unofficial perceptions that often occur, or "impossible" events that are seemingly beyond explanation. *(Pause.)* For now think of your own psyche, which is a <u>consciousized</u> identity, as a kind of "supernatural radio." All of the stations exist at once within the psyche. These do not come through with sound alone, but with all the living paraphernalia of the world. The "you" that you recognize is but one signal on one such station, tuned in to a certain frequency, experiencing that station's overall reality from your own viewpoint—one that is unique and like no other, and yet contributing to the whole life of the station.

(Smile:) The supernatural radio that is your entire psyche contains many such stations, however. These are all playing at the same time. It would be highly confusing in this analogy to experience or hear all of these at once, however, so different portions of the psyche tune in to different stations, concentrate upon them, and tune out the others for immediate practical purposes. Because these stations all operate within the same psyche or supernatural radio, the overall quality of the programs will have much to do with the nature of the psyche itself. Radios are wired and contain transformers and transistors. The overall reception is dependent upon the wiring and the inner workings of the radio—and *(intently)* those workings exist apart from the stations they are meant to pick up. In the same way, the "supernatural psyche" exists apart from the stations of consciousness that it contains. In this case indeed the psyche itself makes the radio, adding ever-new connections and stations.

(10:18.) New paragraph. Pretend that you have a radio with which you can clearly pick up 10 stations. First imagine that during the daily programming there are three soap operas, four news programs, several excellent dramas, a few operas, some popular music, several religious sermons, and some sports programs. Each of these has its own commercials or messages, which may or may not have anything to do with the programs given.

First of all, it would be nearly impossible for you to <u>sample</u> all of these programs with any effectiveness while going about your own affairs. To make matters more complicated, again, these programs do not involve only sound. Each one has its own dimensional realities. Beside that, there is a give-and-take between programs.

For example: Say that you have a certain Wilford Jones, who is a character in one of the soap operas. This Wilford, while carrying on within his own drama as, say, a sickly grocer in

Iowa, with a mistress he cannot support, and a wife that he <u>must</u> support *(with amusement)*—this poor, besieged man on station KYU is also aware of all the other programs going on at the other stations. All of the other characters in all of the other plays are also aware of our grocer. There is a constant, creative give-and-take between the day's various programs. Period.

When our Wilford dramatically cries out to his mistress: "I am afraid my wife will learn of our affair," then the symphony playing on another station becomes melodramatic, and the sports program shows that a hero fumbles the football. Yet each character has its own free will. The football player, unconsciously picking up the grocer's problem, for example, may use it as a challenge and say: "No, I will not fumble the ball." The crowds then cheer, and our grocer in his soap opera may smile and say: "But it will all work out after all."

In other words, there is in the psyche constant interaction between all of the stations, and marvelous, literally unlimited creativity—in which, in your terms, all actions in one station affect all others in the other stations.

Now take a break.

(10:34. Jane's trance had been excellent, her delivery steady and rather quiet for the most part. "I knew what Seth was talking about," she said, "because I had the images to go along with what he was saying. Not that I could repeat him now, word for word. . . ."

(I reminded Jane that during Monday's session, the 710th, Seth had promised to "shortly explain" her hearing his booming voice in her sleep state last Saturday night. See Jane's description of the event preceding that session.

(Resume at 10:54.)

Now: Dictation: Still using the same analogy: As he falls asleep some night our grocer, Wilford, might suddenly hear the full strains of a symphony in his head, or instead catch a quick glimpse of a football player; or on the other hand one of the musicians in the symphony orchestra may suddenly find himself thinking about how difficult it would be to have a mistress and a wife at the same time.

From the point of view of the perceiver these would be unofficial events, and yet they could serve as important clues to the nature of reality. The separate programs existing at once each have their own schedules, and from <u>your</u> reality you could not play them all at once. It seems to you that you are outside of the psyche, so you think of someone as yourself operating this radio from that external position. From your point of view you could not pick up the grocer's escapades and the symphony, for instance, if both came through at 8 o'clock in the evening, without switching from one to the other: You would have to choose which program you wanted.

It is very easy of course to expand our analogy, changing the radio to a television set. In this case the projections on the screen would be fully dimensional, aware of each viewer in each living room. *(Pause.)* Not only this, but the screen people would understand the relationship between you the viewer, and, say, the other viewers in the same town. Behind the scenes not only would the performers, as performers in all of the programs, all know each other, but the <u>characters</u> portrayed by them would know each other and be aware of each other's rolls in the programs, and even now and then stray into one another's dramas.

At levels beyond the comprehension of the viewer, all of the dramas and programs would be related. Again, because of the specific poise of your consciousness, it seems to you that you are outside of all these programs. You tune in to them, making choices, for example, if more than one favorite plays at the same hour.

In greater terms, you are a part of the same "set," and at another level someone sees you as a character in a living room turning on a television set. Intrinsically the psyche, the private psyche, contains all such programs and realities. Certain portions of it, however, choose to take different focuses in order to bring those aspects in more clearly.

(Pause at 11:13.) To some extent, signals from all of the other stations are always in the background of any given program, and by momentarily altering the direction of your own attention you can learn how to bring other stations into focus. Psychically and psychologically, those other stations upon which you do not concentrate form the structure of the psyche as you understand it, from which your earthly experience springs into focus. Studying yourself and the nature of your own consciousness, then, will automatically lead you to some extent to an understanding of the "unknown" reality. The unknown reality is composed of those blocked-out portions of your own psyche, and the corresponding frameworks of experience they form.

(Long pause.) New paragraph. For the sake of imagery, you can imagine your normal consciousness as your connection with this home planet—the familiar station that you tune in to every day. When you project your consciousness away from it, then you will encounter various kinds of atmospheric conditions. Once you understand what these are, and what effects can be expected, such journeys can be undertaken consciously, with the conscious mind that you know acting as the astronaut, for example, and the rest of your consciousness acting as the vehicle. Such journeys lead to quite valid realities, but as an astronaut must know the best landing conditions, so you must learn how to "come in" at the most auspicious time and under the best conditions.

Such journeys take you through the nature of the psyche itself, as well as to those other realities that exist as the result of the psyche's concentration within particular frequencies.

Projecting your consciousness out of your body, therefore, provides at the same time an inner probing of consciousness itself, as well as experience of its manifestations. There are then inner lands of the mind, and other worlds quite as legitimate as your own. They are intimately connected, however, with mental states which are then materialized, and so your own mental processes are highly involved.

Take your break.

(11:28. "He's really going, though, I'm telling you," Jane said, after remarking upon the shorter delivery. "I'm hoping he says something about when I heard his voice in my sleep." Resume at a faster pace at 11:40.)

Now: First of all, I have been speaking of the psyche as if it were a completed thing, with definite boundaries. The private psyche is ever creative, actually—expansive and literally without beginning or end.

Your experience of yourself marks the seeming boundaries of yourself. In a manner of speaking, I am one personality and one program or station. Ruburt is another. We have learned to be aware of each other,* to communicate between stations, to affect each other's programs and to change each other's worlds. I do not speak alone to Ruburt and Joseph, for example, but my words go out to the world that you know. Still within your

---

*See Appendix 7, Volume 2 Part I

framework, Ruburt tunes in to another station, translates it and broadcasts the information. To do this, however, he has to alter his own consciousness, withdraw momentarily from the official station to bring in this one. That means tuning in to other portions of the psyche, as well as another kind of reality. The final translation of my material has to come through his organism, however, or it would be meaningless to you.

Through him I am aware of the nature and condition of your world, and offer from my viewpoint comments meant to help you. Through Ruburt, then, I am permitted to view the earth "again" in your terms. I exist apart from him, as he exists apart from me, yet we are together a part of the same entity—and that simply carries the idea of the psyche further.

The other [Saturday] evening while he was in bed Ruburt had a somewhat surprising experience. He was not dreaming. His body was asleep but his consciousness was drifting. He clearly heard my voice. It seemed to come literally from out of the sky, down into another room outside of *(next-door to, actually)* the one in which his body slept. For a moment the power frightened him, for it sounded like a radio turned up to an incredible degree—louder than thunder. At the time words were clearly distinguishable, though later he forgot what they said. For an instant he was tempted to interpret the power as anger, for in your world when someone is <u>shouting</u> they are usually angry. He realized, however, that something else was involved. He did not sense my presence, but only heard the thunder of the voice. It shocked him because he is used to hearing my words from within his head—he had never before been aware of my voice as existing apart from him. In the dream state he has heard me giving him information. In these instances, however, he was the channel through which my voice came. He has often wondered about the nature of my own independence, and the kind of reality in which I exist.

He as also aware at the time that while the voice literally boomed out, no one else would have heard it. Yet the voice definitely came from outside of himself, and he certainly <u>seemed</u> to hear it with his physical ears.

("Can you tell us what the voice said?"

(Whispering:) Let me continue . . .

Ruburt acts as a receiver when I speak, and so I must make certain adjustments so that my message can be channeled under conditions that involve, among other things, his nervous system and physical apparatus. That evening, through using what I call interior sound,[5] I let Ruburt become acquainted with the power at my disposal so that he could realize that it did, basically now, come from beyond his personality as he understands it.

(12:02.) In regular sessions, as now, he and I again both make adjustments, and so in sessions I am what I call a bridge personality, composed of a composite self—Ruburt and I meeting and merging to form a personality that is not truly either of us, but a new one that exists between dimensions. Beyond that is my real identity.

Ruburt does extremely well with interior sound, and so I use that method rather than, say, an image to make my independent existence known. Now Ruburt called me originally *(last Saturday night)* at unconscious levels because he was upset with "earth programming." He thought that you needed some help from the outside, so to speak. That intent set up certain signals that reached into other realities or stations, an I answered. I was not speaking to Ruburt personally when he heard me, but addressing myself to the world at large in a program that was indeed picked up by others.

This program spread out and was translated by others in dream states. In physical terms, however, the message given that evening is still to be presented through these books.

Give us a moment . . . End of dictation.

(12:09. And so in his own way Seth answered my question of a few minutes ago. Now Jane paused, then came partially out of trance. "I know he said that was the end of book work," she told me, "but I think there's more on it. So if you'll get me a new pack of cigarettes. . . ." Then:)

Continue dictation: Now: In your local programming you have hosts of familiar characters, and at different times, in your terms, you have them play different roles. They take different roles. These often represent strong idealizations alive in the private and mass psyche. *(Humorously:)* Let me give you a brief example that will also show you how well I have learned your culture.

(Seth proceeded to name these currently famous television detectives.)

In their own ways, these are heroes representing the detective who is out to protect good against evil, to set things right. Now these characters exist more vividly in the minds of television viewers than the actors do who play those roles. The actors know themselves as apart from the roles. The viewers, however, identify with the characters. They may even dream about the characters. These have their own kind of superlife because they so clearly represent certain living aspects within each psyche.

The aspects are personified in the character. Through the centuries, in your terms, there have been different personalities, some physical and some not, with whom the species identified. Christ is one of these: in some respects the most ideal detective—in a different context, however—out to save the good and to protect the world from harm. In certain ways man also projected outward the idea of a devil or devils, and for somewhat the same reasons, so that he could identify with what he thought of as the unsavory portions of the psyche as he understood them at any given time. In between there are a multitude of such personalities, all vividly portraying parts of the psyche.

(12:21.) These characters become portions of the inner literature of the mind. Suppose an inhabitant from another reality saw [one of those three programs] and realized that people were watching it. Pretend he wanted to add more depth to the show. He might then come on himself in the guise of [the hero detective], but enlarging upon the characterization, adding more dimension to the plot. So, often when some personality from another station wants to help change the programming, he comes on in the form of a personality already known in fact or fiction. However, you must realize that that personality is larger than fact or fiction. "It" is independent at its own level, yet it is also a part of the portion of the private and mass psyche that is so represented.

I am Seth in those terms.

There are many myths connected with my name.[6] They all represent portions of the psyche as they were understood at various times in man's history. Those portions were originally projected out of the psyche as it began to understand itself, and personified its abilities and characteristics, forming superheroic characters of one kind or another, to which the psyche could then correspond and relate.

End of dictation.

(12:29. Then, after producing a couple of paragraphs on another matter:)

End of session—

("Okay.")

—and a fond good evening. I stop to give you a rest.

("I'm all right."

(With much amusement:) It shows you that I have concern.

("Yes. Well, thank you, Seth. Good night."

(End at 12:35 A.M. As we ate breakfast several hours later, Jane told me that during the night she'd kept waking up with ideas she thought were connected to "Unknown" Reality. When I asked her to write down what she could remember of them, she produced these items, with whatever distortions they may contain:)

"1. Some of the (hypnagogic) images you see in your mind prior to sleeping, and those at other times, are alternates—that is, you could see those pictures physically if you opened your eyes, instead of the ordinary reality you 'know' is there. Inner vision evolves physical sight, lining up exterior data into the kinds of images that correlate.

"2. Each reality is surrounded by its probabilities, but this is obviously relative . . .

"3. Our experience of the present is enriched by our memory of past perceptions. In some systems it works *the other way:* Inhabitants are aware of the future as we are of the past. On the other hand their 'memory' of the past fades almost at once.

"4. Again I received information on Atlantis, only to forget it right away. I'd wanted to tell Rob about it this morning. ... ."

(Jane also came through with material about Atlantis right after the 708th session was held, less than two weeks ago; see Appendix 3 in Volume 2 Part I. We'd described that episode briefly in ESP class the night before this [711th] session was held—so had our doing so caused her second Atlantis pickup? But it's also quite interesting to note that on both occasions Jane turned in to data on Atlantis within hours after Seth had discussed ideas involving alternate realities.)

NOTES: Session 711

1. A note added later: Seth puts the "home station of consciousness" analogy to good use in several more sessions for this volume. See the 716th session in Section 5, for instance.

2. In Note 4 for Session 702, in Volume 1, Seth briefly discussed "space travel" into another probability.

3. Refer to Seth's material on the basic unpredictability of consciousness, and on probabilities, in the 681st session in Volume 1 of *"Unknown" Reality.*

4. In Volume 1, see sessions 685–86, and Appendix 4.

5. See Note 4 for the 708th session.

6. About Seth's reference to the myths connected with his name: Set, or Seth, was an Egyptian god of evil (with an animal's head) whose complicated origins could, it's thought, reach back in antiquity to at least 7500 B.C. In Judaism, of course, Seth was the third son of Adam and Eve, after Cain and Abel (Genesis 4 & 5). (As one correspondent wrote us: "Seth is also a Hebrew name meaning "appointed"—i.e., the appointed one.") However, some very early priestly genealogies omit Cain and Abel, and consider Seth as the oldest son of Adam; in the second century A.D., for instance, the Sethites, who were members of a little-known Gnostic sect, thought of Seth, the son of Adam, as the Messiah. Seth also shows up in writings of the ancient occult religious philosophy, the cabala, which was originated by certain Jewish rabbis who sought to interpret the scriptures through numerical values; the soul of Seth is seen as infusing Moses; he was to reappear as the Messiah. . . .

Perhaps it's been remiss in our parts, but Jane and I haven't concerned ourselves with any connections *her* Seth may have with ancient Seths. We don't believe such relationships exist on any kind of personalized basis, although someday we'll ask Seth to comment here. We think the name of Jane's Seth came about through much more pragmatic needs. In Chapter 1 of *The Seth Material*, Jane quoted Seth-to-be from the 4th session for December 8, 1963, as that personality same through on the Ouija board (which we'd used to initiate these sessions): "You may call me whatever you choose. I call myself Seth. It fits the me of me. . . ." Reincarnation had been mentioned by the 2nd session, but since the concept meant little to us we hardly considered the many names that would be involved. Once Seth gave us a name by which to call him, we simply began using it. I'm sure that at the time Jane had no conscious knowledge about Egyptian, Hebrew, or even Christian origins or uses connected with the name, Seth.

Now I present Seth in part from the ESP class session for April 17, 1973, as he answered students' questions:

"So I ask you: 'What is your name, each of you?' My name is nameless. I have no name. I give you the name of Seth because it is a name and you want names. You give yourselves names . . . because you believe they are important.

"Your existence is nameless. It is not voiceless, but it is nameless. The names you take are structures upon which you hang your images . . . What you are cannot be uttered, and no letter or alphabet can contain it. Yet, now you need words and letters, and names and objects. You want magic that will tell you what you are.

"You believe that you cannot speak to me unless I have a name, so I am Seth . . . I told Ruburt from our earliest sessions that he could call me Seth. I never said, 'My name is Seth,' (but 'I call myself Seth'—my emphasis), for I am nameless. I have had too many identities to cling to one name!''

Seth treats his own reincarnational background both generally and specifically, if rather briefly on both counts, in Chapter 22 of *Seth Speaks*. For the names of three of his past personalities as given in that chapter, see sessions 588–89. A fourth name (as well as names for Jane and me) can be found in the 595th session in the Appendix of *Seth Speaks*.

Session 712

□

October 16, 1974
9:13 P.M. Wednesday

(No session was held Monday night, October 14, as scheduled. Jane was busy instead doing a program for a radio station in a western state, live, via telephone from our living room in Elmira. She sat at her desk and was interviewed by the program's host, then answered questions from listeners. The show went well. In Volume 1, see the notes leading off the 702nd session.

(After supper this evening Jane received from Seth [without subjectively hearing his voice] information that the session would contain material about "probability clusters." We liked the term. but not until Seth began discussing the subject did I realize that Jane had tuned in to it herself following last Wednesday night's session. It appears at the end of that [711th] session as item No. 2 on the list of topics she came up with during the sleep state.

(In ESP class yesterday evening Jane engaged in one of her periodic and unusual "long-sound experiences," as we call them. Seth goes into her adventure in consciousness after first break.)

Good evening.

("Good evening, Seth.")

Now: Dictation: As per Ruburt's notes, each system of reality is indeed surrounded by its probable realities, though any one of those "probable realities" can be used as the hub, or core reality; in which case all of the others will then be seen as probable. In other words, relativity certainly applies here.

The rockbed reality is the one in which the perceiver is focused. From that standpoint all others would seem peripheral. Taking that for granted, however, any given reality system will be surrounded by its probability clusters. These can almost be thought of as satellites. Time and space need not be connected, however—that is, the attractions that exist between a reality and any given probability cluster may have nothing to do with time and space at all. The closest probability satellite to any given reality may, for example, be in an entirely different universe altogether. *(Pause.)* In that regard, you may find brethren more or less like yourselves outside of your own universe—as you <u>think</u> of it—rather than inside it. You imagine your universe as extending outward in space (and backwards in time). You think of it as an exteriorized manifestation, expanding perhaps, but in an exterior rather than an interior fashion.[1]

(Slowly:) Your idea of space travel, for example, is to journey over the "skin of your universe." You do not understand that your system is indeed expanding within itself, bringing forth new creativity and <u>energy</u> (underlined).

Give us time . . . Your universe is only one of many. Each one creates probable versions of itself. When you journey on the earth you move around the outside of it. So far, your ideas of space travel involve that kind of surface navigation. Earth trips, however, are made with the recognition of their surface nature.[2] When you think in terms of traveling to other planets or to other galaxies, though, the same kind of surface travel is involved. As closely as I can <u>around</u> space rather than directly <u>through</u> it.

(9:40.) Give us time . . . You are also viewing your solar system through your own time perspective, which is relative. You "look backward into time," you say, when you stare outward into the universe. You could as well look into the future, of course. Your own coordinates[3] close you off from recognizing that there are indeed other intelligences alive even <u>within</u> your own solar system. You will never meet them in your exterior reality, however, for you are not focused in the time period of their existence. You may physically visit the "very same planet" on which they reside, but to <u>you</u> the planet will appear barren, or not able to support life.

In the same way, others can visit your planet with the same results. There is then a whole great inner dimension even to the space that you know, that you do not perceive. There are intelligent beings outside of your own galaxy, "adjacent" to you. Theoretically, you can visit them with some vast improvements in your technology, but great amounts of time would be involved. Others have visited your own planet in that particular fashion. Yours is still a linear technology. Some intelligent beings have visited your planet, finding not the world you know but a probable one.[4] There are always feedbacks between probable systems. A dominant species in one may appear as a bizarre trace species in another. More will be said about this and your planet later in the book.[5] The <u>closest</u> equivalent to your own kind of intelligence and being can actually be found not by following the outer skin of space, but by going <u>through</u> it, so to speak.

Give us time . . . There are, again, inner coordinates having to do with the inner behavior of electrons. If you understood these, then such travel <u>could</u> be relatively instantaneous. The coordinates that link you with others who are more or less of your kind have to do with psychic and psychological intersections that result in a like space-time framework.

Here I would like to give a very simple example, evocative of what I mean. The other day Ruburt received a telephone call from a woman in California who was in difficulty. Ruburt promised to send [healing] energy. Hanging up, he closed his eyes and imagined energy being sent out from a universal source through his own body, and directed toward the person in need. When he did so, Ruburt mentally saw a long "heavy" beam extending straight to the west from a point between his eyes. It reached without impediment. He felt that this extension was composed of energy, and it seemed so <u>strong</u> that a person could walk upon it without difficulty. Subjectively he felt that this beam of energy reached its destination. And so it did.[6]

Energy was almost instantly transmitted across the continent from one specific individual to another. When you are dealing with that kind of energy, and particularly when you believe in it, space does not matter. Emotional connections are set up and form their own set of coordinates. *[Pause.]* That beam of energy is as strong and real as a beam of steel, through it moves faster than a beam of light.

(10:09.) If Ruburt had tried to visit the woman by plane he would have followed the curve of the earth, but in those terms the energy went through in the "straightest" way.[7]

("But not through the earth?" I asked. Whereupon Seth re-

peated his last sentence three times. That was the answer he wanted to give.)

The psychic and emotional communication, then, cut through physical coordinates. Ruburt was momentarily allied with the woman.

Now: In the same way you can be allied and in tune with other probabilities that do not coincide with your space-time axis. The exterior universe with its galaxies—as you understand it, and on that level of activity—can be encountered on certain rigid space-time coordinates. You can visit other planets only in your present (underlined). Your present may be the past or the future as far as inhabitants of a given planet are concerned. Your physical senses will only operate in their and your present.

"Effective" space travel, creative space travel on your part, will not occur until you learn that your space-time system is one focus. Otherwise you will seem to visit one dead world after another, blind to civilizations that may exist on any of them. Some of these difficulties could be transcended if you learned to understand the miraculous multidimensionality of even your own physical structure, and allowed your consciousness some of its greater freedom.

To some extent you have neurologically blinded yourselves. You accept only a certain range of neurological impulses as "reality."[8] You have biologically prejudiced yourselves. The physical structure is innately aware of many more valid versions of reality than you allow it to be.

Theoretically, a thoroughly educated space traveler in your time, landing upon a strange planet, would be able to adjust his own consciousness that he could perceive the planet in various "sequences" of time. If you land upon a planet in a spaceship and find volcanos, you would, perhaps, realize that other portions of that planet might show different faces. You have confidence in your ability to move through space, so you might then explore the terrain that you could not see from your original landing point. If you did not understand the change in qualities of space, you might imagine that the whole planet was a giant volcano.

You do not understand as yet, however, that in a way you can move through time as you move through space—and until you understand that, you will not know the meaning of a true journey, or be able to thoroughly explore any planet—or any reality, <u>including your own.</u>

You imagine that your own earth is mapped out, and all frontiers known, but the linear aspects of your planet's life represent a most minute portion of its reality.

Take your break.

(10:24. Jane told me that Seth had been "really there," although her delivery hadn't seemed to be any stronger or faster, say, than it usually is when she's under. She added that the material had appeared to be endless, and that Seth had called for a break now only so that we could rest before he launched into the next block of data—for that too was already "there."

(Rain had fallen in a fine drizzle throughout most of the day; and now, I saw from our second-story living room windows, a heavy fog lay over the street corner below and the newly finished Walnut Bridge just south of the intersection. The whole area had a warm dispersed glow from the bridge's lights.

(Resume in the same manner at 10:45.)

The portions of the psyche reflect and create the portions of the universe from this most minute to its greatest part. You identify with one small section of your psyche, and so you name as reality only one small spect of the universe.

New paragraph. In class last evening Ruburt "picked up" messages that <u>seemed</u> to be too slow for his neurological structure. He was convinced that it would take many hours of your time in order to translate perhaps a simple clear paragraph of what he was receiving. He experienced some strain, feeling that each vowel and syllable was so drawn out, in your terms of time, that he must either slow down his own neurological workings to try to make some suitable adjustments. He chose the latter. Messages, therefore, perceptions, "came through" at one speed, so to speak, and he managed to receive them while translating them into a more comfortable, neurologically familiar speed.

One part of Ruburt accepted the "slow" [or "long"] perceptions, while another part quickened them into something like normal speech patterns. Some communication did result.[9]

What he was sensing, however, as an entirely different kind of reality. He was beginning to recognize another synapse [neuronal] pattern not "native"; he was familiarizing himself with perceptions at a different set of coordinate points. Such activity automatically alters the nature of time in your experience, and is indicative of intersections of your consciousness with another kind of consciousness. That particular type of consciousness operates "at different speeds" than your own. Biologically, your own physical structures are quite able to operate at those same speeds, though as a species you have disciplined yourselves to a different kind of neurological reaction. By altering such neurological prejudice,[10] however, you can indeed learn to become aware of other realities that coincide with yours. Period.

Now: Electrons themselves operate at different "speeds." The structure of the atom that you recognize, and its activity, is in larger terms one probable version of an atom.[11] Your consciousness, as it is allied with the flesh, follows the activity of atoms as far as it is reflected in your system of reality.

Ruburt is learning to minutely experience—change that—Ruburt is learning to minutely alter his experience with the probable atomic correlations that exist quite as validly as does the particular kind of atomic integrity that you generally recognize. When he does so, in your terms, he alters atomic receptivity. This automatically brings probabilities to the forefront. To perceive other realities you alter your own coordinates, tuning them in to other systems and attracting those into your focus.

Now take a break or end the session as you prefer.

("We'll take the break."

(11:08 to 11:26.)

Now: To some extent or another there are counterparts[12] of all realities within your psyche. When you slow down, or quicken your thoughts or your perceptions, you automatically begin to alter your focus, to step aside from your officially recognized existence. This is highly important, for in certain terms you are indeed transcending the time framework that you imagine to be so real.

In other terms, certain portions of your own reality have long since "vanished" in the unrecognized death that your own sense of continuity has so nicely straddled. Your personal cluster of probable realities surrounds you, again, on a cellular basis, and biologically your physical body steers its own line, finding its balance operating in a cluster of probabilities while maintaining the focus that is your own. You can even learn to tune in to the cellular comprehension. It will help you realize that your consciousness is not as limited as you suppose. All realities emerge from the psyche, and from the CU's *(the units of consciousness)* that compose it.

(Heartily:) End of dictation. Give us a moment. . . .

*(11:38. Now Jane came through with several pages of material for herself. Some of it was quite personal, but one part consisted of Seth's response to an assessment she'd written after supper tonight, wherein she examined her progress since the inauguration of her psychic abilities late in 1963. Seth, here, adds to our understanding of Jane's reactions to some of the challenges she took up 11 years ago. His material is also an extension of much that he gave in the 679th session for Volume 1 of "*Unknown*" Reality, when he discussed the early background of the probable Jane who chose to live in* this *physical reality, and how* that *Jane began to contend with her strongly mystical nature. See especially Note 8 for Session 679, and Appendix 1.)*

The paper Ruburt wrote this evening is pertinent, and highly significant. Have him show it to you. Indeed, though he dislikes the word, he is finishing the first portion of his "apprenticeship"— in which he became acquainted with a different kind of reality, and had to learn how to equate it with the "normal" one.

Certain strains were involved that in one way were as natural as growing pains. This has nothing to do with so-called psychic phenomena, but the natural growth and development of a personality whenever it tries to go beyond its space and time context, and takes on challenges of such a nature.

In one way, on one level, such a personality seems to be operating "blind," while in another it is aware of its accomplishments and challenges. Often a situation of underbalance is set up that would not exist had the personality not accepted the challenges and, hence, the potentials for an even greater development.

The more prosaic elements of the personality then take whatever measures seem necessary at the time, while new orientation is tried out. These methods may seem to lead to great distortions, particularly in contrast with the sensed possibilities of development. In one way or another, however, they still provide a framework in which the personality feels itself free to pursue its goals. The built-in impetuses provides clue points. When the new sensed reality is strong enough to provide not only greater comprehensions but also to construct a new framework, then the old framework is seen as limiting, and discarded.

Elements in your lives were experienced as negative simply because Ruburt was not sure of himself. Pleas for help *(directed to Jane as well as Seth)* were seen as demands—not as opportunities to use abilities—so he felt hounded. He was not sure enough of his new world; he as still enough a part of the old one so that he often saw his life and abilities through the eyes of the "old world inhabitants"—the others who might scorn him, or set him up for ridicule.[13] They represented portions of his own psyche still at that level of consciousness, not having quite assimilated the greater knowledge or experience, so he felt he needed protection—the protection that would . . . cleverly . . . serve all of his purposes, allowing him to go ahead as he wanted to . . . that would keep him at home working, and yet also serve as a control against too much inner spontaneity until he learned that he could indeed trust the new world of experience.

(Then later:) There is far more I could say. The time this evening does not permit it, though I can talk as long as you can write.

My consciousness does not normally operate at the same speeds as yours, either *(see Note 9),* so in my terms what I am saying has long ago been said, while in your present it is new, or just reaching you.

(And later yet:) Ruburt should have another experience involving me or my voice . . .

And now *(emphatically, but with a smile)* I bid you a fond—and indeed the most fond of good evenings.

("Thank you, Seth. Good night."

(End at 12:01 A.M.

(A note added after Seth had completed his dictation for "Unknown" Reality in April 1975: the 712th session was held on October 16, 1974. In her notes at the beginning of the 710th session, Jane described how she'd heard Seth's very powerful voice in her sleep state during the night of October 5. I can write now that she has yet to have any subsequent, similar kind of encounter with Seth or his voice.)

NOTES: Session 712

1. Jane delivered this material for Seth in the 42nd session for April 8, 1964: "The universe is continually being created . . . as all universe are . . . and the appearance of expansion seen by your scientists is distortive for many reasons.

"Their time measurements, based on camouflage [physical information] to begin with, are almost riotously inadequate and bound to give distortive data, since the universe simply cannot be measured in those terms. The universe was not created at any particular time, but neither is it expanding into nowhere like an inflated balloon that grows forever larger—at least not along the lines now being considered. The expansion is an illusion, based among other things upon inadequate time measurements, and cause-and-effect theories; and yet in some manners the universe could be said to be expanding, but with entirely different connotations than are usually used."

From the 43rd session: "The universe is expanding in the way that a dream does . . . this is a most basic manner is more like the growth of an idea."

At the beginning of Appendix 1 in Volume 2 Part I, see the longer presentation from the 44th session for Seth's discussion of "the value climate of psychological reality"—the "medium" that spontaneously contains within it all of our camouflage constructions of space, time, growth, and durability. Note 2 for Appendix 1 also fits in here, especially Seth's references within it to our endless questions about the beginning and ending of the physical universe.

From the 250th session for April 11, 1966: "The atom you 'see' does not grow larger in mass, or expand outward in your space, and neither does your universe."

Seth's material in those early sessions, given well over a decade ago for the most part, reflected of course his reactions to current astronomical theory about the state—and fate—of our physical (camouflage) universe. The idea of an infinitely expanding universe, with all of its stars ultimately burned out and all life extinct, is still the view largely accepted today; it's based on the red shift measurements of some of the supposedly receding galaxies, their apparent brightnesses, the "missing mass" of the universe, and other very technical data. Yet I find it most interesting to note that now some astrophysicists and mathematicians believe our universe may be destined to contract—indeed, to collapse in upon itself—after all. But again, these ideas aren't based on the kind of thinking Seth espouses (that consciousness comes first, that its creations are continuous), but upon other quite complicated camouflage observations and measurements. One of these is the discovery of at least of that missing mass, thus indicating that gravitational fields may exist among the galaxies, and galactic clusters, strong enough not only to halt the expansion of the universe but to pull all matter back together again.

In scientific terms, it does seem likely that the conflict between the two views will ever be resolved, or any decision reached that our universe may be an oscillating one, forever contracting and expanding. There are too many variables in measurement and interpretation, includ-

ing the difficulties the human mind encounters when it attempts to grasp
the enormous spans of time and space involved.

I hasten to add that it's only of academic interest to us, though,
whether the universe disperses itself through an eternity of frozen expansion or compresses itself into a cosmic fireball of unbelievable proportions. Our scientists have projected either ending many billions of years
into the future, although in the meantime, "only" an estimated five
billion years from now, our own aging, exploding sun will have con-
sumed the inner planets of the solar system—including the earth.

2. Just as he talks here about the surface nature of our travel, in
Volume 1 of *"Unknown" Reality* Seth had a similar observation to
make about our ideas of time; see the 688th session after 10:26: "Again,
you live on the Surface of the moments, with no understanding of the
unrecognized and unofficial realities that lie beneath."

3. Seth began discussing coordinate points in Chapter 5 of *Seth
Speaks*. See the 524th session: "Other kinds of consciousness coexist
within the same 'space' that your world inhabits. They do not perceive
your physical objects, for their reality is composed of a different camouflage structure. This *is* a general statement, however, for various points
of your realities can and do coincide . . . points of what you would call
double reality, containing great energy potential . . . where our realities
merge."

4. For one instance when Seth discussed our coming attempts at space
travel, see Note 4 for Session 702, in Volume 1. Here's part of the
material I quoted from the 40th session: "It is very possible that you
might end up in what you intend as space venture only to discover that
you have 'traveled' to another plane [probability]. But at first you will
not know the difference."

Then, in the Appendix of *Seth Speaks*, see the transcript of the ESP
class session for January 12, 1971. Certain sightings of UFO (unidentified flying objects), Seth told class members, represented the appearance
of visitors from other *realities*, rather than from elsewhere in our own
universe.

5. But, regrettably, it isn't. . . .

6. In this particular case, subsequent correspondence seemed to confirm that the energy sent out by Jane had indeed been on target; its
recipient reported quite beneficial results. I write "seemed to confirm"
because we made no attempt to verify any results here except to check
the time elements involved. Jane and I do our thing by ourselves. It
would take a considerable organization of trained investigators, and
much time, to thoroughly study the results of such projections of energy.
There could be many reasons why the receiver would benefit from
attempts to give that kind of assistance, though; one of them being the
simple knowledge that someone else—the "sender," Jane—cared enough
to try to help. But we do think that more than just suggestion is involved.

7. Of the books on astronomy that I've read (and I'm way short of scanning any great number of them, obviously), only one contains a brief mention of a similar notion in connection with space travel—that is, journeying almost instantaneously in a straight line between planets instead of following the relativistic *curve* of space. The volume's learned author treats the idea as just an idea, however, and a pretty far-out one at that—while here Jane demonstrated her version of the same principle in a practical way. See Note 2 for Session 709.

(An aside: As I wrote this note I asked Jane if she'd seen the appropriate passage in the astronomical text. She wasn't sure. She'd skimmed the whole thing one day recently without trying to read it. "Well," I said, joking, "you've just about lost your chance. The book's overdue at the library and I'm taking it back tomorrow. . . ." But she didn't look at it again.)

A few days after the episode Seth describes in this session had taken place, Jane had another experience with such a beam of energy. This time she lay on her side facing north after we'd retired, for she wanted to send help to a very ill person in a small town in Canada. She felt the transmission go out from her forehead in a straight line toward its destination. She was physically uncomfortable as she lay on her left side, however, so after a few moments she turned over. The movement shut off the beam. After she'd settled down on her *right* side, she felt it go out again—but from the *back* of her head now, and still traveling truly north to its Canadian goal.

Jane is often aware of her "beam of energy," or variations of it, when she's reaching out to others. There's at least an evocative analogy here with the behavior of neutrinos, which are fundamental subatomic "particles." Generated by the nuclear reactions in the cores of stars, neutrinos travel at the speed of light. They have practically no mass, no electric charge, and hardly ever interact with matter. Not only can they pass through the earth, they can traverse the universe itself without losing much of their energy.

8. See Appendix 4 in Volume 1.

9. With some wonder I can write that our average-sized living room had been more than crowded last night: Well over 30 people were present for ESP class. Very few of them had witnessed one of Jane's infrequent "long sound" sessions, as we call them, although a fair number had heard us describe the phenomenon at one time or another. Seth had also referred to it. I seldom take notes in class or use a tape recorder, preferring to be free to engage in the class's spontaneous development. Usually quite a few people will tape a class, yet last night it happened that only two did so. The results were unfortunate, as I'll explain later.

These notes deal with Jane's experiences in this week's class (held in October 1974). I made a verbatim record of her first encounter with

slow, or long, sound in the 612th session for September 6, 1972, just
about a year after she'd finished *Seth Speaks*. Since the material in that
session wasn't covered in *Personal Reality* or *Adventures*, we're publishing most of it as an appendix for this volume.* Not only will it
illuminate these notes; it will also link, if loosely, Seth's reality, Seth
Two, and some other "rapid" effects. There's much to be learned here,
and perhaps eventually we'll be able to do something about that.

Chapter 2 of *Seth Speaks* contains two short passages from Seth that I
find very reminiscent of Jane's expression of long sound. See Session
514 for February 9, 1970: 1. "We can follow a consciousness through
all of its forms, for example, and in your terms, within the flicker of an
eye." 2. ". . . for we can spend a century as a tree or as an uncompli-
cated life form in another reality."

After she'd grappled with her reception of some long-sound material
last night, Jane spoke a few words for Seth. It was then that we began to
glimpse what we could call a "source" of the long material—for Jane
told class that from our physical viewpoint "Seth's true reality had
sounded like a mountain" to her. It had been "that slow, that massive,
that powerful. I slow down . . . like a mountain, and feel trees grow."
By making a strong effort she'd speeded up her reception of him so that
he came through sounding like the familiar Seth. Thus she gained new
insights into Seth and his home environment. And from that much
larger, more encompassing reality, Seth could follow a consciousness in
our camouflage world through all of its forms "within the flicker of an
eye."

Jane had to renew her very strict control each time she tried to
transmit long data, however; I could see that otherwise she'd slide into
an extremely slow delivery. That happened often. Then it would take her
many minutes to contend with a single syllable; her tongue worked
persistently at the "sal" in "universal" for example, but even so all that
issued from her was an elongated hissing sound based upon the "s"
alone.

As the evening passed Jane told class that she'd kept Seth's "true
reality rhythm-speed" to her left and, she hoped, would speak an
understandable translation of it, speeded up for our cognition, to her
right. "But I keep getting pulled back into a more true expression of
Seth's reality. . . ." She could manage only a few words at a time from
the Seth we were used to.

Now for the unfortunate results I mentioned near the beginning of this
note: Of the two cassette tape recorders that had been operated by class
members last night, one malfunctioned throughout the evening, unknown to its owner, and so recorded no class material at all. The other
recorder's tape snapped just before Jane finally succeeded in consistently

---

*See Appendix 8 in Volume 2 Part I

uniting Seth's slow, or long, reality with the accelerated version we ordinarily hear. For a few minutes, then, she was able to speak for Seth about his home environment—but since the information wasn't recorded I have nothing to quote here. By then class was nearly over. I don't want to try reconstructing Seth from memory, but will note that his material took off from some of that in the 612th session (see Appendix 19).

From its owner Jane and I borrowed the one incomplete class tape that had been made. As we'd expected, her long-sound experiences hadn't recorded well at all. The key episodes had been more visible than verbal. While Jane had been straining to compress a long syllable into something recognizable, the tape picked up little except distracting background noises: class people coughing, or moving about or shuffling papers; the sounds of traffic . . . But Jane and I take class events as they come. Otherwise we'd be continually involved in note-taking, making tapes, and so forth.

A note added later: Of course, nowhere in the 712th session did Seth come right out and say that in class the night before Jane had tried to express her version of his "own true reality." Strange it may be, but I didn't catch this during the session, nor did either of us notice it for some time afterward. And for whatever reasons, with the exception of one rather oblique reference at the end of this (712th) session, Seth himself chose to discuss the whole class adventure from quite a detached viewpoint.

10. In Chapter 6 of *Adventures*, see Jane's discussion of "prejudiced perception," which in "our reality is characterized as much by the kind of events it excludes as by those it embraces."

In Volume 1 of *"Unknown" Reality*, see Session 686 at 12:19 for Seth's account of Jane's "Saratoga experience," with its altered neurological connotations.

11. In Volume 1, see these two sessions: the 694th to 10:00 P.M., and the 702nd, with Note 6. In Volume 2 Part I, see Note 24 for Appendix 7.

12. A note added later: See the 721st session, with its Appendix 21.

13. See Appendix 10 in Volume 1. In Volume 2, see the 708th session after 11:40, and (added a few days later) the opening notes for Session 713. All of these passages show Jane's attempts to understand her abilities and beliefs, and to relate them to herself and to the world in general.

Session 713

□

October 21, 1974
9:28 P.M. Monday

("The truth is," Jane said to me the other evening, "I'm alone in this psychic thing. I'm the one who's got to do it. . . ." We were discussing the material Seth had given after 11:38 in the last [712th] session; he'd talked about some of the strains Jane had experienced while serving "the first portion of her apprenticeship" in the development of her psychic abilities. I've heard her say the same thing before, of course; see Note 13 for the 712th session. Basically, her examination of her inner dimensions must be a solitary one. When she began the sessions over 11 years ago, we requested advice and help from a few people,[1] but as we slowly began to understand the very personal nature of her gifts we realized that she'd have to find her own answers as she went along, with whatever help I could learn to offer.

(Those circumstances might have acted as a leavening factor in the early years, perhaps to a mild degree helping determine the direction of some of Jane's psychic explorations, with and without Seth. Much more important is that she's always wanted to do her own thing. Besides, how would she ask advice from another about such an individual, intuitive quality as, say, the next step to take in her psychic growth? These notes make her quest appear to be much simpler than it actually was—and is.[2]

(This afternoon Jane told me that in her sleep last night she'd had bleed-throughs from Seth about the material to come next in his book. She described it to me—and tonight Seth followed that subject matter very closely in the first part of the session. I

suggest the reader review the 711th session in connection with this evening's data to 11:26.)

Good evening.

("Good evening, Seth.")

Dictation. Give us a moment. . . .

(Long Pause.) It might help here if you imagine the psyche again as some multidimensional living television set. In what seems to be the small space of the screen many programs are going on, though you can tune in to only one at a time.

In a manner of speaking, however, all of the other programs are "latent" in the one you are watching. There are coordinates that unite them all. There is a give-and-take quite invisible to you between one program and another, and action within one, again, affects the action within each of the others.

Like this imaginary multidimensional television, the psyche contains within it other programs than the one in which you are acting—other plots, environments, and world situations. Theoretically you can indeed momentarily "walk out of" your program into another as easily, when you know how, as you now move from one room to another. You must know that the other programs exist or the possibility of such action will not occur to you. In larger terms all of the programs are but portions of one, colon: The various sets are real, however, and the characters quite alive.

Now: Actors playing parts are obviously alive, as actors, but in a fictional play, for example, the characters portrayed by the actors are not alive, in your terms, in the same fashion that the actors are. In the psyche, however, and in its greater reality, the characters have their own lives—quite as real as those of the actors.

Think again of the psyche in the manner mentioned, taking it for granted that the program now on the screen is a fully dimensioned reality, and that hidden somehow in its very elements are all of the other programs not showing. These are not lined up in space behind the "front" program, but in a completely different way contained within it. The point of any image at any given time in the picture showing might represent, for example, a top hat on a table. Everyone acting in that scene would view the hat and the table, and react accordingly with their own individual characteristics.

Give us a moment . . . The hat on the table, while possessing all of the necessary paraphernalia of reality for that scene, might also, however, serve as different kind of reference point for one of the other programs simultaneously occurring. In that reality, say program two, the entire configuration of hat and table may be meaningless, while still being interpreted in an entirely different way from a quite different perspective. There in program two the table might be a flat natural plain, and the hat an oddly shaped structure upon it—a natural rather than a manufactured one. Objects in your reality have an entirely different aspect in another. Any of the objects shown in the program you are watching, then, may be used as a different kind of reference point in another reality, in which those objects appear as something else.

(9:50.) We are trying to make an analogy here on two levels, so please bear with me. In terms of your psyche, each of your own thoughts and actions exist not only in the manner with which you are familiar with them, but also in many other forms that you do not perceive, colon: forms that may appear as natural events in a different dimension than your own, as dream images, and even as self-propelling energy. No energy is ever lost. The energy within your own thoughts, then, does not dissipate even when you yourself have finished with them. Their energy has reality in other worlds.[3]

Now imagine that the picture on the television screen shows your own universe. Your idea of space travel would be to send a ship from one planet, earth, outward into the rest of space that you perceive on the "flat" screen. Even with your projected technology, this would involve great elements of time. Imagine here, now, that the screen's picture is off-center to begin with, so that everything is distorted to some extent, and going out into space seems to be going backward into time.

(Pause.) If the picture were magically centered, then all "time" would be seen to flow out from the instant moment[4] of perception, the private now; and in many ways the mass now, or mass perception, represents the overall now-point of your planet. From that now, "time" goes out in all probable directions. Actually it also goes inward in all probable directions.

(Slowly:) The simple picture of the universe that you see on our screen, therefore, represents a view from your own now-perspective—but each star, planet, galaxy or whatever is made up of other reference points in which, to put it simply, the same

patterns have different kinds of reality. True space travel would of course be time-space travel,[5] in which you learned how to use points in your own universe as "dimensional clues" that would serve as entry points into other worlds. Otherwise you are simply flying like an insect around the outside of the television set, trying to light on the fruit, say, that is shown upon the screen—and wondering, like a poor bemused fly, why you cannot. You use one main focus in your reality. In the outside world this means that you have a "clear picture." *(Humorously:)* There is no snow! That physical program is the one you are acting in, alive in, and it is the one shown on the screen. The screen is the part of your psyche upon which you are concentrating. You not only tune in the picture but you also create the props, the entire history of the life and times, hyphen—but in living three-dimensional terms, and "you" are within that picture.

The kind of reality thus created by that portion of your consciousness forms a given kind of experience. It is valid and real. When you want to travel, you do so within the dimensions of the reality thus created. If you drive or fly from one city to another, you do not consider the journey imaginary. You are exploring the dimensions given.

(10:18.) Now: If you alter that picture a little so that the images are somewhat scrambled—and you do this by altering the focus of your consciousness—then the familiar coordination is gone. Objects may appear blurred, ordinary sounds distorted. It seems as if you are on the outskirts of your own reality. In such a state, however, it is easy to see that your usual orientation may be but one of many frames of reference. *(Pause.)* If you did change the focus of your consciousness still further, you might then "bring in" another picture entirely. On the outside this would give you another reality. *(Intently:)* In it your "old" reality might still be somewhat perceivable as a ghost image,[6] if you knew what to look for and remembered your former coordinates. On the inside, however, you would be traveling not around or about, but through one portion of the psyche with its reality, into another portion of the psyche with its reality. That kind of journey would not be any more imaginary than a trip from one city to another.

There are space-time coordinates that operate from your viewpoint—and space travel from the standpoint of your time, made along the axis of your space, will be a relatively sterile

procedure. (In parentheses: Some reported instances of UFO's
happened in the past as far as the visitors were concerned, but
appeared as images or realities in your present. This involves
craft sightings only.*)

Give us time . . . When you change your ordinary television
set from one station to another you may encounter snow or
distortion. If something is wrong with the set you may simply
tune in patterns that seem meaningless and carry no particular
program. You may have sound without a picture, and sometimes
even a picture but sound from another program. So when you
begin to experiment with states of altered consciousness you
often run into the same kind of phenomena, when nothing seems
to make sense.

(10:32.) Currently, physicists have made some important break-
throughs, but they do not recognize their significance. The universe that you know is full of microscopic black holes and white
holes,[7] for example. Since your scientists have themselves given
these labels, then using those terms I will say (*with much gentle
humor*) that there are red, green, orange and purple holes—that
is, the so-called black holes and white holes only represent what
physicists have so far deduced about the deeper properties of
your universe, and the way that certain coordinate points in one
world operate, as providing feed-through into another.

Nothing exists outside the psyche, however, that does not
exist within it, and there is no unknown world that does not have
its psychological or psychic counterpart. Man learned to fly as he
tried to <u>exteriorize</u> inner experience, for in out-of-body states in
dreams he had long been familiar with flight. All excursions into
outer reality come as the psyche attempts to reproduce in any
given "exterior" world the inner freedom of its being.

Men have also visited other worlds through the ages. Others
have visited your world. In dreams, and in altered states through
history as you accept it, men have been taken upon such journeys. On their return they almost always interpreted their experiences in terms of their home programs, intertwining what happened
into what ended up as great myths and stories—real but not real.

Take your break.

*(10:45. "Man," Jane said after quickly leaving an excellent
dissociated state, "is he going to town. There's just tons of*

---

*See Appendix 9, Volume 2 Part I

material there, all ready and waiting. . . ." I could tell that this was the case: Her delivery had reached a steady, quiet yet driving level that she seemed capable of maintaining indefinitely.

(Jane commented here on something I'd also become aware of in recent sessions. For whatever reasons since holding the 709th session, she hasn't had to wait for that certain, more "difficult" kind of trance to develop before launching into Seth's book material; see the note at 10:55 for that session. In some fashion she can't describe, Jane is now able to reach the "right" trance state, or to arrive at it, much more easily. For other contrasting examples, in Volume 1 see the notes closing out sessions 688 and 703, as well as related material in Appendix 4, wherein I wrote about the translation challenges she's often faced since beginning "Unknown" Reality: "—hence her talk before many of these sessions . . . about attaining that 'certain clear focus,' or 'the one clearest place in consciousness,' before she began speaking for Seth."

("I get the strangest feeling of 'folded time' during the sessions," Jane continued. "I'm caught. I can get more on the book, or some on me. I don't know what to do. I know the book stuff is all right there—but it takes time to get it. It's too bad I can't get it instantaneously.[8] I really want both sets of material, so I guess I'll wait and see what happens. . . ."

(Resume in the same manner at 11:01.)

While all of this may sound quite esoteric, it is highly practical, and we are dealing with the nature of creativity itself.

Your thoughts, for example, and your intents, have their own validity and force. You set them into motion, but then they follow their own laws and realities. All creativity comes from the psyche. I [recently] suggested a project to Ruburt's class—one that will ultimately illuminate many of the points I am making in *"Unknown" Reality*. I suggested that Ruburt's students create a "city"[9] at another level of reality. This is not to be a pie-in-the-sky sort of thing, or some "heaven" hanging suspended above, but a very valid meeting place between worlds. A psychic marketplace, for example, where ideas are exchanged, a place of psychic commerce, a pleasant environment with quite definite coordinates, established as an "orbiting satellite" on the outskirts of your world.

Initially, all worlds are created in just that fashion.

In certain terms, then, this involves in a very small way the creation and colonization of a different kind of reality— consciously accepted, however, from your perspective. On an unconscious level, the world as you know it expands in just such a fashion.[10] Several students have had dreams involving their participation in such a project. Ruburt found himself in an out-of-body state, looking at a jacket. It had four rectangular pockets. It was giant-sized. As he looked at it the front flap was open. In the dream he flew through this flap literally into another dimension, where the point of the flap was a hill upon which he landed. From that second perspective, the pockets of the jacket in the first perspective became the windows of a building that existed in a still-further, third dimension beyond the hill. Standing on the hill, he knew that in Perspective One the windows of the building in Perspective Three were jacket pockets, but he could no longer perceive them as such. Looking out from the hill in Perspective Two, Perspective One was invisibly behind him, and Perspective Three was still "ahead" of him, separated from him by a gulf he did not understand.

(11:15) He knew, however, that if the shades were pulled in the windows in Perspective Three, then the jacket-pocket flaps would appear to be closed in Perspective One. He also realized he had been directing the erection of the building in Perspective Three by making the jacket *(in Perspective One).*

When he approached the hill in Perspective Two, he spoke to the contractor who was there before him. Ruburt said that he wanted to change the design. The contractor agreed, and shouted orders to people who were working in Perspective Three, where the building stood.

Now: Ruburt <u>was</u> validly involved in the erection of that building, and he did indeed travel through various dimensions in which the objects in one represented something entirely different in another. He used the particular symbols, however, simply to bring the theory home to him, but it represented the fact that any given object in one dimension has its own reality in another. You cannot move through time and space without altering the focus of your psyche. *(Intently:)* <u>When you so alter that focus</u>, however, you also change the exterior reality that you then experience.

Give us a moment. Rest your hand . . . Later you will realize the startling nature of what has been given this evening.

(Still in trance, Jane poured herself more beer. As Seth, she'd

recited without hesitation all of the difficult, complicated material connected with her own dream.)

The following is for Ruburt, yet also for others, and can serve as a brief essay on the nature of will.

(11:26. But in our opinions a lot of what Seth had to say was pretty personal—so much so that only certain parts of it are given below, along with a few bracketed changes I've made to help tie it together. These excerpts still furnish characteristic insights into aspects of Jane's personality, as well as my own, and I might add that the deleted portions are even more meaningful to us. We're making good use of all of this material.)

Ruburt directed his will in certain areas. Your will is your intent. All of the power of your being is mobilized by your will, which makes its deductions according to your beliefs about reality. Each of you use your will in your own way. Each of you have your own way of dealing with challenges. Ruburt used his will to solve [a series of] challenges.

He was determined to find the kind of mate that would best suit him and his own unique characteristics. That intent was in his mind. When that challenge was met he used his will and mobilized all of his power to fulfill his abilities, and to bring about conditions in which he hoped Joseph *(as Seth calls me)* could also fulfill his. The will, again, operates according to the personality's beliefs about reality, so its desires are sometimes tempered as those beliefs change. In his own way Ruburt always concentrated upon one challenge at a time—boring in, so to speak, and ignoring anything else that might distract him.

He wanted to write, to use his creative and psychic abilities to the fullest, and so he cut down all distractions. His literal mind led him to . . . a rich diet of creativity and psychic experience, and to a situation in which Joseph and he could finally be financially free [to some extent], and not in that way threatened.

To his way of thinking he cut out all excess baggage, so he had a spare diet, physically speaking . . . The power of his will is amazingly strong. He is not one to work in many areas at once. Each person lives by their intent, which springs up about the force of their being. In all of this probabilities are involved, so in all moments of the past he touched points of probable healings.[11] No one can be healed against his or her will. There is no such coercion.

Ruburt does not like [some personal aspects] of his plan on the one hand. On the other it was part of his method, a way of intensifying focus, increasing perception in a small area while also ensuring safety, so that inner excursions would be balanced by [conditions in his exterior environment] . . . he sees that the challenge has been won, and now it is time to take up the next one, to apply the power of the will to certain physical areas.

Now many people never learn to apply the power of the will at all.

You [Joseph] were determined to find the kind of relationship you have with Ruburt, the kind of bond your parents never had,[12] and you applied the power of your will in that direction. At the same time you were determined to set yourself apart from the world to some extent, while still maintaining and developing an emotional contact with a mate that would be unlike any in your earlier experience. Creativity would have to be involved. You were also intrigued, determined to travel into the nature of reality, and at least glimpse a vague picture of what it could be In this probability you provided yourself with a background that included sports and the love of the body, knowing [those qualities] would sustain you.

One of your beliefs, then, was a strong joint one that you had to protect your energy at all costs, and block out worldly distractions. Ruburt with his practical mind interpreted this more literally than you did, and physical restriction was a part of his natural early environment [because of his mother's chronic illness], as it was not in yours. But he is amazingly resilient . . . The power of his will is indeed awesome, and he is just now beginning to feel it. With that awareness, it can be used in a new physically oriented directive. The altered directive is all that is necessary. the rest will unconsciously follow . . . The point of power is in the present[13]; this kind of material and its understanding [by Ruburt and others] is more important than "past" causes.

There has been a series of challenges that Ruburt has met through using the power of his will, and this [physical one] is simply the next one to be conquered. Again, many people are not even familiar with that power.

I bid you a fond good evening.

(End at 12:23 A.M. At the breakfast table some hours later, Jane told me that once again she'd "worked on Seth's book all night."

(And added a year later: Seth also discussed the will in a

personal session that was held just six months after he'd finished dictating "Unknown" Reality in April 1975. As soon as Jane came through with the material, I thought of adding some of its more generalized portions to this session. Seth:)

. . . you cannot equivocate. You have a will for a reason. When you are born, that will is directed toward growth and development. You literally will yourselves alive. That will-to-be triggers all bodily activity, which then operates automatically, with the same power from which the will itself emerged.

In infancy and childhood the will <u>singleheartedly</u> directs the body to go full thrust ahead, sweeping aside obstacles in the great impetus toward growth and development. The will is meant to assess the conditions into which the organism grows, however—to also seek out the best areas for expansion.

There are times in history when the species deals with different kinds of challenges. In programmed societies where "each man or woman knows his or her place," then the will knows which directions to follow, though other conditions and prerogatives might be ignored. Actually, in your own society there are many prerogatives . . .

Ruburt wanted to go in one particular direction, but with no clear-cut known ways of getting there. He wanted to pursue a course that was unconventional. He felt he needed protection while he learned, and until he attained enough wisdom.[14] The search itself would lead to a completely different set of values and a new belief system.

You see about you others dealing with life's challenges, following the old beliefs. They must see for themselves that those beliefs do not work.

The universe is with you and not against you. Your fellow men are with you and not against you. When [each of] you realize that, then you reach those portions of your fellows that are with you. You meet them at a different level that is illuminating to them also, and starts them developing . . . The will's power is impressive, and it is "distributed" throughout the body. The body depends upon it for direction. The will's beliefs, again, activate the body's automatic resources.

End of session.

NOTES: Session 713

1. See the references to the Dr. Instream material (for 1965–67) in Appendix 7 in Volume 2 Part I with its Note 18. In chapters 5 and 6 of *The Seth Material*, Jane described other contacts we made as we sought to understand her psychic growth.

2. A note added six months later: These lines are from a personal session Seth delivered on April 29, 1975, just five days after finishing dictation on *"Unknown" Reality* (in the 744th session): "Our books, and I am including Ruburt's, fall into no neat category . . . In the beginning, particularly, and for that matter now, Ruburt had no accepted credentials. He is not a doctor of anything, for there is no one alive who could give him a degree in his particular line of research, or in yours . . . He hides behind no credentials, or social system, or dogma. . . ."

3. The 453rd session, for December 4, 1968, is printed in its entirety in the Appendix of *The Seth Material*. In that session, I think, Seth came through with one of his most evocative conceptions: "You do not understand the dimensions into which your own thoughts drop, for they continue their own existences, and others look up to them and view them like stars. I am telling you that your own dreams and thoughts and mental actions appear to the inhabitants of other systems like the stars and planets within your own; and <u>those</u> inhabitants do not perceive what lies within and behind the stars in their own heavens."

Seth continued the session by expressing his concern lest this kind of material lead to feelings of insignificance on our parts. (In Volume 1 of *"Unknown" Reality*, see Session 681 at 10:00, with Note 2.) However, in a poem she wrote for me a few years later—at Christmastime 1973—Jane herself dealt equally well with the idea of simultaneous interactions between realities:

Dear Love

Dear Love,
what time unmanifest
in our lives resides
beneath our nights and days?
What counterparts break
within our smiles,
what cracks appear in other skies
as we talk and drink coffee
in quiet domestic grace?

Does the smallest wrinkle
spreading on my face

> *peal like thunder*
> *to molecular identities*
> *who study tissue heavens*
> *with a worried air,*
> *and well in cells, each*
> *private, yet connected?*
> *And when I frown—*
> *or you reading the news,*
> *throw down the paper in disgust—*
> *do storms break out*
> *in miniature worlds inside;*
> *taking precautions*
> *to protect their cellular*
> *heavens, do minute inhabitants*
> *Wave us, rushing with their*
> *tiny antibodies to repair*
> *punctures in a universe*
> *we share?*
> *And when we make love*
> *do their crops grow?*

4. For a definition of the moment point, see Note 11 for Appendix 1 in Volume 2 Part I.

5. See the 712th session to first break, with its appropriate notes.

6. In Volume 1, see Practice Element 1 (in the 686th session) for Seth's description of Jane's projection into a probable past of her own—her "Saratoga experience," as we call it.

7. In Appendix 8 in Volume 2 Part I, see the 612th session after 10:50, and Note 11.

8. Jane has had strong yearnings before to instantaneously receive book material that was "immediately available." See the closing notes for Appendix 7 in Volume 1, in which are described her feelings of intense frustration at her inability to speak all at once the contents of a potential book, *The Way Toward Health.*

9. See Appendix 5 in Volume 2 Part I for Session 711.

10. See Note 1 for the 712th session.

11. See Seth on Jane, her will, her relationship with me, and her physical symptoms in Session 679 for Volume 1. I discussed her symptoms in Note 8 for that session also, besides referring the reader to appropriate material in *Personal Reality.*

12. For some material on the kind of relationship my parents *did* have (one obviously involving their children in the most intimate ways, of course), see the first two sessions in Volume 1: the 679th from 11:37, with Note 9, and the 680th from 9:44, with notes 1–3.

13. In *Personal Reality,* see especially the 657th session in Chapter 15.

14. See the opening notes for this (713th) session.

Session 714

□

October 23, 1974
9:36 P.M. Wednesday

(This afternoon Jane called Tam Mossman, her editor at Prentice-Hall, and told him: "I've got my next book." She's calling it Psychic Politics. *Already she thinks of it as another aspect psychology book, a sequel to* Adventures in Consciousness.[1]

(Jane, in an obvious state of altered or enhanced consciousness, not only outlined all of Politics *today, but wrote four manuscript pages that will either go into its Introduction or Chapter 1. All of the material poured out of her in a most remarkable, unimpeded way— ". . . . as though it was already finished somewhere else, just waiting for me to get it down. But I had to do it just so, right to the last word," she said, then added enthusiastically, "I think it's a classic." Involved with* Politics *is her perception of another version of herself in a psychic "library," from which, evidently, she is to acquire a significant portion of her new book.*

(There were clear-cut connections between her creative performance today and her reception of the outline for The Way Toward Health *last March; see the notes at 10:45, as well as Note 8, for Session 713; and in Volume 1, see Appendix 7. But there was even more creative expression to come through Jane this evening; not only in the session itself, of course, but after it, as I try to explain in the concluding notes.*

(As we sat waiting at 9:32, Jane reported that she was getting her "pyramid" or "cone" effect. At such times she feels that subjective shape come down just over her head—always pointed upward, symbolically perhaps, toward other realities. She also

98

thought she might go into her "massive" feelings at any moment. "But I don't think any of this has to do with Seth Two,"[2] she said. She was still exhilarated from her work on Politics. "I'm getting two things: The sessions's going to be book dictation, which surprises me, but it's also going to be on what's happening to me now . . . And I am getting the massive thing. . . ."

(She had something of a cold, but had told me earlier in the evening that she wanted to hold the session. She fell quiet now after reassuring me that she was all right. The evening was quite warm; we had a window open; the traffic noises rushed up to our second-floor living room. Using many pauses, Jane began speaking very softly for Seth.[3])

Good evening.

("Good evening, Seth.")

This is somewhat of a momentous evening for Ruburt . . . As I speak he is experiencing certain sensations, in which his body feels drastically elongated *(pause)*, the head reaching out beyond the stars, the whole form straddling realities.

Now in a sense the physical body does this always—that is, it sits astride realities, containing within itself dimensions of time and being that cannot be even verbally described. The cells themselves are "eternal," though they exist in your world only "for a time."

The unknown reality and the psyche's greater existence cannot be separated from the intimate knowledge of the flesh, however, for the life of the flesh takes place within that framework. As earlier mentioned,[4] the conscious self generally focuses in but one small dimension. Period. That dimension is experienced as fully as possible, its clear brilliance and exquisite focus possible only because you tune in to it and bring it to the forefront of your attention. In your terms, when you understand how to do this, then you can begin to tune in to other "stations" as well.

You know where physical reality is, then, on the dial of your multidimensional television set. While focused within that living scene you can learn to travel through it, leaving the "surface" picture intact and whole. In a way you program yourself, going about your daily duties as conscientiously and effectively as usual—but at the same time you discover an additional portion of your own reality. This does not diminish the physical self. Instead, in fact, it enriches it. You discover that the psyche has

many aspects. While fully enjoying the physical aspect you find
that there is some part of you left over, so to speak; and that part
can travel into other realities. It can also then return, bringing the
physically oriented self "snapshots" of its journeys. These snapshots are usually interpreted in terms of your home program.
Otherwise, they might make no sense to the physical self.

Throughout the ages people have taken such journeys. The
snapshots[5] are developed in the "darkroom" that exists between
your world and those visited. The people who have journeyed
into the unknown reality have always been adventurous. Yet
many had already seen the snapshots sent to your world by
others, and so they began to clothe their own original visions of
their journeys in the guise of those other pictures. A group of
handy ideas, concepts, and images then formed. The clear vision
of such explorers became lost. Those travelers no longer tried to
make their own original snapshots of the strange environments
and realities through which they passed. It was easier to interpret
their experiences through the psychic penny postcards.

(Pause at 9:59.) At one time these postcards represented
initial original visions and individual interepretations. Later, however, they began to serve as guidebooks consulted ahead of time.
For instance: If you plan to travel to a distant country in your
own world, you can find such publications to tell you what to
expect. When you journey into other realities, or when your
consciousness leaves your body, you can also rely upon guidebooks that program your activities ahead of time. Period.

Instead of telling you that you take an airplane from a certain
airport at a certain time for a particular earthly destination,
leaving one latitude and longitude and arriving at another set;
instead of telling you that you leave your country for another
ruled by a dictator, or a president, or by anarchy, they will tell
you that you leave this <u>astral plane</u> for any one of a number of
others, ruled as the case may be by lords or masters, gods and
goddesses. Instead of pointing out to you, as in earthly travel
booklets, the locations of art galleries and museums, they will
direct you to the Akashic Records.[6] Instead of leading you to the
archaeological sites of your world *(intently)*, and its great ruins
of previous civilizations, they will tell you how to find Atlantis
and Mu[7] and other times in your past.

So you take a psychic guided tour into other realities; the
unknown seems known, so that you are not an explorer after all,

but a tourist, taking with you the paraphernalia of your own civilization, and beliefs that are quite conventional.

There are inner conventions, then, as there are outer ones. As the exterior mores try to force you to conform to the generally accepted ideas, so the interior conventions try to force you to make your inner experience conform to preconceived packaging.

There are good reasons for conventions. Generally, they help organize experience. If they are lightly held to and accepted, they can serve well as guidelines. Applied with a heavy hand they become unnecessary dogma, rigidly limiting experience. This applies to inner and outer activity. Conventions are the results of stratified and rigid "spontaneity." At one time, in your terms, each custom had a meaning. Each represented a spontaneous gesture, an individual reaction. When these become a system of <u>order</u>, however, the original spontaneity is lost, and you project an artificial order that serves to stratify behavior rather than to express it. So there are psychic customs as there are physical ones, religious and psychic dogmas, guided tours of consciousness in which you are told to follow a certain line or a certain program. You become afraid of your private interpretation of <u>whatever</u> reality you find yourself experiencing.

Ruburt has thus far insisted upon his private vision and his unique expression of the unknown reality as he experiences it, and so he brings back bulletins that do not agree with the conventional psychic line.

Take your break.

(10:18. Jane's trance had been good, her delivery quiet and rather fast; her voice had become a little rough because of her cold, though. When Seth talked about Jane's private psychic vision he reminded me of her own remarks on the same subject; see the notes opening the 713th session.

(Jane was aware of the elongated, giant-sized feeling now, as she had been just before the session began. "Everything's in proportion, though," she said. "It's crazy, but I feel that when I stand up my head could go through the ceiling." But she looked quite normal to me, and of course nothing out of character happened when she stood up.

(Resume at 10:25.)

The psychic postcards and travel folders are handy and colorful. They are also highly misleading.

(Long pause.) Once individual travelers took those snapshots,

and they represented original interpretations of other realities. They stood for individual versions of certain travelers taking brief glimpses of strange worlds, and interpreting their experiences to the best of their abilities. As such they were very valid. *(Louder:)* They were as valid as any snapshot that you might take of your backyard in the morning. That picture, however, would vary considerably from one taken by an inhabitant of your planet in a different part of the world, and in a different environment.

If there were discrepancies among the snapshots, however, people worried. While you expect pictures of your own reality to be diverse, those who journeyed into the unknown reality became concerned if their snapshots did not agree, so they tried desperately to make all of the pictures look alike. They touched them up, in other words.

First of all, in your own world those travelers into unknown realms were considered outcasts, so to speak, as if they were picking up television programs that no one else saw.[8] If their stories of their experiences did not jibe, who would believe them? They felt threatened. They felt that they had to tell the same story or they would be considered insane, so they made a tacit agreement, interpreting their experiences in the terms used by those who had gone "before."

You make your own reality. So, programmed ahead of time, they perceived [data] according to the psychic conventions that had been established. There are tigers in Asia, but you can travel through Asia and if you do not want to you'll never see a tiger. It's according to where you go. In the unknown reality your thoughts are instantly made apparent and real, materialized according to your beliefs. There, if you believe in demons, you will see them—without ever realizing that they are part of the environment of your psyche, formed by your beliefs, and thrown out as mirages over a very real environment that you do not perceive. You will believe the psychic tour books and go hunting for demons instead of tigers.

Give us a moment . . . Individually and *en masse,* you form the world that you know, yet it has an overall individual and mass basis so that some things are agreed upon. You view those things through your own unique vision. You form the reality. It is a valid one. It is experience. It is not therefore unreal, but one of the appearances that reality takes. It has a valid basis—an environment that you all accept, in which certain experiences are possible.

The same applies to other realities. You know there is a difference between, say, the picture before your eyes and a postcard, "artificial," rendition of it. So there is a difference between the unknown reality and the postcards that have been given to you to depict it.

In your terms, Ruburt has been out for the real thing—to experience the unknown reality directly through his own perceptions, as divorced from the scenes given him by the postcards. Period.

Give us a moment. . . .

(10:47. "I'm out of it," Jane said abruptly, coughing. Then: "I'm on to something. Wait a minute. I don't know if I can get it, or what. . . ." She coughed again and again; her voice had become very hoarse since break, so much so that a few minutes ago I'd been on the verge of asking her to end the session. Now, over my protests, she wanted a fresh pack of cigarettes. See Note 3 in connection with the following material.)

"If I can get this it'll be something, I'll tell you," Jane said, lighting up. She sipped her beer. "Bob—what I'm getting is something like it would be in real fast, quick beautiful sounds that I can't duplicate—very quick, very musical—connected with the spin of electrons[9] and cellular composition.

"The spin of electrons is faster than the cellular composition. The faster speed of the electrons somehow gives the cells their boundaries. And there's something that's in a trance, say, in crystals, that's alive in the cells.

"Wait a minute," Jane exclaimed again. "What I'm getting is a fantastic sound that's imprisoned in a crystal, that *speaks* through light, that's the essence of personality. I'm getting almost jewel-like colored sounds . . . I'll see what I can do with it. I want to get it in verbal stuff—and I'm getting it fast." Pause.

"—and we're speaking of personality now," Jane said, coughing again. "As the seed falls, blown by the wind in any environment, so there's a seed of personality that rides on the wings of itself and falls into the worlds of many times and places. Falling with a sound that is its own *true tone*, struck in different chords."

(10:58.) "Sounds are aware of their own separateness, gloriously unique, yet each one merging into a symphony. Each

sound recognizes itself as itself, striking the dimensional medium
in which it finds its expression; yet it's aware of the infinite other
multitudinous sounds it makes in other realities—the instruments through which it so grandly plays. Each cell, c-e-l-l,
strikes in the same fashion, *and so does each self*, s-e-l-f, in a
kaleidoscope in which each slightest variation has meaning and
affects the individual notes made by all.

"So we strike in more realities than one, and *I hear* those
notes together yet separately, perhaps as raindrops, and attempt
to put them together and yet hear each separate note . . .

"Seth—or somebody's saying—maybe it's just me—relates to
the people in our time. I've tried to do the same thing, but I
suddenly heard my own true tone, which I'm bound to follow . . .
to go beyond the conventionalized postcards . . . I'm done,
Bob."

*(11:03 P.M. "Wow, I'm out, I'm telling you," Jane said
rather groggily after a few moments. "I don't know how you're
going to put this together with the Seth stuff. It's like a note that
finds its own true tone, and when it does nothing else makes
sense. That's all I can say. But once you strike it, you know
that's it."*

*(Except for a few instances in which I eliminated repetitive
phrases, all of the material Jane gave after 10:47 is unchanged
here. At times, because her delivery had become so steady, even
precise, I'd wondered if she had entered into a Seth trance, but
one without Seth's usual voice effects. I had also been concerned
lest she speak so rapidly that I wouldn't be able to keep up with
her in my notes, but that hadn't happened. Nor had she spoken
for Seth, I realized by the time she finished. Her enhanced state
of consciousness had been her "own."*

*("I know there's a universe between my chair here [in the
living room] and the kitchen floor," Jane said as she got up,
"but I can walk it okay. When you strike your own true tone,
you recognize it and you've got it made. You know your own
meaning in the universe, even if you can't verbalize it. . . ."*

*(Jane told me that her feelings of massiveness had left her by
the time she began her own dissertation. I was surprised to
suddenly notice that her voice was much clearer now, cold or
no. She did feel unsettled. She didn't quite know what to do. She
let our cat, Willy, into the living room from the second apartment we rent across the hall. I suggested she eat something.*

"It's strange," she commented. *"I feel that no matter which way I turn, there's a path laid out for me—and I never felt that way before."* Then she announced that she was going to bed. *"But as soon as I get over there [in the other apartment] I'll turn around and come back here, I'll bet."* She left. I decided to have a snack myself, and to work on these notes while waiting to see if she would return.

(Now here's how I "put this together with the Seth stuff," meaning that from my viewpoint I'll briefly discuss the various states of consciousness Jane enjoyed today, as well as her massive sensations and her psychic perceptions of sound in connection with tonight's session. [The session itself, of course embodied yet another altered state.] At the same time, the reader can make his or her own intuitive connections in assembling such materials, even if "only" in unconscious ways.

(Much of Jane's day had been made up of a series of altered, and at times even near-ecstatic states of consciousness, each one expressing a unique and creative facet of her essentially mystical nature.[10] Even though not at her best, she'd been able to draw upon lavish amounts of energy. I think that her experience with inner sound after the session represented her interpretation of the information Seth gave on feeling-tones, some two years ago; see the 613th session for Chapter 1 of Personal Reality. There are certainly deep connections between Jane's apprehension of her true tone, and Seth's statement in that session that each of us possesses certain qualities of feeling uniquely our own, ". . . that are like deep musical chords." He went on to say at 10:06: "These feeling-tones, then, prevade your being. They are the form your spirit takes when combined with flesh." I also think that Jane's sensing of her true path reflects her understanding of Seth's subsequent remark at 10:16 [in that 613th session]: "The feeling-tone is the motion and fiber—and timbre—of your energy devoted to your physical experience.[11]

(So, given Jane's satisfying yet exhilarating expressions of consciousness throughout the day, I hardly regard it as surprising that she plunged into additional excellent states this evening. Paradoxically, her inspired reception of the material for Psychic Politics came about not only because of her innate knowledge of feeling-tones, but because she gave that basic creative phenomenon expression in Politics.

(And she's quite conscious of the fact that her massive sensa-

tions are one of the ways by which, as she has written, she tries to "view our three-dimensional existence and this universe from outside this framework," or to travel beyond the conventionalized psychic postcards.

(A note in closing out the evening's work: Jane didn't come back to join me in the living room while I ate and wrote. I found her sleeping deeply. . . .)

NOTES: Session 714

1. *Adventures* itself won't be published until next summer. See notes 1 and 3 for Session 705, and the opening notes for Session 708. Right now I'm finishing Diagram 11 of the 16 planned for *Adventures*.

2. In Appendix 8 in Volume 2 Part I, see the 612th session for material on both Seth Two and Jane's feelings of massiveness.

3. A note added later: Jane used certain portions of the 714th session in Chapter 1 of *Politics*, while making her own points there. Since it's obviously part of *"Unknown" Reality* too, however, the entire session is presented in place in Volume 2. The same reasoning applies to the material each of us contributed at session's end.

4. See the 712th session, for instance.

5. Seth offered an analogy involving the camera and the traveling conscious mind in the 710th session after 10:16.

6. In her work on *Politics* today, Jane had already begun writing about the Akashic Records. Her inspiration had been the result of her quite unexpected, humorous, appalling—yet finally illuminating—encounter this morning with a visitor who'd attended her ESP class last night.

In occult terms, the Akashic Records are supposed to contain the complete cosmic account of every action, thought, and feeling that has transpired since creation "began."

"I don't believe in them," Jane said in answer to my question. "At least not in that fashion—so what am I doing tuning in to a psychic library?" She laughed. "I'm having enough trouble explaining my own ideas. I've got to figure it all out."

But see Note 1 (with *its* references) for Session 697 in Volume 1; it contains some of Seth's material on the consciousness connected with any information.

7. Just as legend has it that the continent of Atlantis lay in the Atlantic Ocean between Europe/Africa and the Americas, so the great land of Mu (the Motherland) is said to have existed in the vast Pacific Ocean between the Americas and Asia. Each of those mythical domains eventually sank beneath the waters in a great cataclysm; each perished more than 10,000 years ago. For some Atlantis material and references in Volume 2 of *"Unknown" Reality,* see Appendix 3 in Part I.

8. And "those travelers into unknown worlds" can still be called outcasts, strange, weird—or worse. Jane has had her share of such reactions from others (as have I). When combined with her own natural-enough questions about her psychic abilities, as sometimes happens, such episodes aren't any fun. In accidental ways that would be quite humorous if they weren't so personal, we've also learned what negative ideas others can have about us: A person will inadvertently reveal to us, during a conversation, or in a letter or over the telephone, the unflattering opinions his or her mate, or parents, or friends, really have of Jane and me and the work we're engaged in with the Seth material.

Occasionally we'll meet one or more of our secondhand detractors. Then of course we're greeted with polite smiles; the conversation may touch upon the weather, but hardly ever upon matters psychic. Sometimes we'll discover that the "knowledge" of us held by the skeptic(s) in question is so far removed from our actual beliefs and activities that it would take us a very long time to establish any real understanding among all involved—if it would be possible to begin with, that is. We always elect to pass up such "opportunities."

Even as I wrote this note Jane received a letter: "Do what I ask for me, if you are not a fraud. . . ." I threw the letter away. At the same time I remembered, as I do every so often, the prophetic and amused remarks Seth made way back in the 20th session for January 29, 1964: "As far as publishing this material is concerned, I have no objections. I didn't give it to you, and I'm not giving it to you, simply for your [collective] edification. Because of its source you will probably be called crackpots, but I imagine you know this by now."

Yes . . . And in the face of such skepticism or misunderstanding, Jane and I may at times find ourselves wondering why psychic attributes even exist *in* nature, in those terms, if they're denied any application within that framework. "You [each] must have a basic approval of yourself," Seth told us recently in a personal session. "This is information not only for the two of you, of course, but for others: <u>You must trust your basic being</u>, with its characteristics and abilities. You have them for a reason, in all of their unique combinations. You should also avoid labels, for these can stereotype your perception of yourself."

9. Presented as they are in Appendix 8, Volume 2 Part I, both that portion of Session 612 and its notes contain material on the kinds of fast (and slow) sounds that Jane has been able to perceive so far. See especially notes 7 and 10 there; chromoesthesia, or colored hearing, is defined in the latter. Information on electrons, including electron spin, is either given or referred to in notes 8 and 9 for the 612th session.

10. See the material on Jane and mysticism in Appendix 1 for Volume 1.

11. Of interest here are a few excerpts from a personal session held just a year later, in October 1975. During the session Seth discussed

inner sound in connection with Jane's own physical symptoms. (In
Volume 1 of *"Unknown" Reality*, see the 679th session before 10:31,
and Note 8. The quotations below are also related to the material on
inner sound, light, and electromagnetic values in Chapter 5 of *Personal
Reality*.) Seth, at 11:17 P.M.:

"Give us a moment . . . The movement of the joints makes sound.
The sounds are messages. When hormones are released they make
sounds. Those sounds are messages.

"I say 'sounds'—yet these inner body sounds can only be compared
to an interior body situation where sound operates as light. You are used
to thinking in terms of opaque or transparent color. In those terms there
is opaque light, and transparent light as well. Sound has light value, and
light has sound value. These operate within the body.

"Each frequency, so to speak, functions as a messenger, triggering
body response before an <u>actual</u> reaction is apparent . . . In any body
difficulty, the light and sound frequencies become out of tune, you
might say. The overall 'true tone' is muddied. When Ruburt began
Politics he experienced his 'true tone' mentally and psychically. Though
he did not realize it, this gave him something to go by, so that now . . .
he is unconsciously [still] bringing about the physical equivalent of that
true tone."

Session 715

□

October 28, 1974
9:25 P.M. Monday

(See Note 1 for descriptions of the [two] unusual mental events I experienced Sunday and today: I may have seen myself as a Roman military officer in the first century A.D.

(In the opening notes for last Wednesday's session I described how Jane had started her new book, Psychic Politics, *that same day while she had been immersed in a state of high creativity; I added that at the same time she'd become aware of a slightly different Jane in a psychic library from which, it seemed, she was to get much of the material for* Politics. *Jane visited her library several times on Thursday, without actually transcribing anything from it. Then on Friday morning she received another, shorter passage of library material. I quote in part: "There are ever-changing models for physical reality, transforming themselves constantly in line with new equations instantly set up with each new stabilization . . . We tune in to these models, and our intersections with them alter them at any given point, causing new dimensions of actuality that then reach out from that new focus."*[2]

(Jane didn't really understand what she'd written. Neither of us realized it at the time, but she was to soon embark upon one of the key episodes[3] *of her psychic life: "My later experiences that day were a practical lesson in how models work," she wrote after it was all over.*

(At noontime that Friday, then, Jane told me that she was going into another altered or enhanced state of consciousness. We were eating luch. She compared her feelings with those

109

heightened perceptions she'd enjoyed so much yesterday and Wednesday in connection with the birth of Politics. Even though her state of awareness was still growing, Jane decided that she wanted to ride downtown with me after we'd finished eating; I planned to pick up one of our typewriters at a repair shop, then buy some groceries. Already she was so "loose" that she noticed an unsteadiness in her walking. "It's as though the floor's rising up beneath my feet, supporting my weight, but in a way that I'm not used to," she said. She was enchanted.

("Watch it when we go out to the car," I joked. "If people see you staggering around they'll think you're loaded.")

(As I drove east on Water Street, heading for the center of Elmira, Jane exclaimed again and again over the new beauty she was discovering in her world. A bit later I plan to quote from her own notes some of the details of her transcendent perceptions; but by the time I'd secured the typewriter, then driven over to the supermarket at Langdon Plaza, she didn't think she could get out of the car. Nor did she want to try doing anything that might interrupt the magnificence of her greatly expanded state of consciousness. For all the while she was having the most profound group of experiences in seeing, feeling, and knowing the ordinary physical world about her.

(We searched the glove compartment of the car for paper and a pencil or pen, so that Jane could make notes about some of her perceptual changes—but to my amazement we could find nothing to use in spite of our efforts to keep writing tools in that very place. Among other papers I finally turned up half a sheet of blank paper, and gave Jane the pen I usually used to cross out items on the grocery list. We were parked in front of a drugstore; I hurried in there to buy pens and a notepad for her. So, while I busied myself in the familiar market next door, she sat in the car writing—looking quite ordinary, a small black-haired woman with her head bent forward . . . When I'd finished shopping perhaps 30 minutes later she was still writing. She had covered half a dozen pages.

(Now here are some excerpts from Jane's notes, as I've put them together. [And added later: I remind the reader to see her own much-longer account of the whole experience in Chapter 2 of Politics.])

"Then, between one moment and the next, the world literally changed for me. I'm viewing it from an entirely different perspective. It's like the old world but infinitely richer, more 'now,' built better, and with much greater depth.

"Words aren't describing this at all. Each person who passes the car is more than three-dimensional, super-real in this time, but part of a 'model' of a greater self . . . and each person's reality is obviously and clearly more than three-dimensional. I know I'm repeating myself here, but it's as if before I've seen only a part of people or things. The world is so much more solid right now[4] that by contrast my earlier experience of it is like a shoddy version, made up of disconnected dots or blurred focus. . . ."

And: "Qualitatively, the [supermarket plaza] was so different than usual that I could hardly believe it. While Rob did the shopping I kept looking—and looking—and looking. I knew that each person I saw had free will, and yet each motion was inevitable and somehow there was no contradiction. I could look at each person and sense his or her 'model' and all the variations, and see how the model was here and now in the person. I saw these people as True People in the meaning of a whole people. These people were 'more here,' fuller somehow, more complete. People seemed to be classics of themselves.

"I faced a group of shops and saw these also as models and their variations. The same applied to everything I looked at. I thought: 'I'm being filled to the brim'; and for a moment I wondered if I'd been fitted with a spectacular new pair of glasses. It was an effort to write these notes to begin with. I wanted to just look forever."

(Jane was still deeply within her great experience during our ride back to the apartment house. "Wow," she exclaimed, "I wouldn't touch acid [LSD] for anything after this. Who needs to?" I laughed: "How to go on your own free trip, huh?" She does not use hallucinogenic drugs of any kind.

("What would happen if you opened your eyes and really saw the world?" Jane mused. "It's indescribable. . . ." And later today she wrote: "Driving home with Rob, for example, I felt the earth support the road which supported the tires and the car. I felt this physically, in the same way that we sense, say, temperature; a positive support or pressure that held the road up and almost seemed to push up of its own accord in a long powerful arch, like a giant animal's back."

(Jane's "adventure in consciousness" was so rich,[5] even from

my observor's viewpoint, that my attempts to describe it seem terribly inadequate by comparison. In this session Seth discusses to some extent the whole subject of her psychic growth.)

Good evening.

("Good evening, Seth.")

Give us a moment for dictation.

I said at our last session that the evening was momentous for Ruburt, and that is true for many reasons. This book[6] deals with the unknown reality, and Ruburt began a different excursion into other dimensions last week.

I hope in these sessions to show the indivisible connections between the experience of the psyche at various levels and the resulting experience in terms of varying systems—each valid, each to some extent or another bearing on the life you know.

Ruburt has allowed a portion of his this-life consciousness to go off on a tangent, so to speak, on another path into another system of actuality *(i.e., into his psychic library)*. His life there is as valid as his existence in your world. In the waking state he is able, now, to alter the direction of his focus precisely enough to bring about a condition in which he perceives both realities simultaneously. He is just beginning, so as yet he is only occasionally conscious of that other experience. He is, however, aware of it now in the back of his mind more or less constantly. It does not intrude upon the world that he knows, but enriches it.

The concepts in *"Unknown" Reality* will help expand the consciousness of each of its readers, and the work itself is presented in such a manner that it automatically pulls your awareness out of its usual grooves, so that it bounces back and forth between the standardized version of the world you accept, and the unofficial[7] versions that are sensed but generally unknown to you.

Now as Ruburt delivers this material, the same thing happens in a different way to him, so that in some respects he has been snapping back and forth between dimensions, practicing with the elasticity of his consciousness; and in this book more than in previous ones his consciousness has been sent out further, so to speak. The delivery of the material itself has helped him to develop the necessary flexibility for his latest pursuits.

Clear understanding or effective exploration of the unknown reality can be achieved only when you are able to leave behind you many "facts" that you have accepted as criteria of experience. *"Unknown" Reality* is also written in such a way that it will, I hope, bring many of your cherished beliefs about existence into question. Then you will be able to look even at this existence with new eyes.

Ruburt is taking this new step from your perspective, and from that standpoint he is doing two things.

(At a slower pace:) He is consciously entering into another room of the psyche, and also entering into the reality that corresponds to it. This brings the two experiences together so that they coincide. They are held, however, both separately and in joint focus. As a rule you use one particular level of awareness, and this correlates all of your conscious activities. I told you that the physical body itself was able to pick up other neurological messages beside those to which you usually react.[8] Now let me add that when a certain proficiency is reached in alterations of consciousness, this allows you to become practically familiar with some of these other neurological messages. In such a way Ruburt is able to physically perceive what he is doing in his "library."

He first saw this library from the inside last Wednesday. He was simultaneously himself here in this living room, watching the image of himself in a library room, and he was the self in the library. Period. Before him he saw a wall of books, and the self in the living room suddenly knew that his purpose here in this reality was to re-create some of those books. He knew that he was working at both levels. The unknown and the known realities merged, clicked in, and were seen as the opposite sides of each other.

He has been working with me for some time, in your terms, yet I do not "control" his subjective reality in any way. I have certainly been a teacher to him.[9] Yet his progress is always his own challenge and responsibility, and basically what he does with my teaching is up to him. *(Humorously:)* In parentheses: (Right now I give him an "A.")

(Pause at 10:01.) Like many, however, he was brought up to believe that the intellect's function was mainly to dissect, criticize, and analyze, rather than for instance to creatively unite and build, colon: and analysis was thought of as separating the elements of a concept rather than restricting original concepts. New concepts were thought of as intuitional or psychic, as opposed to the conventional duties of the intellect, so the two

seemed separate. Therefore, Ruburt felt duty-bound to question any intuitive construct most vigorously as a matter of principle. This actually provided an excellent transitory working method, for what he thought of as intuitions would instantly come up with a new psychic construct in answer to what he thought of as intellectual scrutiny and skepticism. Period.

Actually, the intellect and intuitions go hand in hand. In Ruburt's experience,[10] the two finally began to work together as they should. What I call the high intellect then took over, a superb blend of intuitional and intellectual abilities working together so that they almost seem to form a new faculty *(intently)*.

The development freed Ruburt from many old limitations, and allowed him to at last have practical experience with the unknown reality in intimate terms. Ruburt's library does exist as surely as this room does. It also exists as unsurely as this room. It is one thing to be theoretically convinced that other worlds exist, and to take a certain comfort and joy from the idea. It is quite another thing to find yourself in such an environment, and to feel the worlds coincide. Reality is above all practical, so when you expand your concepts concerning the nature of reality, you are apt then to find yourselves scandalized, appalled, or simply disoriented. So in this work I am presenting you not only with probabilities as conjecture, but, often, showing you how such probabilities affect your daily lives, and giving examples of the ways in which Ruburt's and Joseph's lives have been so touched.

For a while, many of you will play with the concepts while avoiding all direct encounters with any other experience, save that already acceptable. Yet the immensities of your own abilities speak in your dreams, in your private moments, as even inaudibly in the knowledge of your own molecules.

There are civilizations of the psyche,[11] and only by learning about these will you discover the truth about the "lost" civilizations of your planet, for each such physical culture coincided with and emerged from a corresponding portion of the psyche that you even now possess.

Take your break.

(10:19 to 10:43.)

Many of you are fascinated by theories or concepts that hint at the multidimensionality of your beings, and yet you are scandalized by any evidence that supports it.

Often you interpret such evidence in terms of the dogmas with which you are already familiar. This makes them more acceptable. Ruburt <u>was</u> often almost indignant when presented with such evidence, but he also refused to cast it in conventionalized guise, and his own curiosity and creative abilities kept him flexible enough so that learning could take place while he maintained normal contact with the world you know.[12]

He has had many experiences in which he glimpsed momentarily the rich <u>otherness</u> within physical reality. He has known heightened perceptions of a unique nature. Never before, however, has he stepped firmly, while awake, into another level of reality, where he allowed himself to sense the continual vivid connection between worlds. He hid his own purpose from himself, as many of <u>you</u> do. At the same time he was pursuing it, of course, as all of you <u>are</u> working toward your own goals.

To admit his purpose, however, to bring it out into the open, would mean for Ruburt a private and public statement of affiliation such as he was not able to make earlier. The goals of each of you differ. Some of you are embarked upon adventures that deal with intimate family contact, deep personal involvement with children, or with other careers that meet ''vertically'' with physical experience. So journeys into unknown realities may be highly intriguing, and represent important sidelights to your current preoccupations. These interests will be like an avocation to you, adding great understanding and depth to your experience.

Ruburt and Joseph chose to specialize, so to speak, in precisely those excursions or explorations that are secondary to others. The focus of each of their consciousnesses therefore was made up of a certain kind of mixture that made such probabilities, in your terms, possible as prime incentives.

(Long pause, eyes closed, at 10:56.) Each person is at his place or her place. You are where you are because your consciousness formed that kind of reality. Your whole physical situation will be geared to it, and your neurological structure will follow the habitual pattern. As you learn to throw aside old concepts you will begin to experience the evidence for other levels of reality, and become aware of other ''messages'' that you have previously blocked. A certain portion of Ruburt's training period is over. The entire focus of his personality now accepts the validity of many worlds—and this means in practical terms.

I have told you many times that your consciousness is not
stationary, but ever-moving and creative, so that each of you
through your life moves through your psyche. Your physical
experience is correspondingly altered.

During these years, then, Ruburt's position within his psyche
has gradually shifted until he found a new, for him better, firmer
point of basis. From this new framework he can more effectively
handle different kinds of stimuli, and form these together to
construct an understandable <u>model</u> of other realities. I will continue to speak from my own unique viewpoint, but in your terms
Ruburt is one of you, and his explorations, taken from your
perspective, can be most valuable.

Give us moment . . . These books, those written and not yet
written, of his and mine, will provide frameworks for others to
follow if they wish, <u>as</u> they wish.

End of dictation.

(11:08.) Give us a moment . . .

*(Seth discussed another matter involving Jane; after delivering
about a page of material he ended the session at 11:19 P.M.)*

NOTES: Session 715

1. Yesterday afternoon, Sunday, I lay down for a nap. Just before I
drifted into the sleep state I had three little experiences involving internal
vision. My eyes were closed. In the episode of interest here, I saw
myself back in the first century A.D.: I was an officer of rather high
rank in a Roman legion, and I was aboard a small galley in the
Mediterranean Sea. I knew that I was on official military business for a
land-based armed force, even though I was on ship. I didn't much like
the blunt, unfeeling "I" that I saw. Briefly through those eyes I looked
out upon twin rows of galley slaves . . . I described the scene and my
feelings about it to Jane, and made small, full-face and profile pen-and-
ink drawings of myself as the officer. I had no name for that other self.
Given Seth's concept of simultaneous time, I thought I might have
glimpsed another existence—whether a reincarnational one or a probable
one—that I was living now.

This afternoon, Monday, I decided upon a nap once again, and once
again I was aware of myself as the Roman officer; at least I thought I
was that individual. I entered into a sequel to the first vision: I felt
myself floating face down in the Mediterranean with my hands tied
behind my back. I knew that I'd been deliberately thrown into the sea. I
cut off my awareness of the experience right there, possibly to avoid
undergoing my own death in that life. From the safety of the cot in my

studio, I didn't panic as that other me faced such a life-threatening situation, yet I was disturbed by it—enough so that I repressed conscious recall of the whole episode until the evening after this (715th) session was held. I'm citing it here so that I can present my "first and second Romans," as I call them, together.

No sooner had I described this second adventure to Jane than she surprised me by saying she might use both of the Roman experiences in *Politics*. She thought she could tie them in with her material on the "ever-changing models for physical reality" that she'd obtained from her psychic library last Friday morning.

After my first Roman, I speculated about whether I might have touched upon a reincarnational self or a probable one. See, therefore, Seth's material on reincarnation in Chapter 4 (among others) of *Seth Speaks*; then see his material on probable selves in Chapter 16 of that book, and in Session 680 for Volume 1 of *"Unknown" Reality*.

For myself, I think of reincarnational selves as having their roots in the physical reality we know (whether in simultaneous or linear terms of time), but of probable selves as having much wider and more complicated ranges of existence: I believe that even though we create them on an individual basis, our probable selves can reach into a multitude of other realities, both physical and nonphysical. I don't remember Seth discussing such "probable" possibilities in just that way, especially, and they would be much too involved to go into here, but I've often felt that some of our probable selves move into realms of being that are literally incomprehensible to us, so different—alien—are they and their environments from our usual conceptions of "solid" physical existence.

2. In Chapter 2 for *Psychic Politics* Jane presents not only her library material, but quotations from the 715th session for *"Unknown" Reality* itself. I wrote this note a month after Session 715 was held in October 1974. By late November, in other words, Jane had signed a contract with Prentice-Hall for the publication of *Politics* in 1976, and had also had time to do considerable work on its early chapters. We already knew that she would initiate some transposition of material from Volume 2 of *"Unknown" Reality* into *Politics*, since she was so intimately and enthusiastically involved in producing both works at the same time: I first wrote about such an exchange in Note 3 for Session 714 (when indicating that she'd used portions of *that* session in Chapter 1 of *Politics*).

But although for *Politics* Jane drew upon the same transcendent experience I described in the opening notes for the 715th session, she did so in her own subjective way; in *"Unknown" Reality* I present my version of the event from an observor's viewpoint. The interested reader might compare the two accounts. I think they're both well worth having on record, since Jane's experience was a profound one—and, in my opinion, very revealing for what it tells us about how we ordinarily view our mundane physical reality, and about the much more powerful versions, or "models," for that reality that exist behind it.

3. In *Dialogues*, her book of poetry, Jane explored several other "key" episodes in her psychic development; see her Preface, then these selections in Part Two: "The Paper and Trips Through an Inner Garden," and "Single-Double Worlds, the Rain Creature, and the Light." She also wrote about those transcendent experiences in *Adventures*; see Chapter 9 for her "paper" perceptions (in March 1972), and Chapter 15 for her encounters with the rain creature and the light (in February 1973). Both Jane and Seth had things to say about the rain creature and the light in *Personal Reality*; see the 639th session for Chapter 10.

4. Jane's declaration of the "super-real" aspects of her ecstatic state, that "The world is so much more solid right now," soon had me hunting for relevant material I remembered Seth giving, but couldn't place. I found two sources in *Seth Speaks*. In Chapter 7, see the 530th session for May 20, 1970, at 10:02: "There are realities that are 'relatively more valid' than your own . . . your physical table [for example] would appear as shadowy in contrast . . . You would have a sort of 'supertable' in those terms. Yours is not a system of reality formed by the most intense concentration of energy . . . Other portions of yourself, therefore, of which you are not consciously aware, do inhabit what you could call a supersystem of reality in which consciousness learns to handle and perceive much stronger concentrations of energy . . ."

In Chapter 16, see the 567th session for February 17, 1971, at 9:24: "You understand that there are spectrums of light. So there are spectrums of matter. Your system of physical reality is not dense in comparison with some others. The dimensions that you give to physical matter barely begin to hint at the varieties of dimensions possible. Some systems are far heavier or lighter than your own. . . ."

5. So far in Volume 2, I've mentioned the inner senses (as described by Seth) in Note 5 for Session 709, and Note 6 for Appendix 7 in Volume 2 Part I. Seth came through with No. 6, *Innate Knowledge of Basic Reality*, in the 40th session for April 1, 1964: "This is an extremely rudimentary sense. It is concerned with the entity's working knowledge of the basic vitality of the universe . . . Without this sixth sense and its constant use by the inner self, you could not construct the physical camouflage universe. You can compare this sense with instinct, although it is concerned with the innate knowledge of the entire universe."

At least to some degree, Jane's exploration last Friday afternoon of those super-real models for our world represented her use of the sixth inner sense—the same one, she wrote in Chapter 19 of *The Seth Material*, that ". . . also shows itself in inspirations, and episodes of spontaneous 'knowing.' Surely this sense was partially responsible for my *Idea Construction* manuscript." In Volume 1, see Note 7 for Session 679.

6. A note added six months later: When Seth referred to "this book" in the 715th session, he meant a one-volume edition of *"Unknown" Reality*, of course. Jane and I didn't decide to publish the work in two volumes until just before the 741st session (for Section 6) was held, in April 1975. See the early Introductory Notes for Volume 2.

·7. For contrast, in Volume 1 see the references to "official" reality that are given in Note 2 for Session 695.

8. See the 686th session in Volume 1; then see Jane's material on other-than-usual neurological messages and speeds in appendixes 4 and 5. And (later) I add here a paragraph from the private session Seth held for us on May 1, 1974—10 days after he'd finished his work on *"Unknown" Reality*:

"He [Ruburt-Jane] has an ability to identify with others, and communicate. He has always been mentally quick and intellectually agile. As a youngster he received the messages from others so quickly that he was diagnosed as having an overactive thyroid gland. Actually, he was receiving "unofficial" messages that are usually neurologically censored. He could not allow them to become conscious in that world . . ."

9. See Appendix 7 in Volume 2 Part I.

In the 4th session, for December 8, 1963, Seth announced his presence to Jane and me through the Ouija board. In the 6th session he told Jane, in connection with our questions: "Begin training." In the 12th session, for January 2, 1964, he informed us that we were his "first lesson class," then added: "At one time or another all of us on my plane give such lessons, but psychic bonds between teacher and pupils are necessary. This means that we must wait until personalities in your reality have progressed sufficiently for lessons to begin . . . although reason is extremely important, and I do not mean to minimize its value, nevertheless what you call emotion or feeling is the connective between us, and it is the connective that most clearly represents the life force on any plane and under any circumstances."

Later, we were to learn about the distortions that could happen as Jane relayed some of Seth's material; given the open-ended nature of time, and considering the idea of probable realities, we came to realize that simultaneously we could and could not be Seth's "first lesson class." But in those early sessions we had no background knowledge out of which to ask meaningful questions. In the 15th session Seth told Jane and me: "I am giving you what may be considered a broad outline to be filled in."

10. See the opening notes for the 713th session.

11. In Note 5 for Session 692, in Volume 1, I refer to Seth's term, "species of consciousness," and the links between his material in that session and this one.

12. Note 25 for Appendix 7 in Volume 2 Part I contains information on *The Coming of Seth*, in which Jane described her burgeoning psychic abilities.

Section 5

□

**HOW TO JOURNEY INTO THE
"UNKNOWN" REALITY:
TINY STEPS AND GIANTS STEPS.
GLIMPSES AND DIRECT ENCOUNTERS**

Session 716

□

October 30, 1974
9:33 P.M. Wednesday

(In Note 1, I described my third "Roman," which took place this afternoon.

("I guess I'm confused," Jane said as we waited for the session to begin. "I think Seth's going to start another section tonight—but I don't think he's quite finished with the last one. . . ." However, Section 4 was finished after all.)

Good evening.

("Good evening, Seth.")

Dictation. The next section *(5)*: "How to Journey Into the 'Unknown' Reality," colon: "Tiny Steps and Giant Steps. Glimpses and Direct Encounters."

This section will deal with various methods that will allow you to come in contact with the unknown reality to one extent or another. We have spoken of probable man, hinted at probable civilizations, and mentioned alternate systems of actuality.[2] Yet these do not exist completely apart from the world that you know, or entirely cut off from the psyche. If you have no experience with such realities, then their existence remains delightful or speculative conjecture.

(Pause.) The unknown reality is a variation of the one that you know, so that many of its features are latent rather than predominant in your own private and mass experience. Any encounter with such phenomena will then include a bringing-into-focus of elements that are usually not concentrated upon. Your consciousness must learn to organize itself in more than one fashion—or rather, you must be willing to allow your consciousness to use

123

itself more fully. It is not necessarily a matter of trying to ignore the contents of the world, or to deny your physical perception. Instead, the trick is to view the contents of the world in different fashions, to free your physical senses from the restraints that your mental conventions have placed upon them.

Each particular "station" of consciousness perceives in a different kind of reality, and as mentioned earlier *(in Session 711, for instance)*, you usually tune in to your home station most of the time. If you turn your focus only slightly away, the world appears differently; and if that slightly altered focus were the predominant one, then that is how the world would seem to be. Each aspect of the psyche perceives the reality upon which it is focused, and that reality is also the materialization of a particular state of the psyche projected outward. You can learn to encounter other realities by altering your position within your own psyche.

In order to begin, you must first become familiar with the working of your own consciousness as it is directed toward the physical world. You cannot know when you are in focus with <u>another</u> reality if you do not even realize what it feels like to be in full focus with your own. Many people phase in and out of that state without being aware of it, and others are able to keep track of their own "inner drifting." Here, simple daydreaming represents a slight shift of awareness out of directly given sense data.

If you listen to an FM radio station, there is a handy lock-in gadget that automatically keeps the station in clear focus; it stops the program from "drifting." In the same way, when you daydream you drift away from your home station, while still relating to it, generally speaking. You also have the mental equivalent, however, of the FM's lock-in mechanism. On your part this is the result of training, so that if your thoughts or experience stray too far this mental gadget brings them back into line. Usually this is automatic—a learned response that by now appears to be almost instinctive. Period.

You must learn to use this mechanism consciously for your own purposes, for it is extremely handy. Many of you do not pay attention to your own experience, subjectively speaking, so you drift in and out of clear focus in this reality, barely realizing it. Often your daily program is not nearly as clear or well-focused as it should be, but full of static; and while this may annoy you,

you often put up with it or even become so used to the lack of harmony that you forget what a clear reception is like. However, in this world you are surrounded by familiar objects, details, and ideas, and your main orientation is physical so that you can operate through habit alone even when you are not as well focused within your reality as you should be.

(9:56.) When you go traveling off into other systems, however, you cannot depend upon your habits. Indeed, often they can only add to your mental clutter, turning into "static"—so you must learn first of all what a clear focus is.

You will not learn it by trying to escape your own reality, or by attempting to dull your senses. This can only teach you what it means not to focus, and in whatever reality you visit the ability to focus clearly and well is a prerequisite. Once you learn how to really tune in, then you will understand what it means to change the direction of your focus.

One of the simplest exercises is hardly an original one, but it is of great benefit.

PRACTICE ELEMENT 11

Try to experience all of your present sense data as fully as you can. This tones your entire physical and psychic organism, bringing all of your perceptions together so that your awareness opens fully. Body and mind operate together. You experience an immediate sense of power because your abilities are directed to the fullest of their capacities. In a physical moment you can act directly on the spot, so to speak.

Sit with your eyes open easily, letting your vision take in whatever is before you. Do not strain. On the other hand, do explore the entire field of vision simultaneously. Listen to everything. Identify all the sounds if you can, mentally placing them with the objects to which they correspond even though the objects may be invisible. Sit comfortably but make no great attempt to relax. Instead, feel your body in an alert manner—not in a sleepy distant fashion. Be aware of its pressure against the chair, for example, and of its temperature, of variations: Your hands may be warm and your feet cold, or your belly hot and your head cold. Consciously, then, feel your body's sensations. Is there any taste in your mouth? What odors do you perceive?

Take as much time as you want to with this exercise. It places you in your universe clearly. This is an excellent exercise to use

before you begin—and after you finish with—any experiment
involving an alteration of consciousness.

Take a brief break.

*(10:19. Jane's delivery had been quite a bit faster than usual—
which means she'd kept me writing at a steady pace even though
I was recording the material with my homemade "shorthand."
She said she felt that in this section Seth would have a series of
exercises related to the one he'd just given; these would help
people glimpse at least some of the alternate or probable realities discussed in Section 4.*

*(Break, though, was hardly brief. Resume in the same manner
at 10:42.)*

Now: Bring all of those sensations together. Try to be aware
of all of them at once, so that one adds to the others. If you find
yourself being more concerned with one particular perception,
then make an attempt to bring the ignored ones to the same clear
focus. Let all of them together form a brilliant awareness of the
moment.

When you are using this exercise following any experiment
with an alteration of consciousness, then end it here and go about
your other concerns. You may also utilize it as an initial step that
will help you get the feeling of your own inner mobility. To do
this proceed as given, and when you have the moment's perception as clearly as possible, then willfully let it go.

Let the unity disappear as far as your conscious thought is
concerned. No longer connect up the sounds you hear with their
corresponding objects. Make no attempt to unify vision and
hearing. Drop the package, as it were, as a unified group of
perceptions. The previous clarity of the moment will have changed
into something else. Take one sound if you want to, say of a
passing car, and with your eyes closed follow the sound in your
mind. Keep your eyes closed. Become aware of whatever perceptions reach you, but this time do not judge or evaluate. Then
in a flash open your eyes, alert your body, and try to bring all of
your perceptions together again as brilliantly and clearly as
possible.

When you have the sense world before you this time, let it
climax, so to speak, then again close your eyes and let it fall
away. Do not focus. In fact, unfocus. Period.

When you have done this often enough so that you are intimately aware of the contrast, you will have a subjective feeling,

a point of knowing within yourself, that will clearly indicate to you how your consciousness feels when it is at its finest point of focus in physical reality.

As you go about your day, try now and then to recapture that point and to bring all data into the clearest possible brilliance. You will find that this practice, continued, will vastly enrich your normal experience. You find it much easier to concentrate, to attend. To attend is to pay attention and take care of. So this exercise will allow you to attend—to focus your awareness to the matters at hand as clearly and vividly as possible. The subjective knowledge of your own point of finest focus will also serve as a reference point for many other exercises.

(Pause at 10:58.)

PRACTICE ELEMENT 12

Exercise two [in the session]. For your benefit, Joseph, this entire section will be made up of practice elements, with comments and directions.

You must work from your own subjective experience, so when you find your own finest focus point, that is your clearest reception for your own home station. You may feel that it has a certain position in your inner vision, or in your head, or you may find that you have your own symbol to represent it. You might imagine it, if you want to, as a station indicator on your own radio or television set, but your subjective recognition of it is your own cue.

In our just-previous exercise, when I spoke of having you let your clear perception drop away, and told you to disconnect vision from hearing, you were drifting in terms of your own home station. Your consciousness was straying. This time begin with the point of your own finest focus, which you have established, then let your consciousness stray as given. Only let it stray in a particular direction—to the right or the left, whichever seems most natural to you. In this way you are still directing it and learning to orient yourself. In the beginning, 15 minutes at most for this exercise; but let your awareness drift in whatever direction you have chosen.

Each person will have his or her own private experience here, but gradually certain kinds of physical data will seem to disappear while others may take prominence. For example, you might mentally hear sounds, while knowing they have no physical origin. You may see nothing in your mind, or you may see images that seem to have no exterior correlation, but you may hear nothing. For a while ordinary physical data may continue to intrude. When it does, recognize it as your home station, and mentally let yourself drift further away from it. What is important is your own sensation as you experience the mobility of your consciousness. If ever you grow concerned simply return to your home station, back to the left or right according to the direction you have chosen. I do not suggest that you use "higher" or "lower" as directions, because of the interpretations that you may have placed upon them through your beliefs.

Do not be impatient. As you continue with this exercise over a period of time you will be able to go further away, orienting yourself as you grow more familiar with the feeling of your mind. Gradually you will discover that this inner sense data will become clearer and clearer as you move toward another "station." It will represent reality as perceived from a different state of consciousness.

The first journey from one home station to another, unfamiliar one may bring you in contact with various kinds of bleed-throughs, distortions, or static. These can be expected. They are simply the result of not yet learning how to tune your own consciousness clearly in to other kinds of focus. Before you can pick up the "next" station, for example, you may see ghost images in your mind, or pick up distorted versions from your own home station. You have momentarily dispensed with the usual, habitual organizational process by which you unite regular physical sense perceptions, so while you are "between stations," you may well encounter mixed signals from each. When you alter your conscious focus in such a fashion, you are also moving away from the part of your psyche that you <u>consider</u> its center. You are journeying through your own psyche, in other words, for different realities are different states of the psyche— materialized, projected outward and experienced. That applies to your home station or physical world as well.

Are you tired?

(11:20. "No," I said. Seth-Jane's pace had been good, though— quiet yet forceful.)

Even your home station has many programs, and you have usually tuned in to one main one and ignored others. Characters in your "favorite program" at home may appear in far different guises when you are between stations, and elements of other programs that you have ignored at home may suddenly become apparent to you.

(Pause.) I will give you a simple example. At home you may tune in to religious programs. That means that you might organize your daily existence about highly idealistic principles. You may try to ignore what you consider other programs dealing with hatred, fear, or violence. You might do such a good job of organizing your physical data about your ideal that you shut out any emotions that involve fear, violence, or hatred. When you alter your consciousness, again, you automatically begin to let old organizations of data drop away. You may have tuned out what you think of as negative feelings or programming. These, however, may have been present but ignored, and when you dispense with your usual method of organizing physical data they may suddenly become apparent.

If you tell yourself that sexual feeling is wrong, and organize your daily programming in that fashion, then when you "meditate," or dispense with that orientation, you may suddenly find yourself presented with material that you consider unsavory. You cannot deny the reality of the psyche, or those natural feelings that you experience in the flesh. When you begin to alter your perception, then, and your habitual picture of reality drops away, you may well find yourself encountering in distorted fashion elements of your own reality that you have up to then studiously denied or ignored.

This is most apparent with those who use the Ouija board or automatic writing as methods to alter consciousness.

Do you want a break?

(11:34. "No," I said again, in answer to Seth-Jane's obvious concern. It was a warm night for the end of October, and we had the windows open; the traffic noise from the busy intersection just one house removed was bothering me more than anything else.)

In your home station, events are encountered clearly in space and time. When you move away, however, you may meet events in time but not in space, and reality that you have tried to deny may then appear vividly. If you understand this you can gain immeasurably, for as you move your focus away from your organized reality, other portions of it upon which you have not concentrated will come into view.

This can show you what was missing from your home station if you know how to read the clues. You form your home station according to your beliefs. If you firmly believe, again, that sex is wrong, then your home station may involve you in a life "programming" in which you constantly try to deny the vitality of the flesh. The sight of a nude body might upset you. You might undress in the dark, or think, if you are married, of the sexual act of intercourse as dirty. If you are a man, you might be ashamed of what you consider to be your need.

I have an example in point. A young man I will call Joe wrote Ruburt a letter. He left his home in San Francisco to travel to India to study with a guru. He has been told that sexual desire mitigates against spiritual illumination. His home program involves him with no sex whatsoever. Joe tries desperately to abstain. At the same time, when he meditates and alters his consciousness, he immediately finds himself with a blinding headache, images of nude women, and fantasies of female goddesses out to tempt him from his celibate state.

Joe thinks of such images as very wrong. Instead, they are telling him something—that his home program is impoverished, for he has been denying the reality of his being.[3] If he ignores the advice of his psyche, then his journeys into the unknown reality will be highly distorted. Seductive goddesses will follow him wherever he goes.

Take your break or end the session as you prefer.

(11:46 P.M. Break turned out to mark the end of the session, though. Jane was surprised at the time; she'd been in trance for over an hour. "My God—he's got the whole thing all laid out," she exclaimed. She too had been bothered by the rush and clatter of traffic, even in trance, and we talked about moving to quieter surroundings before next summer.[4]

(Jane wanted to continue the session, but she was also hungry. "I feel guilty," she laughed. "I want a nice big snack, but I feel all this stuff that Seth's got ready, right on the line . . . Oh, to hell with it—let's eat!")

NOTES: Session 716

1. In Note 1 for Session 715, I described my "first and second Romans"—internal visions or perceptions that had come to me as I lay down for afternoon naps last Sunday and Monday. Each time I'd evi-

dently seen myself as a Roman military officer living early in the first century A.D. In the first episode I was aboard a galley in the Mediterranean; in the second, I floated face down in that sea with my hands bound behind me.

As I prepared to sleep this afternoon I had my third vision in the series. Presumably this will be the last one—for now, closely following upon my precarious circumstance in the water, I saw myself as dead. When I woke up I made another little drawing: I showed my Roman-captain self still face down in the water, but entangled with the branches projecting from a waterlogged tree trunk—I'd been caught that way for a while, before a group of fishermen on a North American beach hauled body and tree ashore in their net. At least, I thought as I described the experience to Jane, I dared face my death in that life *after* the fact of its happening, even if I didn't care to undergo the actual process.

And added later: Jane did use my three Roman experiences in her *Psychic Politics*: she'd mentioned doing so after the second one had taken place, and ended up quoting my own accounts of them in Chapter 4. (As I wrote up my third vision, incidentally, I called myself "captain," automatically using present-day terminology to denote a certain military rank. Then I began to wonder if such a classification had even existed in the Roman armed forces in those ancient times. I learned that it had: A captain was called a "centurio.")

2. Seth discussed probable man and probable civilizations, and mentioned alternate systems of actuality, in various portions of Volume 1. See the 687th session (which bridges sections 1 and 2), for instance, and Appendix 6 for that session.

3. Later, in Chapter 10 of *Politics*, Jane elaborated upon Seth's "Joe" material. She also related Joe's limited model of his nature to some of her own ideas about disciplining her "writing self."

4. A note added four and a half months later: And we did!

Session 718

□

November 6, 1974
9:50 P.M. Wednesday

(On Monday, November 4, I mailed to Jane's publisher all of the art due for her Adventures in Consciousness: An Introduction to Aspect Psychology: *the 16 diagrams I'd just finished, plus two older pieces of work. All are in "line," or pen-and-ink. I thought it interesting that as I was completing work for Jane's first book on aspect psychology, she was starting* Psychic Politics, *the second one in the series. But now I can return to my longer project—the 40 line drawings for Jane's book of poetry,* Dialogues of The Soul and Mortal Self in Time. Adventures *and* Dialogues *are to be published by Prentice-Hall in the spring and fall, respectively, of 1975. Other references to both books can be found in Note 1 for Session 714.*

(Our last session, the 717th, is deleted from "Unknown" Reality. *For it was and wasn't a Seth session, and it was and wasn't book dictation, as the following notes will show.*

(Before what we expected to be our regular session for Monday evening, Jane told me that she'd awakened in the middle of the previous night with insights about two practice elements[1] Seth would discuss—but we didn't hear from Seth even though she felt him "around" as we prepared for the session.

(Instead a development took place that left us puzzled, intrigued, and more than a little upset. Yet at this writing [immediately following the 718th session], I can note that we've been somewhat relieved by subsequent events. Now, in fact, I'm veering toward the idea that Monday night's session marked a

132

distinct step in the further development of Jane's abilities. She may also use some of that new material in Politics.[2]

(*It seems that a combination of factors led to those oddly disturbing yet challenging events in the 717th session. One is probably just the state of Jane's recent exceptional psychic receptivity. Another is my own longtime interest in the American psychologist and philosopher, William James [1842–1910]; he wrote the classic* The Varieties of Religious Experience.[3] *A third is a letter received last week from a Jungian psychologist who had been inspired by Seth's material on the Swiss psychologist and psychiatrist, Carl Jung [1875–1961], in Chapter 13 of* Seth Speaks. *And a fourth factor would be a most evocative experience Jane had Monday afternoon, in which she found herself experiencing consciousness as an ordinary housefly*[4]: *From that minute but enthralling viewpoint she knew "herself" crawling up a giant-sized blade of grass. She was exploring the "world view" of a fly. This adventure was certainly a preparation for developments in the 717th session.*

(*Other reasons must enter in, of course. But for now let's say that Jane knows of James and his work; she's read parts of his* Varieties, *for instance, but seemed rather put off by it, where I reread passages from it frequently.*

(*The letter from the Jungian psychologist evidently provided the immediate impetus for the fly episode and for Monday evening's events, though. The author requested additional material from Seth on Jung or his works. I hardly think it accidental now that such an inquiry came just when Jane's abilities seemed about to ripen in the particular way they did that night.*

(*We were discussing the letter and half-facetiously wondering whether Seth might respond in any way, when Jane suddenly told me that she was picking up material on the "essence" of William James. Because of his own persistent melancholy, she said, James had been able to understand others with the same kind of disposition. As she continued to give her impressions, though, I wondered: Why James? He wasn't mentioned in the psychologist's letter, for instance. Why this picking up on, and identifying with, a famous dead personality? Most likely my own interest in James's work exerted some kind of influence upon Jane's newly developing abilities, I thought; but still, that didn't answer my questions.*

(*What had happened to Seth? That individual would have to*

wait. "I was getting just now," Jane said at 8:58, "that James called his melancholy 'a cast of soul.' " Her eyes were closed. "Now I'm getting a book. Why, it's a paperback. I see this printed material, only it's very small, almost microscopic, and oddly enough the whole thing is printed on grayish-type paper. I see it really small, in my mind."

(And with that, in an altered state of consciousness, Jane began delivering last Monday evening the material from the book she mentally saw. Before I fully realized what was happening, I was taking her words down verbatim.

(The material itself was beautifully done, rather quaint in expression but of excellent quality. When I typed it the next day [yesterday], there were over 10 pages of double-spaced prose. Here's a small quotation from it, dealing with part of a vision "James" had following his physical death:

("There was a procession, a procession of the gods that went before my very eyes. I wondered and watched silently. Each god or goddess had a poet who went in company, and the poets sang that they gave reason voice. They sang gibberish, yet as I listened the gibberish turned into a philosophical dialogue. The words struck at my soul. A strange mirror-image type of action followed, for when I spoke the poets' words backwards, to my intellect they made perfect sense."

(At one of our breaks Jane said that she had picked up the title of the James book from which she'd been "reading": The Varieties of Religious States—*with only* States *differing from* Experience *in the name of James's book in our physical reality. She'd also felt Seth around, like a supervisor, perhaps. She added: "I felt as if the James stuff was coming from a person who was very intent about trying to say something."*

(Which pointed up our dilemma, I thought at the time. I said little to Jane, but I was most uneasy that she was delivering material supposedly from a member of the famous dead. Actually, we'd always thought that such performances were somehow suspect. Not that mediums, or others, couldn't communicate with the "dead"—but to us, anyhow, exhibitions involving well-known personages usually seem . . . psychologically tainted. So our feelings about the night's affair weren't of the best at that point.

(The events to come didn't help matters any, either. No sooner had Jane finished with the lengthy James material than she promptly began to get impressions from "Carl Jung." This time

she was almost apologetic. We decided to go ahead, though. Jane didn't see a book or have any visual data. The words just came to her along with strong emotional feelings that she connected with Jung.

(The material seemed endless. It was a few minutes before midnight when Jane just stopped, saying that she'd more or less "had it" for the evening. The Jung material felt much more animated, she added, with a lot of vitality and energy to it: " 'He' really seemed excitable." Neither of us found the Jung passages as evocative as the James material, however. This is a brief Jungian excerpt:

("Numbers have an emotional equivalent, in that their symbols originally arose from the libido that always identifies itself with the number 1, and feels all other numbers originating out of itself. The libido knows itself as God, and therefore all fractions fly out of the self-structure of its own reality."

(Jane said she had the impression of someone very compact, loaded with energy, almost wildly adolescent in a way, going off in too many directions at once.

(We both wondered right then if Jane was going off in too many directions at once. She'd always refused to try to "reach the dead" in this way before. Both of us were more than a little troubled—but as usual, we were intrigued even as we questioned our own reactions. We were also quite aware of the humorous aspects of the situation, since Jane does speak for at least one of the "dead": Seth. And of course, as we sat for tonight's session we wondered if Seth would discuss what had happened Monday night.

(I'd just begun typing the "James and Jung" material, so from my original notes I read the rest of it to Jane as we waited for Seth to come through. I also thought she discussed an excellent idea of her own, saying that she believed the James-Jung episode itself was an exercise in making the unknown reality known. She'd already done some writing yesterday, for Psychic Politics, leading toward this view [5]; so whatever we learned through Seth this evening, we already felt reasonably sure that in usual trite terms Jane hadn't been communicating directly with two such famous personalities. Instead, she was involved in something quite a bit different—and much more believable.)

Good evening.

("Good evening, Seth.")

Now. This section [of *"Unknown" Reality*] deals with the various exercises that will, I hope, provide you with your own intimate glimpses into previously unknown realities.

I said *(in sessions 711 and 716, for instance)* that your normal focus of consciousness can be compared to your home station. So far, exercises have been described that will gently lead you away from concentration upon this home base, even while its structure is strengthened at the same time. You can also call this home station or local program your world view, since from it you perceive your reality. To some extent it represents your personal focus, through which you interpret most of your experience. As I mentioned *(in Session 715, for instance)*, when you begin to move away from that particular organization, strange things may start to happen. You may be filled with wonder, excitement, or perplexity. You may be delighted or appalled, according to whether or not your new perceptions agree or disagree with your established world view.

Instead of a regular session *(last Monday night)*, the framework of the session was used in a new kind of exercise. It was meant as an example of what <u>can</u> happen under the best of circumstances, when someone leaves a native world view and tunes in to another, quite different from the original.

You always form your own experience. Ruburt picked up on the world view of a man known dead. He was not directly in communication with William James.

(Slowly:) He was aware, however, of the universe through William James's world view. Period. As you might dial a program on a television set, Ruburt tuned in to the view of reality now held in the mind of William James. Because that view necessarily involved emotions, Ruburt felt some sense of emotional contact—but only with the validity of the emotions. Each person has such a world view, whether living or dead in your terms, and that "living picture" exists despite time or space. It <u>can</u> be perceived by others.

(Pause, one of many.) Each world view exists at its own particular "frequency," and can only be tuned in to by those who are more or less within the same range. However, the frequencies themselves have to be adjusted properly to be brought into focus, and those adjustments necessitate certain intents and sympathies. It is not possible to move in to such a world view if

you are basically at odds with it, for example. You simply will not be able to make the proper adjustments.

Ruburt has been working with alterations of consciousness *(for Psychic Politics)*, and wondering about the basic validity of religion. He has been trying to reconcile intellectual and emotional knowledge. James is far from one of his favorite writers, yet Ruburt's interests, intent, and desire were close enough so that under certain conditions he could experience the world view held by James. The unknown reality is unknown only because you believe it must be hidden. Once that belief is annihilated, then other quite-as-legitimate views of reality can appear to your consciousness, and worlds just as valid as your own swim into view.

To do this, you must have faith in yourself, and in the framework of your known reality. Otherwise you will be too afraid to abandon even briefly the habitual, organized view of the world that is your own.

Even in your life as you understand it, if you are insecure or frightened, you cannot properly see your family or your neighbors. If you are afraid, then your own fear stands between yourself and others. You do not dare take your eyes off yourself for a second. You cannot afford to be friendly, for instance, because you are terrified of being rebuffed.

In the same way, if you are overly concerned about the nature of your own reality, and if you are looking to others to justify your existence, you will not be able to abandon your own world view successfully, for you will feel too threatened. Or, traveling in psychic exercises even slightly away from your own home station, you will still try to take your familiar paraphernalia with you, and interpret even entirely new situations of consciousness in the light of your own world view. You will transpose your own set of assumptions, then, into conditions in which they may not really fit at all.

(10:22.) Ruburt picked up on William James's world view because their interests coincided. A letter from a Jungian psychologist helped serve as a stimulus. The psychologist asked me *(deeper and with humor)* to comment about Jung. Ruburt felt little correspondence with Jung. In the back of his mind he wondered about James, mainly because he knew that Joseph *(Rob)* enjoyed one of James's books.

It is quite possible to tune in to the world view of any person, living or dead in your terms. The world view of any individual, even <u>not yet born</u> from your standpoint, exists nevertheless. Ruburt's experience simply serves as an example of what is possible.

Quite rightly, he did not interpret the event in conventional terms, and Joseph did not suppose that James himself was communicating in the <u>way</u> usually imagined *(but see the opening notes for this session)*. Joseph did recognize the excellence of the material. James was not aware of the situation. For that matter, James himself is embarked upon other adventures. Ruburt picked up on James's world view, however, as in your terms at least it "existed" perhaps 10 years ago.[6] Then, in his mind, James playfully thought of a book that he would write were he "living," called *The Varieties of Religious States*—an altered version of a book he wrote in life.

He felt that the soul chooses states of emotion as you would choose, say, a state to live in. He felt that the chosen emotional state was then used as a framework through which to view experience. He began to see a conglomeration of what he loosely called religious states, each different and yet each serving to unify experience in the light of its particular "natural features." These natural features would appear as the ordinary temperaments and inclinations of the soul.

Ruburt tuned in to that unwritten book. It carried the stamp of James's own emotional state at that "time," when he was viewing his earthly experience, in your terms, from the standpoint of one who had died, could look back, and see where he thought his ideas were valid and where they were not. At that point in his existence, there were changes. The plan for the book existed, and still does. In Ruburt's "present," he was able to see this world view as expressed within James's immortal mind.

To do this, Ruburt had to be free enough to accept the view of reality as perceived by someone else. To accomplish this, Ruburt allowed one portion of his consciousness to remain securely anchored in its own reality while letting another portion soak up, so to speak, a reality not its own.

(Pause.) The unknown reality, colon: Again, because of your precise orientation you are often theoretically intrigued by the contemplation of worlds <u>not</u> your own. And while you may often yearn for some evidence of those other realities, you are just as

apt to become scandalized[7] by the very evidence that you have so earnestly requested.

Ruburt has embarked upon his own journeys into the unknown reality. I cannot do that for him. I can only point out the way, as I do for each reader. In his own new book *(Politics)* Ruburt has his personal way of explaining what he is experiencing, and since he shares the same reality with you, then you will be able to relate—perhaps better, even—to his explanations than to mine.

However, it is quite possible for him to tune in to James's complete book if he desires to, for that work is indeed a psychic reality, a plan or a model existing in the inward order of activity *(as Jane had explained to me in similar terms this afternoon).*

Such creative "architect's plans" are often unknowningly picked up by others, altered or changed, ending up as entirely new productions. Most writers do not examine their sources that closely. The same applies, of course, to any field of endeavor. Many quite modern and sophisticated developments have existed in what you think of now as past civilizations. The plans, as models, were picked up by inventors, scientists, and the like, and altered to their own specific directions, so that they emerged in your world not as copies but as something new. Many so-called archaeological discoveries were made when individuals suddenly tuned in to a world view of another person not of your space or time. Before you have the confidence to leave your own particular home station, however, you must be secure within it. You must know it will "be there" when you get back.

Take your break.

(10:52. Jane's trance had been deep, her delivery for the most part just about as fast as I could write. I told her that Seth's material was excellent, that it backed up her ideas as to the nature of the James-Jung "communications," and added more data as well.

("I felt out of the James thing until you read it to me before the session," she said, "then a lot of aspects about it came back. We won't bother doing that book of his, I know, but I could get it—the whole thing. It's right there in the library. . . ." We talked about what an interesting product The Varieties of Religious States *would be, and the many implications involved, without intending to do anything more about such a work.*

(We also discussed the parallels—and differences—revolving around Jane's perception of the James book this week, and her

*development eight months ago of the outline and chapter head-
ings for the possible book,* The Way Toward Health. *Two months
later, in May, she produced the summary for* The Wonderworks,
*which would be a shorter dissertation on her own dreams, Seth,
and the dream-formation of the universe as we know it. [See
appendixes 7 and 11 in Volume 1 of* "Unknown" Reality.*] Jane
hasn't taken the time to concentrate upon either of those projects, interesting as they are, although she would if one—or
both—of them "caught fire" for her. Neither Jane nor Seth had
delivered their respective world-view ideas when she came through
with* Health *and* Wonderworks, *so another significant aspect of
her abilities has since become conscious. Once more questions
arise. For instance: Whose world view was Jane tuning in to for
the health book? Her own? In turn, of course, all three potential
endeavors—Religious States, Health, and Wonderworks—must
have origins that are closely related to the source of information
behind the "psychic library" Jane tells of visiting in* Politics.

(Resume in the same manner at 11:14.)

Now: Ruburt has trained himself to deal with words as a
writer. When he picks up a world view that belongs to someone
else, he can quite automatically translate it faithfully enough in
that idiom of language. Many artists do the same thing, translating inner "models" into paint, lines, and form.

So do scientists and inventors often tune in to the world views
of others—living or dead, in your terms—that correlate with
their own intents, talents, and purposes.[8]

These "other," reinterpreted world views form a matrix from
which new creativity emerges. The same thing applies in more
mundane endeavors in ordinary life. For example: You may be
in a predicament that seems beyond solving. It may be highly
individual, since it is yours. It is unique, and has happened in no
other way before. No one else has viewed your particular dilemma through your eyes, yet others have been in similar situations, solved the challenges involved, and gone on to greater
creativity and fulfillment. If you can momentarily abandon your
private world view, that focus from which you experience reality, then you can allow the experience of others who have had
similar challenges to color your perception. You can tune in to
their solutions and apply them to your particular circumstances.
You often do this unconsciously. I do not want you to think,
then, that such occurrences work only in esoteric terms.

Many people working with the Ouija board or automatic writing receive messages that seem, or purport, to come from historic personages. Often, however, the material is vastly inferior to that which could have been produced by the person in question during his or her existence. Any comparison with the material received to the written books or accounts already existing would immediately show glaring discrepancies.

Yet in many such instances, the Ouija board operator or the automatic writer is to some extent or another tuning in to a world view, struggling to open roads of perception free enough to perceive an altered version of reality, but not equipped enough through training and temperament, perhaps, to express it.

(Long pause at 11:30.) The most legitimate instances of communication between the living and the dead occur in an intimate personal framework, in which a dead parent makes contact with its offspring[9]: or a husband or wife freshly out of physical reality appears to his or her mate. But very seldom do historic personages make contact, except with their own intimate circles.

(Emphatically:) There is great energy, however, in those who have persevered enough to become generally known in their time, and the great impetus of that psychic and mental energy does not cease at death, but continues. In their way others may tune in to that continuing world view; and, picking it up, can be convinced that they are in contact with the physical personality who held it.

Give us a moment . . . You are so used to your own private interpretation of reality that when you allow yourselves to stray from it, you immediately want to interpret your new experience in terms that make sense to your familiar orientation. You are also highly involved with symbols. In ordinary life you often hamper your own creativity. When you use the Ouija board or trance procedures, you frequently free philosophical areas of your mind that have been frozen. The resulting information then definitely seems to come from outside of yourself, and because you are literal-minded you try to interpret such experiences in a literal way. The material must come from a philosopher, therefore *(amused)*, and since it certainly seems profound to your usual mundane organization, then it appears that such information must originate with a profound mind certainly not your own.

You may signify this to yourself symbolically, so that the
board or the automatic writing designates its origin as being
Socrates[10] or Plato. If you are spiritualistically oriented, the
information may come from a famous psychic recently dead.
Instead, you yourself have momentarily escaped from your accustomed world view, or home program; you are reaching out
into other levels of reality, but still interpreting your experience
in old terms. Therefore much of its creativity escapes you.

You are each as valid as Socrates or Plato. Your influences
reach through the entire framework of actuality in ways that you
did not understand. Socrates and Plato—and William James
(note that I smiled)—specialized in certain fashions. You know
those individuals as names of people that existed—but in your
terms, and in your terms only, those existences represented the
flowering aspects of their personalities. *(Louder:)* They often
dwelled nameless upon the face of the earth, as many of you do,
in your terms only, now, before reaching what you think of as
those summits.

Wait a moment. End of dictation—though I will have something to say about Ruburt's experience as a fly.

*(11:49. Jane rested a minute or so, still in trance. Her fly
experience of last Monday afternoon is mentioned in the opening
notes for this session. When Seth returned, he delivered half a
page of material for Jane and me, including this passage: "He
[Ruburt] has made an extraordinary leap into his [psychic] library, and it is freeing him physically. You have made as vital a
leap, and it is freeing you artistically. The library is valid, and
in the most legitimate of terms it is far more important, for
example, than a physical library. . . ." Seth finished his personal material at 12:10 A.M., and we thought the session was
over. Jane was very tired, much more so than she usually is after
a session. She wanted only to sleep.*

*(We keep our typewritten transcripts of the sessions in a series
of three-ring binders. I not only record the current session in the
latest one, of course, but have in there a page or two of
comments and questions so that from time to time I can ask Seth
to clear them up. In closing the notebook tonight, I noticed the
query I'd written following the 697th session for May 13, 1974,
in Volume 1. In that session Seth told us: "Because you are now
a conscious species, in your terms, there are racial idealizations
that you can accept or deny."*

*(I've never really forgotten that statement of almost six months
ago, nor Seth's saying at the end of the 699th session that he'd
go into my questions about it "when your material will fit."*

*("What," I wrote at the time, "would a state other than a
conscious one be? I have difficulty conceiving of such a situation—
which, perhaps, is more revealing of the way I think than of
anything else. But how could the species, or its individual members, not be 'conscious'? Since I think our collective and individual actions are self-consciously designed for survival, in the best
meaning of that word, I'm curious to know in what other state
these functions could be performed, for existence's sake . . .
There are many ramifications here, as I discovered when I
started making notes about this concept, so I'm purposely keeping them short."*

*(When Jane first read my question after she'd held the 697th
session, she told me that she "didn't get it"—that perhaps I was
drawing inferences from Seth's material that weren't intended. I
tried to explain the point at issue to her on several different
occasions, and discovered each time that it was an oddly elusive
one to put into words.*

*(Idly now, not intending that Jane do any more work this
evening, I read my question aloud. She raised a hand in dismay.
"I'm tired," she said, "but wait a minute—I've got the answer.
Seth's all ready. Get me a pack of cigarettes, and I'll do
it. . . ."*

(12:14.) Now: I have been using your terms as I understood
your meaning of them.

There are, in those terms, gradations. When I used the word
"conscious" (or "consciousness"), I meant it as I thought you
understood it. I thought that you meant: conscious of being
conscious, or placing yourself on the one hand outside of a
portion of your own consciousness—viewing it *(intently)* and
then saying, "I am conscious of my consciousness."

Consciousness is always conscious of itself, and of its validity
and integrity, and in those terms there is no unconsciousness.

When I use the term time-wise, I refer it to the formation of a
structure from which one kind of consciousness then views itself,
sees itself as unique, and then tries to form other kinds of
conscious structures. A fly is conscious of itself, fulfilled within
that reality, and feels no need to form an "extension" of that
awareness from which to view its own existence.

In your terms, time considerations involved extensions of that kind of consciousness, in which separations could occur and divisions could be made. In terms of an <u>organic</u> structure, this could be likened to developing another arm or leg, or protrusion or filament—another method of locomotion through another kind of dimension.

The fly is intensely conscious, at every moment engrossed in itself and its environment, precisely tuned to elements of which <u>you</u> are "unconscious." There are simply different kinds of consciousness, and you cannot basically compare one to the other any more than you can compare, say, a toad to a star to an apple to a thought to a woman to a child to a native to a suburbanite to a spider to a cat. They are <u>varieties</u> of consciousness, each focused upon its own view of reality, each containing experience that others exclude.

(Louder, humorously:) <u>End of explanation</u>.

(With a laugh: "Thank you very much." 12:19 A.M. And so it turned out that I brought up my questions about self-consciousness, and Seth answered them, when that material did fit.

(A note added in December 1977: The 718th session on world views proved to be a cornerstone in Jane's own development, and in Seth's thematic structure as well. Jane's The World View of Paul Cézanne: A Psychic Interpretation, *was published earlier this year, and as I type this final manuscript for Volume 2 of* "Unknown" Reality *I can add that she's also completed* The Afterdeath Journal of an American Philosopher: The World View of William James. *It came out in 1978.*

(In a sense, both world-view books were "born" in the 718th session and the odd previous one that took place under Seth's auspices. I write this although Jane had no idea of producing such works when those two sessions were held [but see my speculations in Note 6]. Nothing has been forthcoming on any additional material concerning Carl Jung, however—nor has Jane tried for this.

(The entire world-view concept is extremely interesting, of course, and worthy of continuous investigation.

(Oddly enough, the original pages of the James material that Jane saw mentally during the 717th session [and later presented in Chapter 6 of Psychic Politics] *never appeared in* Afterdeath Journal. *There were two different James books in her "library," Jane said. She transcribed only one of them.)*

NOTES: Session 718

1. Jane remembered part of one of the two practice elements she'd tuned in to Sunday night; perhaps we'll get them later. She said that Seth had designed them to follow those he'd given in the 716th session. At the moment, even the fragment she recalled is well worth trying: Seth instructed the reader to immerse himself or herself in an old photograph of a person—and then to look out at our current physical reality through that individual's eyes. An interesting way to gain a fresh perspective on our present time.

2. A note added several months later: I see now that I should enlarge upon Note 2 for the 715th session, in which I wrote that Jane "would initiate the transposition of material from Volume 2 of *'Unknown' Reality* into *Politics*, since she was so intimately and enthusiastically involved in producing both books at the same time." For her to work this way is entirely in keeping with her spontaneous nature; she intuitively seeks to use whatever sources of information—including Seth himself—she has at hand for whatever project she may be engaged in. In the early chapters of *Politics* especially, then, she both quotes and paraphrases material from Volume 2, beginning with the 714th session, which contains her account of her original inspiration for that work.

However, Jane's use of material in this manner is quite natural in another way also: for *Politics* represents her personal exploration of the unknown reality that Seth has been so graphically describing in his own work.

I always indicate in Volume 2 when such a movement of material into *Politics* has taken place. Yet Jane did no blind copying, and almost always she quoted an excerpt rather than a complete passage from a session, for instance. Jane and Seth each say what they want to say from their unique, respective viewpoints—and it becomes obvious that her book should be read as an adjunct to Seth's.

For example, Jane began *Politics* by describing how impatient she was, how "disconnected" she felt, because she hadn't been inspired since finishing *Adventures* two months previously. Indeed, she was very upset over this, and quite serious in her feeling, as she later wrote in her new book, of being abandoned by her inner self. In Volume 2, now, the reader can note the many events Jane was actually involved in before she began *Politics* (on October 23), and see just how objective her perception of her activities was—or see, really, the demanding standards of creativity against which she constantly judges herself.

In my own notes, of course, I described those events dealt with by Jane and Seth from my own perspective, as I watched them happen. "In *'Unknown' Reality* the reader should focus upon the material from Seth's viewpoint," Jane said. "Yet it might be fun now and then to look at the daily events in our lives *first*, as recorded in Rob's notes—and see the dictation in the sessions as emerging from those humble sources. What I've said in *Psychic Politics* should certainly add a lot of insight there."

3. Longmans, Green and Co., London, 1908.

4. The contents of this note flow out of what I wrote in Note 2: Seth mentions Jane's fly experience in this (718th) session, and Jane discussed it in more detail in Chapter 5 of *Politics*. Then in Chapter 6 of her book she presented long excerpts from the James-Jung material as it developed in the 717th session.

5. See Jane's "library" material at the beginning of Chapter 7 of *Politics*. And again: For her own purposes she quoted in the same chapter the appropriate Seth material from the 718th session.

6. Since William James died in 1910, this means that in our terms Jane picked up on his world view as it existed some 54 years after his physical death. We could easily ask Seth a dozen questions about the ideas he's given in just this one paragraph of material. Very lengthy answers could result, leading to more queries. A book on world views could even develop. But the questions always pile up ahead of us; often they're never voiced, no matter how interesting they may be. Whether Seth will ever deal with this latest batch, implied as they are, is very problematical.

7. See the 715th session after 10:43.

8. Seth's information here, that scientists and inventors often tune in to the world views of other such individuals, at once reminded me that a similar long-term situation could have existed within the Butts family.

In Volume 1, see Session 680, with notes 1–3. My father, Robert Sr., who died in 1971, was very gifted mechanically. According to Seth, a still-living probable self of Robert Butts, Sr., is "a well-known inventor, who never married but used his mechanically creative abilities to the fullest while avoiding emotional commitment." Although my father's "sole intent" was the very challenging one of raising a family in this reality, still he may have often exchanged ideas about automobiles, motorcycles, welding torches, cameras, and so forth, with that other inventor-self.

Do probable selves actually communicate with each other through their world-view frameworks, then, or can such an interchange of idea or emotion take place more "directly" at times—simply between the probable personalities involved? Either situation can apply, it seems to me, or the two methods may merge at any given "time." We plan to ask Seth to elaborate.

9. Nine months ago, in February 1974, Seth mentioned the few tentative contacts I'd evidently made with my deceased mother through dreams; see the 683rd session after 11:30, then see my account of one such dream in Note 5 for that session. Two months later, in the 693rd session, Seth described how I reacted (on a cellular, or "unconscious" level) to communications from my mother as Jane and I considered

buying a certain house in my childhood neighborhood in Sayre, Pennsylvania. So far, Jane has nothing to report about meetings of any kind with her late mother or father. (All of our parents died between February 1971 and November 1973.)

10. I'd like to dwell a bit upon a point I made in the opening notes for this (718th) session, when I wrote about mediums, or others, contacting the well-known dead. I mean it kindly—but Jane and I have never believed that a living individual could be in contact with a famous dead person, especially through the Ouija board or automatic writing. Although we haven't scoffed at such instances when we heard of them, we've certainly regarded those encounters through very skeptical eyes. The gist of our attitudes is that we find it most difficult to believe that "Socrates"—wherever he is and whatever he may be doing, in our terms—is willing to drop everything to give very garbled information to a well-intentioned, really innocent person living in, say, a small town in Virginia. There must be other things he wants to do! Seth's world-view concept, and Jane's own experiences with it, make the accounts of such happenings much more understandable.

Session 719

☐

November 11, 1974
9:36 P.M. Monday

(Jane was so relaxed and "floppy" before the session that I asked her if she'd rather not have it. She decided that she wanted to try. She's been experiencing many muscular changes and releases in recent days. I read parts of the last session to her, to remind us both of what Seth had discussed. At 9:30 Jane said: "There—I'm just beginning to feel him around. . . .")

Now: Good evening—

("Good evening, Seth.")

—and dictation. I consider my own book, *The Nature of Personal Reality: A Seth Book,* as a prerequisite for the exercises given here in this volume.

In that previous book I discussed the ways in which you form your private experience through your beliefs. You have certain pet ideas, therefore, and you use them to structure your own world view of the reality you know. It is important that you understand what your own beliefs are. Many of them might work quite well "at home," but when you begin to journey away from that home station you may find that those same ideas impede your progress.

Other concepts are really not basically workable even in your own physical reality. A rigid, dogmatic concept of good and evil will force you to perceive physical existence as a battleground of opposing forces, with the poor unwary soul almost as a buffer. Or you will think of the poor soul as a blackboard eraser, slapped between two hands—one good and one evil.

Upon the blackboard, in this homey analogy, would be written the soul's earthly experiences. With the eraser the"evil hand" would try to rub out all of the good, and at the same time the "good hand" would be trying to erase all of the evil. In such a case all of your experience becomes suspect. You will have a tendency to consider the body with its natural appetites wrong, and deny them, while at the same time the physical part of you will look upon your "good intents" as wrong, and infringements upon its own existence.

If you do not understand the natural grace of your being,[1] then when you try some of the exercise given here you may automatically translate them into a quite limiting set of beliefs.

You are familiar with your own view of the world. As you leave your usual orientation, however, altering the focus of your consciousness, you may very well structure your new experience just as you do your physical one. At the same time, you _are_ more free. You have greater leeway. You are used to projecting your beliefs onto physical objects and events. When you leave your home station, those objects and events no longer present themselves in the same fashion.

(Intently:) You often find yourself encountering your own structures, no longer hidden in the kind of experience with which you are familiar. These may then appear in quite a different light. You may be convinced that you are evil simply because you are physical. You may believe that the soul "descends" into the body, and therefore that the body is lower, inferior, and a degraded version of "what you really are." At the same time your own physical being knows better, and basically cannot accept such a concept.[2] So in daily life you may project this idea of unworth outward onto another person, who seems then to be your enemy; or upon another nation. In general, you might select animals to play the part of the enemy, or members of another religion, or political parties.

In any case, in your _private_ life you may hardly ever encounter your belief in your own unworth, or evil. You will not realize that you actually consider _yourself_ the enemy. You will be so convinced that your projection (onto others) is the enemy that there will be no slack to take up, for all of your feelings of self-hate or self-fear will be directed outward.

When you begin to leave your home station and alter your focus, however, you leave behind you the particular familiar receptors for your projections. Using the Ouija board or auto-

matic writing, you may find yourself immediately confronted
with this material that you have suppressed in the past. When it
surfaces you may then project it outward from yourself again,
but in a different fashion. Instead of thinking you are in contact
with a great philosopher or "ancient soul," you may believe that
you are instead visiting with a demon or a devil, or that you are
possessed of an evil spirit.

In such a case, you will have already been convinced of the
power of evil. Your natural feelings, denied, will also carry the
great charge of repression. You may be filled with the feeling
that you are in the midst of a great cosmic struggle between the
forces of good and evil—and indeed, this often represents a valid
picture of your own view of the world.

(Long pause.) None of this is necessary. There is no danger in
the exercises I suggest. You are in far greater danger the longer
you inhibit your natural feelings, and alterations of consciousness often present you with the framework in which these come
to light. If they do not in one way or another come to your
attention, then it is very possible that the denied energy behind
them will erupt in ruptured relationships or illnesses.

Long pause at 10:11.) "Psychic explorations" never cause
such difficulties, nor do they ever compound original problems.
On the contrary, they are often highly therapeutic, and they
present the personality with an alternative—an alternative to
continued repression that would be literally unbearable.

If you are normally capable of dealing with physical reality,
you will encounter no difficulties in alterations of consciousness, or leaving your home station. Be reasonable, however: If
you have difficulties in New York City, you are most apt to
encounter them in a different form no matter where else you
might travel. A change of environment might help clear your
head by altering your usual orientation, so that you can see
yourself more clearly, and benefit. The same applies when you
leave your home station. Here the possible benefits are far
greater than in usual life and travel, but you are still yourself. It
is impossible not to structure reality in some fashion. Reality
implies a structuring.

If you take your own world view with you all of the time,
however, as you travel, even in your own world, then you never
see the "naked culture." You are always a tourist, taking your
homey paraphernalia with you and afraid to give it up. If you are

American or English, or European, then when you visit other areas of the world you stay at cosmopolitan hotels. You always see other cultures through your own eyes.

Now when you leave your home station and alter your consciousness, you are always a tourist if you take your own baggage of ideas along with you, and interpret your experiences through your own personal, cultural beliefs. There is nothing unconventional about gods and demons, good spirits or bad spirits. These are quite conventional interpretations of experience, with religious overtones. <u>Cults simply represent counterconventions, and they are as dogmatic in their way as the systems they reject</u>. Underline that sentence.

Give us a moment . . . When you try these exercises, therefore, make an honest attempt to leave your conventional ideas behind you. Step out of your own world view. There is an exercise that will help you.

PRACTICE ELEMENT 13

Close your eyes. Imagine a photograph of yourself (in parentheses: Yes, we are finally back to photographs).[3] In your mind's eye see the photograph of yourself on a table or desk. If you are working mentally with a particular snapshot, then note the other items in the picture. If the photograph is strictly imaginary, then create an environment about the image of yourself.

Look at the image in your mind as it exists in the snapshot, and see it as being aware only of those other objects that surround it. Its world is bounded by the four edges of the picture. Try to put your consciousness into that image of yourself. Your world view is limited to the photograph itself. Now in your mind see that image walking <u>out</u> of the snapshot, onto the desk or table. *(Pause.)* The environment of the physical room will seem gigantic to that small self. The scale and proportion alone will be far different. Imagine that miniature image navigating in the physical room, then going outside, and quite an expanded world view will result.

Take your break.

(10:37. Jane's delivery had been rather fast throughout, except for an occasional long pause. She felt more alert now, she said, but still wasn't as wide-awake as usual. She'd been taking a little wine during her trance. At her request I got her a glass of milk—which she didn't finish before Seth returned.

(During break I saw a certain look pass across Jane's tired face. I couldn't describe the expression, but it reminded me of the internal "vision" I'd had this afternoon when I lay down to sleep: I found myself looking at a very old, very probable future manifestation of myself in this life, who rested quietly in bed. Just before supper tonight I finished writing an account of what I'd seen, and Jane read it while we ate. See Note 4. Now as we discussed the event in a little more detail, I made a quick sketch of that possible self of mine.

(Resume at 11:01.)

Dictation: Many of you do not really want to step out of the photograph, or leave your world view, yet in the dream state you are far freer. You can pretend that dreams are not "real," however, so you can have your cake and eat it too, so to speak.

Different varieties of dreams often provide frameworks that allow you to leave your own world view under "cushioned conditions." You step out of the normal picture that you have made of reality.

(As Seth, Jane took a swallow of milk. She promptly made a most disapproving face. Her features wrinkled up, her lips drew back distastefully. She held the half-empty glass of milk up to me, her Seth voice booming out:)

This is far different from any milk that I ever drank! It is like a chalk with chemicals, far divorced from any cow!

(Still in trance, Jane set the milk aside. She didn't return to it, but sipped her wine for the rest of the session. I was tempted to ask Seth to explain his idea of what good milk was like, and in what life [or lives] he'd enjoyed such a potion, but I didn't want to interrupt the flow of the material. While tasting the milk during break, however, Jane "herself" had had no such reaction.)

Your alterations of consciousness frequently occur in the dream state, therefore, where it seems to you at least that your experiences do not have any practical application. You imagine that only hallucinations are involved. Many of your best snapshots of other realities are taken in your dreams.[5] They may be over-or-underdeveloped, and the focus may be blurred, but your dreams present you with far more information about the unknown reality than you suppose. In the most intimate of terms your body is your home station, so when you leave it you often hide this fact from yourselves.

In your sleep, however, your consciousness slips out of your body and returns to it frequently. You dream when you are out of your body, even as you dream inside it. You may therefore form dream stories about your own out-of-body travel, while your physical image rests soundly in bed. The unknown reality, you see, is not really that mysterious to you. You only pretend that it is. Sometimes you have quite clear perceptions of your journeys, but the actual native territories that you visit are so different from your own world that you try to interpret them as best you can in the light of usual conditions. If you remember such an episode at all it may well seem very confusing, for you will have superimposed your own world view where it does not belong.

(11:16.) In dream travel it is quite possible to journey to other civilizations—those in your past or future, or even to worlds whose reality exists in other probable systems. There is even a kind of "cross-breeding," for you <u>affect</u> any system of reality with which you have experience. There are no closed realities, only <u>apparent</u> boundaries that seem to separate them.*[6] The more parochial your own world view, however, the less you will recall of their dreams or their activities, or the more distorted your "dream snapshots" will be.

Now here is another brief but potent exercise.

PRACTICE ELEMENT 14

Before you go to sleep, tell yourself that you will mentally take a dream snapshot[7] of the most significant dream of the night. Tell yourself that you will even be aware of doing this while asleep, and imagine that you have a camera with you. You mentally take this into the dream state. You will use the camera at the point of your clearest perceptions, snap your picture, and—mentally again—take it back with you so that it will be the first mental picture that you see when you awaken.

You will, of course, try to snap as good a picture as possible. Varying results can be expected. Some of you will awaken with a dream picture that presents itself immediately. Others may find such a picture suddenly appearing later in the day, in the middle of ordinary activities. If you perform this exercise often, however, many of you will find yourselves able to use the camera consciously even while sleeping, so that it becomes an element of your dream travels; you will be able to bring more and more pictures back with you.

These will be relatively meaningless, however, if you do not learn how to examine them. They are not to be simply filed away and forgotten. You should write down a description of each scene and what you remember of it, including your feelings both at the time of the dream, and later when you record it. The very effort to take this camera with you makes you more of a conscious explorer, and automatically helps you to expand your own awareness while you are in the dream state. Each picture will serve as just one small glimpse of a different kind of reality. You cannot make any valid judgment on the basis of one or two pictures alone.

Now this is a mental camera we are using. There is a knack about being a good dream photographer, and you must learn how to operate the camera. In physical life, for example, a photographer knows that many conditions affect the picture he takes. Exterior situations then are important: You might get a very poor picture on a dark day, for instance. With our dream camera, however, the conditions themselves are mental. If you are in a dark mood, for example, then your picture of inner reality might be dim, poorly outlined, or foreboding. This would not necessarily mean that the dream itself had tragic overtones, simply that it was taken in the "poor light" of the psyche's mood.

(Pause at 11:40.) Inner weather changes constantly, even as the exterior weather does. One dream picture with a dreary cast, therefore, is not much different from a physical photograph taken on a rainy afternoon.

Many people, however, remembering a dark dream, become frightened. You even structure your dreams, of course. For that matter, your dream world is as varied as the physical one. Each physical photographer has an idea of what he wants to capture on film, and so to that extent he structures his picture and his view. The same applies to the dream state. You have all kinds of dreams. You can take what you want, so to speak, from dream reality, as basically you take what you want from waking life. For that reason, your dream snapshots will show you the kind of experience that you are choosing from inner reality.

(Pause at 11:46.) Give us a moment . . . End dictation.

(Seth spent the next six minutes or so giving some personal material for Jane. Then, as he was about to wind up the session:

("Can I ask a question?")

You may indeed.

("What about my little view of myself this afternoon, as a very old man?")

Now: It represented two things: an association with a definite past old-age sensation, and a "precognitive" moment in this life that you have not as yet encountered. Because you were [psychically] open, the position of your body and head acted as the associative bridge between the two events. You were not senile in either.

My heartiest regards and a fond good evening.

("Thank you very much, Seth. Good night."

(11:56 P.M. Seth's comments on my experience certainly illustrate his notions of simultaneous time to some extent, since from my "present" I perceived aspects of myself in the reincarnational "past" as well as in the "future" in this life. See Note 4.

(In ordinary terms I can only wait, of course, to see if I decide to create that distant probable moment in this reality. In the meantime, I have no conscious memory of being an old man, let alone one in the specific, dependent situation in which I saw myself. However, aside from the idea of simultaneous time, I do believe that an individual can touch upon at least some of his or her earlier lives, provided enough long-term effort is given to the endeavor. Since through my internal vision I evidently looked in upon a particular past life of my own, however unaware I was of what I was doing, it seems that the knowledge of that existence may not be too deeply buried within my psyche. I might try jogging my memory through suggestion, to see what else about that life I can recall. It would also be interesting to see whether the same technique could help me tune in to my future in this life.

(But the big thing is finding the physical time to try everything I'd like to do—just as it is with Jane.)

NOTES: Session 719

1. In *Personal Reality*, see the 636th session in Chapter 9, and much of the material in the four sessions making up Chapter 12.

2. When I come across material that puts down the physical body, I sometimes try to counter such negative projections by turning to one of the technological accomplishments of our "degraded" species: I study photographs of minute portions of the human body, taken with a scanning electron microscope. Then I experience a series of steps in thinking—

not all of them good, I'm afraid—and I'd like to mention each one in turn.

At this writing, an electron microscope can magnify the surfaces of tissue samples from 20,000 to 60,000 times. Always the resulting photographs obtained leave me groping as I try to appreciate the beauty, order, and complexity of the human organism at just the greatly enlarged levels shown. (If we could plunge "down" into the body's molecular and atomic stages, and *see* those, we'd find intricacies that are even more unbelievable.)

Next, I ask myself how such a marvelously structured being can think of its image as inferior to *anything*, especially since we're far from understanding it even on a "mere" physical basis, let alone from any sort of nonphysical standpoint. Jane's own abilities, for instance, raise questions about certain biological attributes as well as mental ones; in large part our society still doesn't want to contend with such challenges at this time.

Yet, the awe I invariably feel when I study a microphotograph of the retina of the eye, magnified "only" 20,000 times, is hardly an unalloyed blessing. For next I wonder how the human creature, whose bodily components each possess such a ceaseless, rational integrity, can often function so *ir*rationally as a whole, through the creation of war, poverty, pollution, disease, and so forth. Jane and I hope that her work with Seth is offering insights into these enormous questions about our species' individual and collective behavior. Surely we don't think that atoms or cells, or livers or eyeballs, are irrational.

Finally, the incredibly complex physical assemblage of the human being—or of any organism, to confine ourselves to just "living" entities—always reminds me that according to evolutionary theory life on earth arose by chance alone. We must remember that through Darwinism or Neo-Darwinism science tells us that life has no creative design, or any purpose, behind it; and that, moreover, this ineffable quality called "life" originated (more than 3.4 billion years ago) in a *single* fortuitous chance combination of certain atoms and molecules in a tidal pool, say, somewhere on the face of the planet. . . .

Aside from whatever difficulties I may have about resolving the internal beauties of our physical construction with our external behavior, I hope my deep skepticism about this little "official" scenario on evolution is apparent here. See Appendix 1 in Volume 2 Part I.

3. In Volume 1 of *"Unknown" Reality*, Seth incorporated the use of photographs in practice elements 3–5 and 7.

After tonight's session, Jane told me that his Practice Element 13 was one of the two she'd had insights on during the night preceding the deleted 717th (James-Jung) session. Practice Element 14 didn't seem at all familiar to her, though. See Note 1 for Session 718.

4. I lay down for a nap as usual at 4:30 this afternoon (Monday,

November 11). As I started drifting toward sleep I became aware that I was looking at my own head; the image lasted for several seconds and was quite clear, without being needle-sharp. My view was from my right side as I lay face up on the cot. This is a bit difficult to describe, but the glimpse of my own head came from a point usually invisible to me—centered perhaps two inches or so above and behind my right ear.

I saw the head of a very old man, in his late 80's or early 90's. I had no doubt that this was a definitely probable version of myself in this reality. How strange to peek at the curve of my own skull from that odd viewpoint. I saw short, almost wispy white hair, but I wasn't bald. Through the hair I could see the pulsing bluish veins in the skin as it lay over the bone—and in some fashion this sight alone was most evocative of the very young and the very old. I lay face up, bony arms folded across my chest, just as my present "me" did. I knew that I was resting, and that I wasn't senile. I don't believe I was bedridden, but that I was being cared for somehow.

My eyes were closed, and something about my bearing or pose reminded the present me of my father in *his* old age. When he lay dying, early in February 1971, I stood so that I had a view of him similar to the one I'd just experienced of myself. I was sure that this old man was me, though, and no one else. I was very thin beneath the blanket, which I believe was an ivory color.

The whole experience had a hard-to-define childlike or naive quality, as several members of Jane's ESP class remarked the next night when I read this account to them, and showed the sketch around.

5. All in Volume 1: Note 1 for Session 698 contains quotations from the dream material Seth gave in the 92nd session for September 28, 1964. Then see the equally interesting information on dreams in Session 699; I especially like Seth's statement that "In a way, one remembered dream can be compared to a psychological photograph. . . ." Jane's poem, *My Dreaming Self*, is presented in the notes following that session, along with references to other dream material.

6. See Note 2 for Session 688, in Volume 1.

7. See the 710th session for Seth's material on dreams, and the "snapshots" the conscious mind can learn to take during out-of-body travel.

Session 720

□

November 13, 1974
9:55 P.M. Wednesday

(Just as she had this afternoon, Jane "picked up" a little material from Seth at 9:00 this evening. I'll cover both episodes in the notes at the end of the session.)

Good evening.

("Good evening, Seth.")

Dictation *(whispering)*. Now, if you take a physical camera with you today and snap pictures as you go about your chores, walk, or talk with friends, then you will have preserved scenes from the day's activities.

Your film, however, will only take pictures today, of today. No yesterday or tomorrow will suddenly appear in the snapshots of the present. The photographer in the dream world, though, will find an entirely different situation, for there consciousness can capture scenes from entirely different times as easily as the waking photographer can take pictures of different places. Unless you realize this, some of your "dream albums" will make no sense to you.

In waking life you experience certain events as real, and generally these are the only ones that can be captured by an ordinary photographer. The dream world,[1] however, presents a much larger category of events. Many [events] may later appear as physical ones, while others just as valid will not. The dream camera, therefore, will capture probable events also.

When you awaken with a dream photograph in mind, it may appear meaningless because it does not seem to correlate with the official order of activities you recognize. You may make one

158

particular decision in physical and waking consciousness, and that decision may bring forth certain events. Using your dream camera, you can with practice discover the history of your own psyche, and find the many probable decisions experienced in dreams, These served as a basis from which you made your physical decision. There is some finesse required as you learn to interpret the individual pictures within your dream album. This should be easy to grasp, for if you tried to understand physical life having only a group of snapshots taken at different places and in different times, then it would be rather difficult to form a clear idea of the nature of the physical world.

The same applies to dream reality, for the dreams that you recall are indeed like quick pictures snapped under varying conditions. No one picture alone tells the entire story. You should write down your description of each dream picture, therefore, and keep a continuing record, for each one provides more knowledge about the nature of your own psyche and the unknown reality in which it has its existence.

Give us a moment . . . When you take a physical photograph you have to know how your camera works. You must learn how to focus, how to emphasize those particular qualities you want to record, and how to cut out distracting influences. You know the difference between shadows, for example, and solid objects. Sometimes shadows themselves make fascinating photographer studies. You might utilize them in the background, but as a photographer you would not <u>confuse</u> the shadows with, say, the solid objects. No one would deny that shadows are real, however.

Now, using an analogy only, let me explain that your thoughts and feelings also give off shadows *(intently)* that we will here call hallucinations.[2] They are quite valid. They have as strong a part to play in dream reality as shadows do in the physical world. They are beautiful in themselves. They add to the entire picture. A shadow of a tree cools the ground. It affects the environment. So hallucinations alter the environment, but in a different way and at another level of reality. In the dream world hallucinations are like conscious shadows. They are not passive, nor is their shape dependent upon their origin. They have their own abilities.

Physically, an oak tree may cast a rich deep shadow upon the ground. It will move, faithfully mirroring the tiniest motion of the smallest leaf, but its freedom to move will be dictated by the motion of the oak. Not one oak leaf shadow will move unless its counterpart does.

Following our analogy, in the dream world the shadow of the oak tree, once cast, would then be free to pursue its own direction. Not only that, but there would be a creative give-and-take between it and the tree that gave it birth. Anyone fully accustomed to inner reality would have no difficulty in telling the dream oak tree from its frisky shadow, however *(humorously)*, any more than a waking photographer would have trouble distinguishing the physical oak tree from its counterpart upon the grass.

When you, a dream tourist, wander about the inner landscape with your mental camera, however, it may take a while before you are able to tell the difference between dream events and their shadows or hallucinations. So you may take pictures of the shadows instead of the trees, and end up with a fine composition indeed—but one that would give you somewhat of a distorted version of inner reality. So you must learn how to aim and focus your dream camera.

(Pause.) In your daily world objects have shadows, and thoughts or feelings do not, so in your dream travels simply remember that there "objects" do not possess shadows, but thoughts and feelings do.

Since these are far more lively than ordinary shadows, and are definitely more colorful, they may be more difficult to distinguish at first. You must remember that you are wandering through a mental or psychic landscape. You can stand before the shadow of a friend in the afternoon, in waking reality, and snap your fingers all you want to, but your friend's shadow will not move one whit. It will certainly not disappear because you tell it to. In the dream world, however, any hallucination will vanish immediately as soon as you recognize it as such, and tell it to go away. It was cast originally by your own thought or feeling, and when you withdraw that source, then its "shadow" is automatically gone.

Do you want a break?

(10:40. "No," I said, although Seth's pace had been good.)

Give us a moment . . . A stone's physical shadow will faithfully mirror its form. In those terms, little creativity is allowed it. Far greater leeway exists, however, as a thought or feeling in the dream world casts its greater shadow out upon the landscape of the mind.

Moods obviously exist when you are dreaming as well as when you are waking. Physically the day may be brilliant, but if you are in a blue mood you may automatically close yourself off from the day's natural light, not notice it—or even use that natural beauty as counterpoint that only makes you feel _more_ disconsolate. Then you might look outward at the day through your mood and see its beauty as a meaningless or even cruel façade. Your mood, therefore, will alter your perception.

The same applies in the dream state; but there, the shadows of your thoughts may be projected outward into scenes of darkest desolation. In the physical world you have mass sense data about you. Each individual helps form that exterior environment. No matter how dark your mood on any given sunny day, your individual thoughts alone will not suddenly turn the blue skies into rainy ones. You alone do not have _that_ kind of control over your fellows' environment. In the dream world, however, such thoughts will definitely form your environment.

Stormy dream landscapes are on the one hand hallucinations, cast upon the inner world by your thoughts or feelings. On the other hand, they are valid representations of your inner climate at the time of any given dream. Such scenes can be changed in the dream state itself if you recognize their origin. You might choose instead to learn from such hallucinations by allowing them to continue, while realizing that they are indeed shadows cast by your own mind.

Take your break.

_(10:52 to 11:12.)_

Now: If you are honest with your thoughts and feelings, then you will express them in your waking life, and they will not cast disturbing shadows in your dreams.

You may be afraid that a beloved child or mate will die suddenly, yet you may never want to admit such a fear. The feeling itself may be generated because of your own doubts about _yourself_, however. You may be depending upon another such person too strongly, trying to live your own life secondhandedly through the life of another. Your own fear, admitted, would lead you to other feelings behind it, and to a greater understanding of yourself.

Unencountered in waking life, however, the fear might cast its dim shadow, so that you dream of your child's death, or of the death of another close to you. The dream experience would be cast into the dream landscape and encountered there. Period.

If you remembered such a dream, therefore, you might think that it was precognitive, and that the event would become physical. Instead, the whole portent of the dream event would be an educational one, bringing your fear into clear focus. In such cases you should think of the dire dream situation as a shadow, and look for its source within your mind.

Shadows can be pleasant and luxurious, and on a hot sunny day you are certainly aware of their beneficial nature. So some dream hallucinations are beautiful, comforting, refreshing. They can bring great peace and be sought after for themselves. You may believe that God exists as a kindly father, or you might personify him as Christ or Buddha. In your dreams you might then encounter such personages. They are quite valid, but they are also hallucinations cast by your own thoughts and feelings. Dreams of Heaven and Hell alike fall into the same category, _in those terms,_ as hallucinations.

Now: The physical shadow of a tree bears witness to the existence of a tree, even if you see only the shadow; so your hallucinations appearing in dreams also bear witness to their origin, and give testimony to a valid "objective" dream object that is as "solid" _(slowly)_ in _that_ reality as the tree is in your world.

(Long pause at 11:32.) In physical reality there is a time lag that exists between the conception of an idea, say, and its materialization. Beside that, other conditions operate that can slow down an idea's physical actualization, or even impede it altogether. If not physically expressed, the thought will be actualized in another reality. An idea must have certain characteristics, for example, that agree with physical assumptions before it turns into a recognizable event. It must appear within your time context.

In the dream world, however, each feeling or idea can be immediately expressed and experienced. The physical world has buildings in it that you manufacture—that is, they do not spring up naturally from the ground itself. In the same way, your thoughts are "manufactured products" in the dream world. They are a part of the environment and appear within its reality, though they change shape and form constantly, as physically manufactured objects do not.

The earth has its own natural given data, however, and you

must use this body of material to form all of your manufactured products. The dream world also possesses its own natural environment. You form your dreams from it *(long pause)*, and use its natural products to manufacture dream images. Few view this natural inner environment, however.

Give us a moment . . . End of dictation.

(11:44. Speaking as Seth, Jane now delivered two pages of material for herself and me. Embedded within it were these lines: "Ruburt's idea did come from me, about your reincarnational episodes involving the Roman officer, and your personal experience illustrates what I am saying in "Unknown" Reality—the individual's history <u>is</u> written in the psyche, and can indeed be uncovered." Note Seth's heading for this Section 5, for example.

(Twice today Jane had tuned in to very similar concepts while going about her daily business. "I'm sure I got that from Seth," she told me after the first such instance had taken place this afternoon. "Not only about your reincarnational stuff, but your thing as the old man [as described in Note 4 for the 719th session]. And the history of the species is written in the mass psyche in just the same way. . . ."

(My "three Romans" are presented in the first notes for sessions 715–16. I'm quite concerned by some of the questions these experiences have raised—especially the possible time contradictions with some of my other supposed past lives. [I plan to soon explain these rather cryptic references.] In the meantime, my little psychic adventures continue to flow. I regret that I seldom seem to find the physical time for more than very quick sketches relative to any of them.

(Tonight's session ended, then, at 12:04 A.M.)

NOTES: SESSION 720

1. The reader can also refer to Seth's material on dreams in chapters 8 and 10 in *Seth Speaks*, and chapters 10 and 20 in *Personal Reality*.

2. Seth's creative use of "hallucinations" here is certainly at variance with the concepts ordinarily associated with the word. In a dictionary, for instance, hallucinations may be described as sights and sounds *apparently* perceived. Hallucinations are tied in with some mental disorders; with objects not actually present. Logically enough, then, in the dictionary one of the synonyms for hallucination will be a word like "delusion": a belief not true, a persistent opinion without corresponding physical evidence.

Session 721

□

November 25, 1974
9:14 P.M. Monday

(At the conclusion of the 720th session I mentioned the Roman-soldier visions I'd had near the end of October, and added that I would soon go into my questions about them. Before I could do so, however, I had another experience with psychic perceptions three days later—on November 16—that led to more questions. This one wasn't a "Roman," though, but a series of very vivid impressions of myself as a black woman on the island of Jamaica, in the Caribbean Sea. The time period was—is—the 19th century. See Note 1.

("Jamaica" took place on a Saturday, and Seth referred to it briefly in the next session, on Monday night. That session turned out to be private, rather than one for book dictation. Seth came back to Jamaica in Jane's ESP class the next evening [on November 19]; at the same time he began discussing his concept of "counterparts," which he formally introduces in tonight's [721st] session for "Unknown" Reality. His material enhances my Roman and Jamaican visions [and others]—which saves me considerable effort in figuring them out for myself, of course. And, obviously, Seth does a much better job of putting them all together than I could.

(I'd like to add that I hardly think it a coincidence, however, that within less than a month from my "first Roman," Seth was to initiate a body of information in which he began to clarify many of the questions I had about certain of my own psychic adventures. I don't think those events directly led Seth into beginning his new material, but in retrospect Jane and I agree

164

that they certainly played some considerable part in establishing a foundation, or impetus, for such a development.

(Last Wednesday night's scheduled session wasn't held, giving Jane some rest the day after class. Then yesterday, Sunday, she gave a very long session on her own for a visiting scientist. When I write "on her own," I not only mean that Seth didn't come through, but that Jane wasn't aware of his presence even though she didn't give voice to it.

(Yesterday's "Jane" session seemed to run itself, to take place outside of time as we usually think of that quality. It lasted from 2:00 P.M. until after 12:30 A.M., with interruptions only for a casual supper of scrambled eggs, and an occasional short break. We estimate, then, that in a slightly altered state of consciousness Jane gave impressions for something like nine hours out of the actual ten and a half involved.

(She enjoyed the exchange a great deal; she made sketches while speaking on such subjects as the many facets of the electron and its behavior; time and its variations; gravity, its changes with motion, and its attributes in the past, present, and future; the velocities of light; mathematical equations; astronomy, including perceptions by telescope of the future as well as of the past; the structure of the earth's core; earthquakes and "black" sound/light; language, including glossolalia and her own Sumari; pyramids, coordination points, and so forth. Our guest recorded it all and is to send us a transcript [which he did]. Jane plans to quote parts of it in Psychic Politics.[2] *These bits are from her material about gravity and age: "There is a different kind of gravity that surrounds older objects than that which surrounds younger ones, but we don't perceive this at the level of our instruments. We can pick it up, however, if we know where to look. Age affects gravity . . . Older objects are heavier. This is ordinary gravity—not some new kind."*

(I asked Jane to write a paragraph about the predominant mode of consciousness she'd experienced during the long session, and here's what she produced:)

"It seems to be an easy natural state for me to take; I go into it 'like a duck takes to water,' I guess, but it's difficult to explain. It's a state in which hardly any resistance is encountered; answers are 'just there.' The only problem is in getting the information across to another person in terms of his or her vocabulary. I enjoy this particular 'alteration of consciousness,' although I don't really recognize it as alien to my regular one; it's just different. It's an accelerated condition mixed with passivity; poised. If [our scientist's] attitude had been critical, I probably wouldn't have done as well, though.''

(I'll finish the references to yesterday's session by quoting the comments Seth made at the end of some material we've deleted from the 712th session in Section 4. A few weeks ago, through a magazine we subscribe to, Jane joined a science club. Now each month she receives a little kit to be assembled; this in turn is used to carry out the scientific experiment for the month. Seth: "Ruburt's science kit is something picked up, in your terms, from another probability—in which he learned all there is to know about science as you know it. That is why he can enter into the reality of electrons so easily."[3]*

(And separately: Over the weekend Jane remarked more than once that "Unknown" Reality might prove to be so long that it could go into two volumes—a probable development I hardly took seriously. [Her statements turned out to be exactly prophetic, of course, as I noted five months later in the 741st session. Also see the beginning of the Introductory Notes for Volume 1.])

Good evening.

("Good evening, Seth.")

Now: Dictation: When you look into a mirror you see your reflection, but it does not talk back to you. In the dream state you are looking into the mirror of the psyche, so to speak, and seeing the reflections of your own thoughts, fears, and desires.

Here, however, the "reflections" do indeed speak, and take their own form. In a certain sense they are freewheeling, in that they have their own kind of reality. In the dream state your joys and fears talk back to you, perform, and act out the role in which you have cast them.

If, for example, you believe that you are possessed of great inner wealth, you may have a dream about a king in a fine palace. The king actually need not look like you at all, nor need you identify with him in the dream. Symbolically, however, this would represent one way of expressing your feelings. Inner wealth would be interpreted here in the same terms as worldly luxury. The dream, once created, would go its own way. If you have conflicts over the ideas connected with good and evil, or wealth and poverty, then the king might lose his lands or goods, or some catastrophe might befall him.

If you suspect that abundance is somehow spiritually dangerous,[4] then the king might be captured and punished. All kinds of other events might be involved: groups of people, for example, representing bands of "rampaging" desires. The entire drama would involve the "evolution" of an emotion or belief. In the dream state you set it free and see what will happen to it, how it will develop, where it will go.

The reflections of your ideas and intimate emotions are then projected outward in a rich drama. You can observe the play, take a role in it, or move in and out of its acts as you prefer. You will use your own private symbols. These represent your psychic shorthand. They are connected with your personal creativity, so dream books will not help you in deciphering those meanings if they attach a specific significance to any given symbol. Symbols themselves change. If you had before you your entire dream history and could read—as in a book—the story of all of your dreams from birth, you would discover that you changed the meaning of your symbols as you went along, or as it suited your purposes. The content of a dream itself has much to do with the way you employ any given symbol.

The king, for example, may be at one time the symbol of great inner wealth. He may be kingly but poor, signifying the idea that wealth does not necessarily involve physical goods. He might at another time appear as a dictator, cruel and overbearing, where he would represent an entirely different framework of feeling and belief. He might show himself as a young monarch, signaling a belief that "youth is king." At various times in history the same image has been used quite differently. When people are fighting dictatorial monarchs then often the king appears in dreams as a despicable character, to be booted and routed out.

Give us a moment . . . Whether or not you remember your dreams, you are educating yourself as they happen. You may suddenly "awaken" while still within the dream state, however, and recognize the drama that you have yourself created. At this point you will understand the fact that the play, while seeming quite real, is to a certain extent hallucinatory. If you prefer, you can clear the stage at once by saying, "I do not like this play, and so I will create it no longer." You may then find yourself facing an empty stage, become momentarily disoriented at the sudden lack of activity, and promptly begin to form another dream play more to your liking.

If, however, you pause first and wait a moment, you can begin to glimpse the environment that serves as a stage: the natural landscape of the dream reality. In waking life, if you want to disconnect yourself from an event or place, you try to move away from it in space. In dream reality events occur in a different fashion, and places spring up about you. If you meet with people or events not of your liking, then you must simply move your attention away from them, and they will disappear as far as your experience is concerned. In physical reality you can move fairly freely through space, but you do not travel from one city to another, for example, unless you want to. Intent is involved. This is so obvious that its significance escapes you: but it is intent that moves you through space, and that is behind all of your physical locomotion. You utilize ships, automobiles, trains, airplanes, because you want to go to another place, and certain vehicles work best under certain conditions.

(9:53.) In the waking state you travel to places. They do not come to you. In dream reality, however, your intent causes places to spring up about you. They come to you, instead of the other way around. You form and attract ''places,'' or a kind of inner space in which you then have certain experiences.

This inner space does not ''displace'' normal space, or knock it aside. Yet the creation of a definite inner environment or location is concerned.

Those of you who are curious, try this experiment.

PRACTICE ELEMENT 15

In a dream, attempt to expand whatever space you find yourself in. If you are in a room, move from it into another one. If you are on a street, follow it as far as you can, or turn a corner. Unless you are working out ideas of limitations for your own reasons, you will find that you can indeed expand inner space. There is no point where an end to it need appear.

(Long pause.) The properties of inner space, therefore, are endless. Most people are not this proficient in dream manipulation, but surely some of my readers will be able to remember what I am saying, while they are dreaming. To those people I say: ''Look around you in the dream state. Try to expand any location in which you find yourself. If you are in a house,

remember to look out the window. And once you walk to that window, a scene will appear. You can walk out of that dream house into another environment; and theoretically at least you can explore that world, and the space within it will expand. There will be no spot in the dream where the environment will cease.''

Now: What you think of as exterior space expands in precisely the same manner. In this respect, dream reality faithfully mirrors what you refer to as the nature of the exterior world.

Earth experience, even in your terms, is far more varied than you ever consciously imagine. The intimate life of a person in one country, with its culture, is far different from that of an individual who comes from another kind of culture, with its own ideas of art, history, politics or religion or law. Because you focus upon similarities of necessity, then the physical world possesses its coherence.[5]

There are unknown gulfs that separate the private experience of a poor Indian, a rich Indian, a native in New Guinea, an American tailor, an African nationalist, a Chinese aristocrat, an Irish housewife. These differences cannot be objectively stated. They bring about qualitative differences, however, in the experience of space and time.

There are jet travelers and those who have never seen a train, so your own system of reality contains vast contrasts. The dream state, however, involves you with a kind of communication that is not physically practical, for there *(intently)* no man or woman is caught without a given role; no individual's ideas in the dream state are limited by his or her cultural background, or physical experience.

Even those who have never seen an airplane can travel from place to place in the twinkling of an eye, and the poor are fed, the ignorant are wise, the sick are well. The creativity that may be physically hampered is expressed. It is true that the hungry man, awakening, is still hungry. The ill may awaken no healthier than they were before. In deeper terms, however, in the dream state each person will be working out his or her own problems or challenges. Dreaming, a person can cure himself or herself of a disease, working through the problems that caused it. Dreaming, the hungry individual can discover ways to find food, or to procure the money to buy it. Dreaming is a practical activity. If it were understood as such, it would be even more practical in your terms.

Animals also dream, for example, and whole herds of starving animals will be led by their dreams to find better feeding grounds. In the same way, the dreams of starving people point toward the solution of the problem. Such data are largely ignored, however. *(With emphasis:)* In the dream state <u>any</u> individual can find the solution to whatever challenge exists.

The great natural cooperation that exists between the waking and the dreaming self has been mostly set aside. The conscious mind is quite equipped to interpret dream information.

You may take your break.

(10:26 to 10:39.

(Humorously:) You <u>forget</u> that dreaming is a part of life. You have disconnected it in your thoughts, at least, from your daily experience, so that dreams seems to have no practical application.

You live in a waking and dreaming mental environment, however. In both environments you are conscious.

Give us a moment . . . Your dream experience represents a pivotal reality, like the center of a wheel. Your physical world is one spoke. You are united with all of your other simultaneous existences through the nature of the dream state. The unknown reality is there presented to your view, and there is no biological, mental, or psychic reason why you cannot learn to use and understand your own dreaming reality.

In your dreams, in your terms, you find your personal past appearing in the present, so in those terms the past of the species also occurs. *(Long pause.)* Future probabilities are worked out there also so that individually and *en masse* the species decides upon its probable future. There is a feeling, held by many, that a study of dream reality will lead you further away from the world you know. Instead, it would connect you with that world in most practical terms.

I said *(in connection with Practice Element 15)* that inner space expands, but so does inner <u>time</u>. Those of you who can remember, try the following experiment.

PRACTICE ELEMENT 16

When you find yourself within a dream, tell yourself <u>you will know what happened before you entered it</u>, and the past will grow outward from that moment. Again, there will be no place where time will stop. The time in a dream does not "displace" physical time. It opens up from it. Exterior time, again, operates in the same fashion, though you do not realize it.

(Pause at 10:52.) Give us a moment . . . Now *(with a smile)*: in your own book.[6] There will be no gap in <u>this</u> book if you do not use it here.[7]

Time expands in all directions, and away from any given point.[8] The past is never done and finished, and the future is never concretely <u>formed</u>. You choose to experience certain versions of events. You then organize these, nibbling at them, so to speak, a bit "at a time."

The creativity of any given entity is endless, and yet all of the potentials for experience will be explored. The poor man may dream he is a king. A queen, weary of her role, may dream of being a peasant girl. In the physical time that <u>you</u> recognize, the king is still a king, and the queen a queen. Yet their dreams are not as uncharacteristic or apart from their experiences as it might appear. In greater terms, the king has been a pauper and the queen a peasant. You follow in terms of continuity one <u>version</u> of yourself at any given "time."

Many people realize intuitively that the self is multitudinous and not singular. The realization is usually put in reincarnational terms, so that the self is seen as traveling through the centuries, moving through doors of death and life into other times and places.

The fact is that the basic nature of reality shows itself in the nature of the dream state quite clearly, where in any given night you may find yourself undertaking many roles simultaneously. You may change sex, social position, national or religious alliance, age, and yet know yourself <u>as</u> yourself.

Lately Joseph has found himself embarked upon a series of episodes that seem to involve reincarnational existences. There was a catch, however. He saw himself as a woman—black. Last month he also saw himself as a Roman soldier aboard a slave ship. He previously had experience that convinced him that he was a man called Nebene.[9] All of this could have been accepted quite easily in conventional terms of reincarnation, but Joseph felt that Nebene and the Roman soldier had existed during the same general time period, and he was not sure where to place the woman *(but see Note 1)*.

In all of these episodes definite emotional experience was

involved. Also connected was an indefinable but unmistakable sense of familiarity. Space and time continually expand, and all probabilities of any given action are actualized in one reality or another. All of the <u>potentials</u> of the entity are also actualized.

(11:11.) Give us a moment . . . Quite literally, <u>you live more than one life at a time</u>. You do not experience your century simply from one separate vantage point, and the individuals alive in any given century have far deeper connections than you realize. *(Intently:)* You do not experience your space-time world, then, from one but from many viewpoints.

(Pause at 11:13.) If you are glutted—sated—with a steak dinner, for example, in America or Europe, then you are also famished in another portion of the world, experiencing life from an entirely different viewpoint. You speak of races of men. You do not understand how consciousness is distributed in that regard. You have counterparts[10] of yourself.

Give us a moment . . . Generally speaking, the people living within any given century are related in terms of consciousness and identity. This is true biologically and spiritually, through interrelationships you do not understand.

Joseph was ''picking up'' on lives that ''he'' lived in the same time scheme. In this way and in your terms, he was beginning to recognize the familyship that exists between individuals who share your earth at any given time.

(11:20.) Give us a moment . . . because this is difficult to explain. . . .

Each identity has free will, and chooses its environment as a physical <u>stance</u> in space and time. Those involved in a given century are working on particular problems and challenges. Various races do not simply ''happen,'' and diverse cultures do not just appear. The greater self ''divides'' itself, materializing in flesh as several individuals, with entirely different backgrounds— yet with each embarked upon the same kind of creative challenge.

The black man is somewhere a white man or woman <u>in your time</u>. The white man or woman is somewhere black. The oppressor is somewhere the oppressed. The conqueror is somewhere the conquered. The primitive is somewhere sophisticated—and, in your terms, somewhere on the face of the same earth in your general time. The murderer is somewhere the victim, and the other way around—and again, in <u>your</u> terms of space and time.

Each will choose his or her own framework, according to the intents of the consciousness of which each of you is an independent part. In such a fashion are the challenges and opportunities inherent in a given "time" worked out.

You are counterparts of yourselves, but as Ruburt would say *(amused)*, living "eccentric"[11] counterparts, each with your own abilities. So Joseph "was" Nebene, a scholarly man, not adventurous, obsessed with copying ancient truth, and afraid that creativity was error; authoritative and demanding. He feared sexual encounter, and he taught rich Roman children.

At the same time, in the same world and in the same century, Joseph was an aggressive, adventurous, relatively insensitive Roman officer, who would have little understanding of manuscripts or records—yet who also followed authority without question.[12]

In your terms, Joseph is now a man who questions authority, stamps upon it and throws it aside, who rips apart the very idea structures to which he "once" gave such service.

In greater terms, these experiences all occur at once. The black woman followed nothing but her own instincts *(and very vividly, too)*. I do not want to give too much background here, and hence rob our Joseph of discoveries that he will certainly make on his own—but *(louder)* the woman bowed only to the authority of her own emotions, and those emotions automatically put her in conflict with the [British colonial] politics of the times.

Give us a moment . . . Joseph's focus of identity is his own. He will follow it. He was <u>not</u> Nebene, or the Roman officer or the woman. Yet they are versions of what he <u>is</u>, and he is a version of what they "were," and at certain levels each is aware of the others. There is constant interaction.[13]

The Roman soldier dreams of the black woman, and of Joseph. There is a reminiscence that appears even in the knowledge of the cells, and a certain correspondence.[14] There are connections then as far as cellular recollection is concerned, and dreams. Now the Roman soldier and Nebene and the woman went their separate ways after death, colon: They contributed to the world as it existed, in those terms, and then followed their own lines of development, elsewhere, in other realities. So each of you exists in many times and places, and versions of yourselves exist in the world and time that you recognize. As you are part of a physical species, so you are a part of a species of consciousness. That species forms the races of mankind that you recognize.

<u>Now</u>: Give us a moment . . . and shortly we will end. This material is indeed endless (*as Jane had remarked at break*).

(11:44. Seth proceeded to deliver a block of material for Jane and me, which is deleted from this record. At 12:06 he presumably closed out the session, after remarking that I had access to as much energy as he did. I said good night. Then Jane told me that Seth could "continue forever"—whereupon he returned to touch upon Jane's and my reincarnational "history" from another angle:)

Now: <u>In your terms only</u>, [neither of] you . . . has a reincarnational future. Give us a moment . . . You have accepted this as your breaking-off point. In <u>other</u> terms there are three future lives, but your greater intents, as of now, break you off from this system of reality, and you have already journeyed, both of you, into another; and from that other reality I speak. In those terms I am a part of both of your realities. Think of this in terms of other information given this evening, and you may see what I mean.[15]

(End at 12:08 A.M. Jane's trances had been excellent.

("Well," I said after discussing the session with her, "it's my understanding that our whole self or entity experiences a group of simultaneous physical lives in various historical periods, and that in ordinary terms we think of those lives as following one after another. That includes so-called future lives, too. But each of those incarnations will have its cluster of counterpart lives, revolving around it like planets around a sun. Within that context, of course, each counterpart personality thinks of itself as being the sun, or the center of things. . . ."[16] Yawning, Jane agreed.

(I fell asleep almost at once when we went to bed. Sitting up beside me, though, smoking a cigarette, Jane got more material on reincarnation and counterparts. "In fact," she told me the next morning, "I was getting stuff on 'Unknown' Reality each time I woke up during the night. I was also reading solid copy in the dream state." In those cases she received the material "herself," while knowing that it came from Seth.

(Jane's own counterpart material included variations of Seth's basic concept. Here's one of her examples as she described it to me: "We can span a period like a century if we want to. We can

be a child at one end of it and an old man or woman at the other . . . Michelangelo [who lived for 89 years, from 1475 to 1564] decided to span a century himself, instead of as three counterparts, say. Since there aren't any laws about all of this, a great man could choose to do it that way in order to affect our world more with his gifts, from his own personal angles. He wouldn't necessarily want or need the counterparts, at least for those purposes. He'd have more than enough to offer on his own.''

(This session on counterparts represents a key point in Seth's discussion of the unknown reality. The reader is directed to Appendix 21 for related material from the recent past, which anticipated tonight's new concept. Some earlier intimations of the counterpart concept are also briefly discussed there.)

NOTES: Session 721

1. The series of visions that made up my overall perception of the black woman in Jamaica were the most vivid I've experienced yet. For me they had a most unique, thrilling, immediate quality, and strong emotional involvement. As I sat at the typewriter in my studio, I was flooded with perceptions of myself as such a woman: Pursued by an armed English military officer, she ran for her life down a hilly village street. She wasn't especially young. Her—my—name? Maumee, or Mawmee—an illiterate but shrewd, very strong personality who was acting in rebellion against the colonial authority of England in the early 1800's. She escaped that time, and lived to struggle often against such forces on the island.

After the experience was over I wrote a description of it, and made two pen-and-ink drawings—full-face self-portraits that hardly look like the me I know. One of the drawings is very successful, and I plan to do an oil painting from it.

I'm most gratified that some of the Jamaican visions were externalized, that I didn't see all of them within as I did for the Roman series. That is, with open eyes I *saw* fleeting hectic images in the studio. I *felt* emotions. I was exhilarated by the whole thing.

And added later: Jane presented my account of the Maumee episode, as well as portions of the 721st session itself, in Chapter 12 of *Politics*.

2. And eventually Jane did describe her day's work in *Politics*. See the opening pages of Chapter 11.

3. Both Jane and I think Seth's statement, that in another probability "Ruburt . . . learned all there is to know about science . . ." is pretty strong, but since it came through that way we let it stand. However, as

Jane wrote later in Chapter 11 of *Politics*: "Finding out what's happening to electrons, say, is something I really enjoy. I admit I feel much more free than I do when I have people's emotions to deal with. I'd rather 'find' a lost electron than a lost person any day, for example."

In Volume 1 of *"Unknown" Reality*, see her material on electron spin in the 702nd session after 10:22.

4. See the first two sessions in Chapter 13 of *Personal Reality*.

5. See Appendix 1 in Volume 2 Part I. In it I quote Seth from the class session for June 23, 1970, as excerpted in the Appendix for *Seth Speaks*: "In this reality, (each of] you very nicely emphasize all the similarities which bind you together; you make a pattern of them, and you very nicely ignore all the dissimilarities . . . If you were able to focus your attention on the dissimilarities, merely those that you can perceive but do not, then you would be amazed that mankind can form any idea of an organized reality."

6. Here Seth refers to *Through My Eyes*—the book he suggested (in December 1972) that I write on the Seth phenomenon and other subjects. In Volume 1, see item No. 3 at 11:35, in Session 683. Replying to all of those who have asked: So far I haven't had the time to do more than short essays on art, Seth, the fairly recent deaths of my parents, and a few other topics for *Through My Eyes*. Certainly I won't be able to work steadily on the project until Volume 2 of *"Unknown" Reality* is ready for publication.

7. A note added later: Considering what was to come in *"Unknown" Reality*, though, I'm very glad I *did* decide to present "the following material" here.

8. See the quotations from Seth about the moment point in Note 11 for Appendix 1 in Volume 2 Part I. One of the references also included in that note can be traced back to his material on reincarnation, moment points, and dreams in the 668th session for Chapter 19 of *Personal Reality*.

9. In those terms, my supposed "Nebene" life took place in Greece, Palestine, Rome, and other locations in the Middle East during the earlier part of the first century A.D. See Chapter 5 of Jane's *Adventures in Consciousness*.

10. This note is as much for my own edification as it is for anyone else's. The definitions are from *Webster's New World Dictionary of the American Language*, Second College Edition, © 1970 by The World Publishing Company, New York and Cleveland:

counterpart 1. a person or thing that corresponds to or closely resembles another, as in form or function 2. a thing which, when added to another, completes or complements it 3. a copy or duplicate, as of a lease

11. With some humor, Seth borrowed the word "eccentric" from Jane's own *Psychic Politics*. In her book she uses the term in connection with personality, to mean that each physical self is a creative—and unpredictable—version of an inner "heroic" model.

12. My Roman-soldier self might have "followed authority without question," as Seth states in this (721st) session, yet he must have behaved with more than a little guile. In a private session held some time after he'd finished *"Unknown" Reality*, Seth again referred to the Roman—doing so because of additional material I'd produced about that first-century personality. Seth:

"As a Roman, you pretended to be a follower while you were a man of rank in the military. You had no belief in the conventional gods, yet you were supposed to be conquering lands in their names. You traveled even to Africa. You had a disdain for leaders as liars, and of the masses as followers, and so you were always in one kind of dispute or another with your fellows, and even with the authorities. You were of a querulous nature, yet highly curious, and, again, physically involved.

"Your curiosity did not concern philosophies, but had to do with the physical world, and particularly with its water passageways. . . ."

I've also accumulated more graphic information about my other first-century counterpart, Nebene. Eventually I hope to discuss all of my reincarnational data in *Through My Eyes*. (See Note 6.)

13. The "constant interaction" that Seth mentioned as involving myself, Nebene, the Roman soldier, and the black woman, Maumee, obviously takes place on other-than-usual conscious levels—at least in my case, that is. For while I was having experience as the Roman, for instance, I had no feeling for Nebene, or Maumee—no idea of reincarnation, or of counterparts either. Each "time" I tuned in to one of those personalities I was too caught up in that particular role to be aware of any of the others. Now, however, as I write this I can at least feel ideas about them in the back of my mind. . . .

14. For one example of Jane and Seth on cellular memory (among other subjects), see the 653rd session as it bridges chapters 13 and 14 in *Personal Reality*. Jane also discussed some of the material in that session in Chapter 17 of *Adventures*.

15. In Appendix 7 I discussed to some extent the relationships involving Jane, Seth, and me. I chose not to study this paragraph of material in Appendix 7 because in it Seth mentions what I take to be probable lives involving Jane and me (when he speaks of our future lives), rather than reincarnational involvements we've had with Seth that "actually happened."

Seth refers to evocative situations here, though—one of them possibly being a kind of counterpart relationship among the three of us in another reality.

16. As Jane wrote in Chapter 16 of *Adventures*: "In one way, each person *is* at the center of the universe and at the center of the psyche."

APPENDIX 1
(For Session 705)

(Originally I planned this appendix on evolution to contain just three widely separated excerpts from Seth's material: an early unpublished session, a few passages in Seth Speaks, *and one in Volume 1 of* "Unknown" Reality. *The appendix, however kept growing as I worked on it; I found myself adding quotations from other sessions, along with comments derived from my own reading and from conversations Jane and I had on the subject.*

(I learned that "evolution" can mean many things. Like variations on a theme, it can be progressive or relatively sudden, convergent or divergent. I also learned that once I began to study it, a great amount of material presented itself, seemingly without effort on my part; the information ranged all the way from paleontological studies to current biological research on recombinant DNA, and I found it in newspapers, scientific journals and popular magazines, in books and even on television. [I'm sure others have had similar experiences: Once a subject is focused upon, data relative to it seem to leap out from the background welter of daily events and "facts" surrounding one's life.] Almost automatically, many of the notes for this appendix came to deal with the scientific thinking about evolution, and I realized that I wanted them to show the differences [as well as any similarities that might emerge] between Seth's concepts and those "official" views prevailing in our physical reality.

(Our beliefs and intents cause us to pick "from an unpredictable group of actions," or probabilities, those that we want to happen, as Seth tells us in the 681st session in Volume 1; therefore, from my physically oriented probability the considerable work I've put into this paper is an examination of evolution in connection with a number of Seth's concepts. Religious questions connected with evolution aren't stressed as much as some might like, although they aren't ignored either—but to go very

far into religious history would lead away from the focus I've chosen.

(I found some of the excerpts, notes, and comments very difficult to assemble and interpret, and others easy to do. The Seth material is incomplete, of course; new information "intrudes" constantly, and in so doing often takes off from a given subject in fresh directions. Some of this process has to do with Jane's own character: She likes new things, new ideas. Yet in her own way she—and Seth as well—eventually returns to earlier material. Interpretation of old and new together calls for a system of constant correlations, then, and I use that approach as often as I can.

(Even so, as I worked on this appendix I wondered again and again why I was investing so much time in it. The answers proved to be simple once I understood them: I ended up shocked to discover how little real evidence there is to back up the idea of evolution, and fascinated by the limits of scientific thinking. I was quite surprised at my reactions. Somehow Jane and I always understood, to make an analogy, that Seth's kind of "simultaneous" reincarnation [or anyone else's kind, for that matter] wasn't acceptable in our Western societies at this time in history; we could trace out many reasons why this is so. But some time passed before I realized that our ruling intellectual establishments were advancing notions about evolution that were not proven in scientific terms—then teaching these "facts" to succeeding generations. Finally, the humor of the whole situation got through to me: As some have very clearly noted, in the biological and earth sciences especially, circular reasoning often predominates: The theory of evolution is used to prove the theory of evolution.

(The first quotes I've put together, then, are from the 44th session for April 15, 1964. In that session Seth gave us his interpretations of some of the basic laws or attributes of the inner universe, but it will be quickly seen that he was really discussing space and time,[2] as those qualities are perceived in his reality and in ours. In our world, of course, space and time form the environment in which conventional ideas of evolution exist. For that matter, all of the material in this appendix shows the interrelationship between our ideas of serial time and Seth's simultaneous time. Connected here also is the philosophical

concept known as "naive realism," which will be discussed briefly later.

(This presentation from the 44th session shows clearly just how much of his philosophy Seth had given Jane and me by then. He spoke very forcefully:)

I have said that the mind cannot be detected by your instruments at present. The <u>mind</u> does <u>not</u> take up space, and yet the mind is the value that gives power to the brain. The mind expands continuously, both in individual terms and in terms of the species as a whole, and yet *(with amusement)* the mind takes up neither more nor less space, whether it be the mind of a flea or a man.

I have also said that basically the universe has <u>no more</u> to do with space <u>in your terms</u> than does the dream world.

Your idea of space is some completely erroneous conception of an emptiness to be filled. Things—planets, stars, nebulae—come into being in this physical [camouflage] universe of yours, according to your latest theories, and this universe expands—pushed so that its sides bulge, so to speak, the outer galaxies literally bursting into nowhere. True inner space is to the contrary vital energy, itself alive, possessing abilities of transformation, forming all existences, even the camouflage reality with which you are familiar, and which you attempt to probe so ineffectively.

This basic universe of which I speak expands constantly in terms of intensity and quality and value, in a way that has nothing to do with your idea of space. The basic universe beneath all camouflage does not have an existence in space at all, as you envision it. Space is a camouflage . . . This tinge of time is an attribute of the physical camouflage form only, and even then the relationship between time and ideas, and time and dreams, is a nebulous one . . . although in some instances parts of the inner universe may be glimpsed from the camouflage perspective of time; only, however, a small portion.

If the dream world, the mind, and the inner universe do exist, but not in space, and if they do not exist basically in time, though they may be glimpsed <u>through</u> time, then your question will be: In what medium or in what manner <u>do</u> they exist; and without time, how can they be said to exist in duration? I am telling you that the basic universe exists behind <u>all</u> camouflage universes in the same manner, and taking up no space, that the mind exists behind the brain. The brain is a camouflage pattern. It takes up space. It exists in time, but the mind takes up no space and does not have its basic existence in time. Your camouflage universe, on the other hand, takes up space and exists in time.

Nevertheless the dream world, the mind, and the basic inner universe do exist . . . in what we will call the value climate of psychological reality. This is the medium. This takes the place of what you call space. It is a quality which makes all existences and consciousness possible. It is one of the most powerful principles behind or within the vitality that itself composes from itself all other phenomena.[3]

One of the main attributes of this value climate is spontaneity, which shows itself in the existence of the only sort of time that has any real meaning—that of the spacious present.

The spacious present does not contradict the existence <u>of a future</u> as you conceive it. Now this may appear contradictory, but later I hope that you will understand this more clearly. The spacious present, while existing spontaneously, while <u>happening</u> simultaneously, still contains within it qualities of duration.

Growth in your camouflage universe often involves the taking up of more space. Actually, in our inner universe . . . growth exists in terms of the value or quality expansion of which I have spoken, and does not—I repeat—does <u>not</u> imply any sort of space expansion. Nor does it imply, as growth does in your camouflage universe, a sort of projection into time.

I am giving it [this material] to you in as simple terms as possible. If growth is one of the most necessary laws of your camouflage universe, value fulfillment corresponds to it in the inner-reality universe.[4]

Now, the so-called laws of your camouflage physical universe do not apply to the inner universe. <u>They do not even apply</u> to other camouflage planes. However, the laws of the inner universe apply to <u>all</u> camouflage realities. Some of these basic laws have counterparts known and accepted in various camouflage realities. There are diverse manifestations of them, and names given to them.

These fundamental laws are followed on many levels in your own universe. So far I have given you but one, which is value fulfillment. In your physical universe this rule is followed as physical growth. The entity follows it through the cycle of [simultaneous] reincarnations. The species of mankind, and all other species in your universe on your particular horizontal plane, follow this law [value fulfillment] under the auspices of <u>evolution</u> *(my emphasis).*[5] In other camouflage realities, this law is carried through in different manners, but it is never ignored.

The second law of the inner universe is energy transformation.[6] This occurs constantly. Energy transformation and value fulfillment, both existing within the spacious present [or at once], add up to a durability that is at the same time spontaneous . . . and simultaneous.

You may see what we are getting at here. Our third law is spontaneity, and despite <u>all</u> appearances of beginning and end, of death and decay, all consciousnesses exist in the spacious present, in a spontaneous manner, in simultaneous harmony; and yet within the spacious present there is also durability.

Durability is our fourth law. Durability within the framework of the spacious present would not exist were it not for the laws of value fulfillment and energy transformation. These make duration within the spacious present not only possible but necessary. . . .

(The "value climate of psychological reality," first mentioned in the [44th] session just quoted, is also dealt with through analogy in the 45th session. Portions of that material are given as Appendix 8 in Volume 1; in that session also Seth stated that "value expansion becomes reincarnation, and evolution and growth." [Seth's own kind of simultaneous time, of course, easily accommodates all three concepts, although this appendix isn't concerned with reincarnation.]

(Seth material on evolution is presented twice in the 582nd session for Chapter 20 of Seth Speaks—*not only in the session proper, but from an ESP class delivery given a few days later, on April 27, 1971. In class, Seth discussed Charles Darwin and his theory of evolution,[7] and that material, some of which wasn't published in the 582nd session, is the source for my second group of excerpts:)*

He [Darwin] spent his last years proving it, and yet it has no real validity. It has a validity within very limited perspectives only; for consciousness does, indeed, evolve form. Form does not evolve consciousness. It is according to when you come into the picture, and what you choose to observe . . . Consciousness did not come from atoms and molecules scattered by chance through the universe . . .

Now, if you had all been really paying attention to what I have been saying for some time about the simultaneous nature of time and existence, then you would have known that the theory of evolution is as beautiful a tale as the theory of Biblical creation. Both are quite handy, and both are methods of telling stories, and both might seem to agree within their own systems, and yet, in larger respects they cannot be realities . . .

Within you, concepts and actions are one. You recognize this, but your mental lives are often built around concepts that, until recently, have been considered very modern and very "in," such as the idea of evolution . . . In actuality, life bursts apart in all directions as consciousness does. There is no one steady stream of progress.

(To a student:) Now last week, when Ruburt [Jane] was speaking about the natives who are such expert dreamers, you asked: "But why are they not more progressive?" Yet I know you realize that your own progress as a civilization will, in your terms, come to a halt unless you advance in other directions. This is what your civilization is learning: that you cannot rape your planet, that life did not begin as some isolated [substance], that in the great probabilities of existence met another [similar substance], and another, and then another, until a chain of molecules could be made and selves formed. Using an analogy, neither does consciousness exist as simple organisms separated by vast distances, but as a complicated gestalt.

(From the beginning, then, Seth has referred to evolution in his material. He attaches his own meanings to it, however, and as I show in this appendix, does not imply that all life as we know it on this planet evolved from a single primeval source. [See notes 5 and 7.]

(I think it more than a coincidence that in these excerpts from Seth Speaks, *Seth mentions Darwin's theory of evolution and the Biblical story of creation in the same sentence, for those systems of belief represent the two poles of the controversy over origins in our modern Western societies: the strictly Darwinistic, mechanistic view of evolution, in which the weakest of any species are ruthlessly eliminated through natural, predatory selection; and the views of the creationists, who hold that God made the earth and all of its creatures just as described in the Bible.*

(Many creationists believe that the Bible is literally true. [An undetermined number of scientists hold creationist views, by the

way, but I have no statistics to offer on how many do.] The Bible
certainly advocates at least a relative immutability of species,
rather than a common ancestry in which a single cell evolved
into a variety of ever more complex and divergent forms. In
between these opposites there range all shades of meaning and
interpretation on evolution. Theistic evolutionists and progres-
sive creationists, for example, try to bring the two extremes
closer together through postulating various methods by which
God created the world and then, while remaining hidden, either
helped it to evolve to its present state in the Darwinistic tradi-
tion, or, through a series of creative acts, brought forth each
succeeding "higher" form of life.

(Ironically, Charles Darwin's natural selection, "the survival
of the fittest," [a phrase that Darwin himself did not originate,
by the way], allows for all sorts of pain and suffering in the
process—the same unhappy facts of life, in Darwin's view, that
finally turned him into an agnostic, away from a God who could
allow such things to exist! As I interpret what I've read, Darwin
didn't deny the existence of a god of some kind, but he wanted
one that would abolish what he saw as the "upward" struggle
for existence. According to the geological/fossil record, this
conflict had resulted in the deaths of entire species. Darwin
came to believe that he asked the impossible of God. Instead, he
assigned the pain and suffering in the world to the impersonal
workings of natural selection and chance variation [or genetic
mutation]. For Darwin and his followers—even those of today,
then—nature's effects gave the appearance *of design or plan in*
the universe without necessitating a belief in a designer or a
god; although, as I wrote in Note 7, from the scientific stand-
point this belief leaves untouched the question of design in
nonliving matter, which is vastly more abundant in the "objec-
tive" universe than is living matter, and had to precede *that*
living matter.

(As counterpoint to Darwin's ideas, here briefly are some of
Seth's comments on the human condition, and that of the ani-
mals. The material is from two sessions. The first one is the
580th [for April 12, 1971] from, once again, Chapter 20 of Seth
Speaks. *Seth talked about the innate creative ability of human*
beings—even in creating *war. Then he continued:)*

Illness and suffering are not thrust upon you by God, or by All
That Is, or by an outside agency. They are a by-product of the

learning process, created by you, in themselves quite neutral . . .
Illness and suffering are the results of the misdirection of creative energy. They are a part of the creative force, however.
They do not come from a different source than, say, health and
vitality. Suffering is not good for the soul, unless it teaches you
how to stop suffering. That is its purpose . . .

I have mentioned before that everyone within your system is
learning to handle this creative energy; and since you are still in
the process of doing so, you will often misdirect it. The resulting
snarl in activities automatically brings you back to inner questions.

*(The second session quoted is the 634th [for January 22, 1973]
in Chapter 8 of* Personal Reality. *Seth discussed the repression
of natural aggression, and mentioned the sense of guilt that
arose in early man with the birth of compassion. Then:)*

Animals have a sense of justice that you do not understand,
and built into that innocent sense of integrity there is a biological
compassion, understood at the deepest cellular levels . . .

A cat playfully killing a mouse and eating it is not evil. It
suffers no guilt. On biological levels both animals understand.
The consciousness of the mouse, under the innate knowledge of
impending pain, leaves its body. The cat uses the warm flesh.
The mouse itself has been hunter as well as prey, and both
understand the terms in ways that are very difficult to explain.

At certain levels both cat and mouse understand the nature
of the life-energy they share, and are not—in those terms—
jealous for their own individuality . . . Man, pursuing his own
way, chose to step outside of that framework—on a conscious
level . . .

*(This kind of material from Seth is deceptively simple, but
upon reflection it can be seen to offer much. Jane and I think its
implications are often missed by many who write us with questions about the pain and suffering in the world. Undoubtedly
Seth has much more to say on the subject, and we hope to
eventually obtain that information. Certainly individual and mass
beliefs will be involved [along with the natural and unnatural
guilt Seth discussed in the sessions making up Chapter 8 of*
Personal Reality]. *I'd say that just understanding the complicated relationships between mass beliefs and illness alone, for
example, will require much material from Seth and much time
invested upon our parts.*

(For the most part Seth's ideas are far away from thoughts of

replicating genes or the second law of thermodynamics. Through Jane, he grapples with the mysteries of existence in emotional terms, rather than through the impersonal, "scientific," and really unproven concepts that life originated by accident [more than 3.4 billion years ago,[8] to give a late estimate], and perpetuates itself through chance mutations. Darwin's objective thinking, then, cut him off from such comprehensions as Seth advocates. The same was true for many scientists and theistic thinkers in succeeding generations, and in my opinion this holds today. I suggest that the entire 634th session in Personal Reality *be read with this appendix, for in it Seth explored some connections between animal and man—including the* evolution *[my emphasis] by man of "certain animal capacities to their utmost." At practically the same time, in the 637th session for the following chapter [9], he could tell us: "Note: I did not say that* man emerged from the animals."

(Over a year later Jane supplemented such remarks by Seth with some trance material of her "own"; see Appendix 6 in Volume 1 of "Unknown" Reality. *According to her, if man didn't emerge from the animals, there were certainly close relationships involved—a dance of probabilities between the two, as it were. As I noted at the beginning of this appendix, the Seth material is still incomplete, and new information requires constant correlation with what has come before. Jane's own material— including whatever she comes up with in the future—ought to be integrated with Seth's, also, and eventually we hope to find time to do this. Although she left Appendix 6 unfinished, it contains many ideas worth more study: "Some of the experiments with man-animals didn't work out along our historic lines, but the ghost memories of those probabilities still linger in our biological structure . . . The growth of ego consciousness by itself set up both challenges and limitations . . . For many centuries there was no clear-cut differentiation between various aspects of man and animal . . . there were parallel developments in the emergence of physical man . . . there were innumerable species of man-in-the-making, in your terms. . . ." [I can add that just as Jane supplemented Seth's material on early man, he in turn has added to hers in a kind of freewheeling exchange; his information is presented later in this appendix.]*

(The third excerpt I'd originally planned to use is from the 690th session in Volume 1, and shows that even when Seth talks

of evolution in our terms of ordinary time, he means something quite different from that conventional definition of linear change: Precognition is one of the attributes of the growth through value fulfillment that he described in the [already quoted] 44th session. I also want to use this material to lead into short discussions of "naive realism," and evolution at the level of molecular biology. Seth:)

I have said that evolution does not exist as you think of it, in any kind of one-line ape-to-man sequence. No other species developed in that manner, either. Instead there are parallel developments. Your time perception shows you but one slice of the whole cake, for instance.

In thinking in terms of consecutive time, however, evolution does not march from the past into the future. Instead, precognitively the species is aware of those changes it wants to make, and from the "future" it alters the "present" state of the chromosomes and genes *(see Note 14)* to bring about in the probable future the specific changes it desires. Both above and below your usual conscious focus, then, time is experienced in an entirely different fashion, and is constantly manipulated, as physically you manipulate matter.[9]

(Seth's ideas aside for the moment, biologists faithful to Darwin's theories don't want to hear anything about the precognitive abilities of a species, nor do they see any evidence of it in their work. In evolutionary theory, such attributes violate not only the operation of chance mutation and the struggle for existence, but our ideas of consecutive time [which is associated with "naive realism"—the belief that things are really as we perceive them to be]. Not that scientifically the concept of a far more flexible time—even a backward flow of time—is all that new. In atomic physics, for example, no special meaning or place is given to any particular moment, and fundamentally the past and future all but merge in the interactions of elementary particles—thus at least approaching Seth's simultaneous time.[10] At that level there's change, or value fulfillment, but no evolution. To Jane's and my way of thinking, if there's value fulfillment there's consciousness, expressed through CU's, or units of consciousness.

(But to some degree many scientists outside physics regard such esoteric particle relationships as being of theoretical interest mainly within that discipline; the concepts aren't seen as

posing any threat to biology, zoology, or geology, for instance, nor do they tinker with naive realism. The biological sciences can cling to mechanistic theories of evolution by employing the conservative physics of cause and effect to support their conclusions while being aware, perhaps, of the tenets of particle physics. Such "causal analysis" then proves itself over and over again—a situation, I wryly note, that's akin to the criticism I've read wherein the theory of evolution is used to prove the theory of evolution. [I mentioned such circular reasoning near the beginning of this appendix.]

(I find it very interesting, then, to consider that the theory of evolution is a creature of our coarser world of "physical" construction. Our ordinary, chosen *sensual perceptions move us forward, within "the time system that the species adopted," as Seth commented in Chapter 8 of* Personal Reality. *And Seth's explanation of the moment point[11] encompasses the seeming paradox through which consecutive time can be allowed expression within simultaneous time.*

(Naive realism, the philosophical concept that's been mentioned a few times in this appendix, enters in here. It could, however, be considered at just about any time, since its proponents believe that it's unconsciously involved in practically all of our daily activities. Simply put, naive realism teaches that our visual and bodily sense reveal to us an external world as it really is—that we "see" actual physical objects, for instance. Disbelievers say that neurological evidence contradicts this theory; that from the neurological standpoint the events in our lives and within our bodies depend upon interpretation by the brain; that we can know nothing directly, but only experience transmitted through—and so "colored" by—the central nervous system. The perceptual time lag, caused by the limited speed of light, is also involved in objections to naive realism. I merely want to remind the reader that in ordinary terms naive realism, or some mind-brain idea very much like it, is habitually used whether we're considering evolution within a time-oriented camouflage universe, painting a picture, or running a household. And after many centuries, the debate over the relationship between mind and brain continues, if first the existence of the mind is even agreed upon!

(Is there really *"something out there?" That was one of the questions I asked Jane not long after she began giving these*

sessions late in 1963. I'd say that we still have but a partial answer [the same situation that applies to a lot of our other questions, too], although Seth came through with what I think of as a key passage in the 23rd session for February 5, 1964:)

Because I say that you actually create the typical camouflage patterns of your own physical universe yourselves, by use of the inner vitality of the universe in the same manner that you form a pattern with your breath on a glass pane, I do not necessarily mean that you are the creators of the universe. I am merely saying that you are the creators of the physical world as you know it—and herein, my beloved friends, lies a vast tale.

(And a decade later we're still unraveling that tale, with Seth's help. I'll digress here for a moment to note that we expect to be so occupied for the rest of our lives: The intellectual and emotional challenges posed by the Seth material are practically unlimited.

(Yet, as far as he went in Chapter 5 of Personal Reality, *Seth was pretty definite in his ideas about physical reality. It seems to me that he combines certain aspects of naive realism with some of the objections to it; see the 625th session for November 1, 1972:)*

Because you are flesh and blood creatures, the interior aspects of perception <u>must</u> have their physical counterparts. But material awareness and bodily response to it would be impossible were it not for these internal webworks . . . I am saying that all exterior events, including your own bodies with their insides, all objects, all physical materializations, are the outside structures of inside ones that are composed of interior sound and invisible light, interwoven in electromagnetic patterns.

Beneath temporal perception, then, each object and event exists in these terms, in patterns that interact with each other. On a physical level you seem to be separated from everything that is not yourself. This is not true, but in your day-to-day existence it seems to be, and it is an assumption that you usually take for granted . . .[12]

Again, we run into difficulties in explanation simply because there are few verbal equivalents for what I am trying to say.[13]

(Within that temporal framework, investigators have recently discovered great biochemical differences among human beings at the molecular level: The genetic structures of numerous proteins [see Note 5] have been shown to be much more varied than was

suspected. Even more pronounced are the differences among proteins between species. Each of us is seen to be truly unique—but at the same time those studying biological evolution express concern about whether their discoveries will challenge Darwinistic beliefs. Instead, I think that what has been learned so far offers only possible variations within the idea of evolution, for the talk is still about the origin of life out of nonlife, followed by the climb up the scale of living complexity; most evolutionists think that natural selection, or the survival of the fittest, still applies.

(Any role that consciousness might play in such biochemical processes isn't considered, of course, nor is there any sort of mystical comprehension of what we're up to as creatures. No matter how beautifully man works out a hypothesis or theory, he still does so without any thought of consciousness coming first. Through the habitual (and perhaps unwitting) use of naive realism, he projects his own basic creativity outside of himself, or any of his parts. He also projects upon cellular components like genes and DNA[14] learned concepts of "protection" and "selfishness": DNA is said to care only about its own survival and "knowledge," and not whether its host is man, plant, or animal. Only man would think to burden such pervasive parts of his own being, and those of other entities, with such negative concepts! Jane and I don't believe the allegations—in its own terms, how could the very stuff controlling inheritance not care about the nature of what it created? I'm only half joking (is there a gene for humor?) when I protest that DNA, for example, doesn't deserve to be regarded in such a fashion, no matter how much we push it around through recombinant techniques.[15]

(I'm projecting my own ideas here, but I think that in all of its complexity DNA has motives for its physical existence [as mediated through Seth's CU's, or units of consciousness] that considerably enlarge upon its assigned function as the "master molecule" of life as we know it. Deoxyribonucleic acid may exist within its host, whether man, plant, or animal—or bacteria or virus—in cooperative altruistic ventures with its carrier that are quite beside purely survival ones. Some of those goals, such as the exploration of concepts like the moment point [see Note 11], or probabilities [and reincarnation[16]], really defy our ordinary conscious perception. In terms we can more easily grasp, social relationships within and between species may be explored, start-

ing at that biochemical level and working "upward." Basically, then, an overall genetics of cooperation becomes a truer long-run concept than the postulated deadly struggle for survival of the fittest, whether between man and molecules, say, or among members of the same species. Once again we have consciousness seeking to know itself in as many ways as possible, while being aware all of the time, in those terms, of the forthcoming "death" of its medium of expression, DNA, and of DNA's host, or "physical machine."

(I continue my projections by writing that to a molecule of DNA the conventional notion of evolution—could such an entity grasp that idea, or even want to—might be hilarious indeed, given its own enhanced time scheme.[17] Actually it would be more to the point if, perhaps with the aid of hypnosis and/or visualization, we tried from our giant-sized viewpoints to touch such minute consciousnesses with our own,[18] and so extend our knowledge in unexpected ways. Some probable realities might be reached—potential conscious achievements that I think are already within the reach of certain gifted individuals, Jane among them.[19] Jane and I would rather say that the variability among humans [or the members of any other species] at the molecular level is a reflection of Seth's statement that we each create our own reality, with all that that implies.

(I want to add here that our real challenge in knowing our own species, and others, may lie in our cultivating the ability to understand the interacting consciousnesses involved, rather than to search only for physical relationships supposedly created through evolutionary processes. The challenge is profound. The consciousnesses of numerous other species may be so different from ours that we only approximately grasp the meanings inherent in some of them, and miss the essences of others entirely. To give just two examples, at this time we are surely opaque to the seemingly endless search for value fulfillment that consciousness displays through the "lowly" lungfish and the "unattractive" cockroach. Yet those entities are quite immune to our notions of evolution, and they explore time contexts in ways far beyond our current human comprehension: As far as science knows, both have existed with very little change for over 300 million years.

(It should be clear, then, that in our camouflage reality the ordinary concept of evolution becomes very complex if one chooses to make it so. The process can be discussed from many view-

*points; Jane and I think that such inquiries could easily "evolve"
[to make a pun] into a book, either to bolster Seth's ideas on the
subject, for instance, or to refute them. I now have on file
materials that support or reject any stance on evolution that one
cares to take. But it never fails, as "they" say: The members of
each "pressure group," whatever its orientation, want to see
things their way—very human performances, I'm afraid. Once
it's created, each school of thought takes upon itself, and often
with great intellectual and emotional arrogance, the right to
advance its own belief systems in the world at the expense of its
rivals.*

*(But, I asked Jane recently, why do our sciences and religions
take it all so seriously? I wasn't really too earnest. If we truly
owe our physical existence to the chance conglomeration of
certain atoms and molecules in the thickening scum of a primordial pond or ocean [to discuss only mankind here], then certainly
we'll never come this way again in the universe; and moreover,
our emotional and intellectual attributes must rest upon the same
dubious beginning. Aside from the lack of evidence to back up
such "scientific" speculations, what thinking or feeling values, I
wonder, can make such a belief system so attractive? Surely very
limited ones in linear terms, fated to never get beyond those
incessant questions about what came before the beginning. To
paraphrase some other material Jane wrote not long ago: "But
the earth and all upon it are given. To imagine that such an
entire environment is an accident is intellectually outrageous and
emotionally sterile."*

*(And this is the ideal place to insert the poem she wrote not
long afterward:*

Science Convinces Me of Magic

*Science convinces me of magic
More each day.
To think that you and I,
The tiniest blade of grass
And highest mountain,
The smallest ant
And the Empire State Building
(and all the shops, streets,
and people in modern-day Manhattan)*

> All exist because
> Some elemental dice
> Just happened to
> Fall together right!
> Dice thrown by no hand
> Or intent,
> Because neither were
> Invented yet.

(Jane and I certainly do not hold creationist views [see Note 1]. As I wrote near the beginning of this appendix, to go very far into religious history would lead away from the subject matter I planned to cover; but to us science is as far away from Seth's philosophy in one directions as religion is in the opposite direction. The species' religious drives have been around a lot longer than its scientific ones, however, so I found myself looking for broad correlations between the two, in that under each value system the individual carries a very conscious sense of personal vulnerability. Before Darwinism, to use that concept as an example, man at least felt that God had put him on earth for certain purposes, no matter how much man distorted those purposes through ignorance and war. According to Judaism and Christianity, among many religions, man could seek forgiveness and salvation; he had a soul. After Darwin, he learned that even his physical presence on earth was an accident of nature. He was taught—he taught himself—that ideas of souls and gods were ridiculous. Either way, this very fallible creature found himself vulnerable to forces that consciously he couldn't understand—even though, in Seth's view, down through the millenia man had chosen all of his religious and antireligious experiences.

(As far as I can discover, science pays very little attention to any philosophical questions about why we're here, even while most definitely telling us what's true or not true. And while postulating that life is basically meaningless or goal-less [DNA doesn't care what its host looks like, for instance], science fights awfully hard to convince everyone that its right—thus attaching the most rigid kind of meaning or direction to its professional views! [If I were very cynical, I'd add here that to Jane and me it often seems that science wants only what science believes.] At the same time, in mathematical and biological detail much too

*complicated to go into here, the author of many a scientific work
in favor of evolution has ended up by undermining, unwittingly,
I'm sure, the very themes he so devoutly believes in. I've hinted
at some of those paradoxes in certain notes [mainly 5 through 8]
for this appendix.*

*(In the current literature I read that a typical famous scientist—
one of many leaders expressing such views these days—is very
pessimistic about the state of the human species, given its many
dilemmas. I also note that he seems to be most unhappy while
stressing his agnosticism,[20] which is the kind of belief system that
perpetuates standard evolutionary doctrines. Building upon those
limited assumptions, the individual in question tells us how
ironic it is that the "new" portions of the human brain, those
that have evolved within the last two million years, are responsible for the moral and technological problems our species now
faces. The brain's great creative neocortex is held especially
accountable for problems that may lead to humanity's self-
destruction. None of these challenges, as Jane and I habitually
call them, are seen as distorted expressions of the kind of
creativity Seth has described many times.[21]*

*(Within such a gloomy framework, then, I think it legitimate to
ask how the species can consciously stress its accidental presence in the cosmos, yet demand that its members be the most
"moral" of creatures. If science insists that there was, and is,
no design or planner behind man's emergence, then how can
man be expected to act as if there was, or is? Seth hasn't said so
yet, but I think such contradictions play an important negative
role in present world conditions. The attitude that life is a
godless thing is so pervasive—and not only in Western cultures—
that in Seth's terms it can be called an invisible mass core belief.*

*(I'm happy to note that Seth's ideas oppose much of the
"modern" thinking that we're fated to bring about our own end
as a species, whether by nuclear warfare or in some other
equally devastating way. From his own viewpoint, Seth recently
discussed such fears in a session given for Jane's ESP class:)*

. . . in certain terms the theory of evolution, as it is conventionally held, has caused unfortunate beliefs. For how can you
look at yourselves with self-respect, with dignity or with joy, if
you believe that you are the end product of forces in which the
fittest survive? Being the fittest implies those given most to what

would appear to be murderous intent—for you must survive at the expense of your fellows, be you leaf, frog, plant, or animal.

You do not survive through cooperation, according to that theory, and nature is not given a kind or creative intent, but a murderous one. And if you see yourselves as the end result of such a species, then how can you expect goodness or merit or creativity from yourselves, or from others? How can you believe that you live in a safe universe when each species exists because it survives through claw, if it must hunt and kill out of murderous intent, as implied in the theories of evolution and of reality itself?

So when you think of your beliefs and who you are, you must also think of your species, and how you are told your species came to be. For your private beliefs are also based upon those theories, and the beliefs, culturally, of your times.

It is seldom that you really question your biological origins, what they mean, and how you interpret them. Are you physically composed of murderous cells, then, each spontaneously out to get the others? If so, your physical being is more miraculous a product than even I have ever told you! If your cells did not cooperate so well, you would not be listening to this voice, and it would make no sound. As you listen to me, the cooperative, creative adventure within your bodies continues, and in terms of continuity reaches back prehistorically and into the future. Because consciousness creates form with joy, there is no murder that you have not projected out of misunderstanding and ignorance of the nature of that consciousness.

Roots do not struggle to exist. One species does not fight against the others to live. Instead creativity emerges, and cooperatively the environment of the world is known and planned by all the species. What appears to be struggle and death to you at those levels is <u>not</u>, now, for the experience of consciousness itself is different there, as is the experience of your own cellular composition.

(Then soon afterward, Seth had this to say in a private session:) Your body knows how to walk. The knowledge is built in and acted upon. The body knows how to heal itself, how to use its nourishment, how to replace its tissues—yet in your terms <u>the body itself has no access</u> to the kind of information the mind possesses. Being so ignorant, how does it perform so well?

If it were scientifically inclined, the body would know that such spontaneous performance was impossible, for science cannot explain the reality of life itself in its present form, much less its origins. Consciousness within the body knows that its existence is within the body's context, and <u>apart</u> from it at the same time.

(I repeat that when Seth discusses evolution his meaning differs considerably from the scientific one—which, with various modifications, is even accepted by a number of religious thinkers. As I show at the end of this appendix, Seth allows for a much greater range of simultaneous origins; in our reality these imply growth and development out of that "basic" group of species for the most part, with multidimensional purposes operating inside an enhanced time scheme that includes probabilities, reincarnation, counterparts,[22] precognition, and other concepts, meanings, and beliefs. All of these qualities are manifestations of All That Is, or consciousness, or energy, or whatever. Probabilities aside, when Seth talks about cells [or their components] recombining as parts of plant or animal forms, as he does in the 705th session, Jane and I don't take that to mean the evolution, alteration, of one species into another—but that a unity of consciousness pervades all elements in our environment, whether "alive" or "dead." With the concept of probabilities in mind, however, much of the "thrust for development and change" that Seth also mentions as existing inside all organisms, could just as well take place in those other realities. Early in this appendix, I described how Seth continually built upon material that he'd given before, and that processes of correlation between old and new resulted. At this time, my ideas there represent a correlation between Seth's material on evolution in the 705th session [which led to this appendix], and his later statements on origins, referred to above. We hope to learn much more about the whole business of evolution. And behind all, Seth insists upon the condition that each of us chose to experience this camouflage reality within this historical context.

(My thought is that because of that choosing, common denominators must lie beneath the clashing beliefs about evolution, and that a good place to start looking for such unifying factors is within the theory, or the framework or idea, of simultaneous time—however one wants to try to express such a quality within serial terms. The search would be a complicated one. At the same time, I admit that ideas like this always remind me of

Seth's comments in the class session for June 23, 1970, as excerpted in the Appendix for Seth Speaks:)

In this reality, [each of] you very nicely emphasize all the similarities which bind you together; you make a pattern of them, and you very nicely ignore all the dissimilarities . . . If you were able to focus your attention on the dissimilarities, merely those that you can perceive but do not, then you would be amazed that mankind can form any idea of an organized reality.

(However, collectively we do share an agreed-upon reality, even if one subject to many stresses. The next two excerpts to be presented from Seth came through in a couple of sessions delivered some time after he'd finished "Unknown" Reality. I've put them together for easy reading. Their inspiration was my work here and the discussions on evolution that Jane and I led in ESP class. As noted with the quotations given in Note 13, eventually this material will be published in its entirety as part of a Seth book; perhaps then it can be used as a guide for the sort of investigation just mentioned. In the meantime, the thoughts below can at least help orient some fresh thinking about the beginning of our planet, of all the species upon it, and indeed of the universe itself. Seth began:)

There are verbal difficulties having to do with the definition of life. Because of the psychological strength of preconceived notions, I have to work around many of your concepts. Your own kind of conscious mind is splendid and unique. It causes you, however, to interpret all other kinds of life according to your own specifications and experiences.

There is no such thing, in your terms, as nonliving matter. There is simply a point that you recognize as having the characteristics that you have arbitrarily ascribed to life, or living conditions. For there is no particular point at which life was inserted into nonliving matter.

If we must speak in terms of continuity, which I regret, then <u>in those terms</u> you could say that life in the physical universe, on your planet, "began" spontaneously in a given number of species at the same time. Words do nearly forsake me, the semantic differences are so vast. <u>In those terms</u> there was a point where consciousness, through intent, impressed itself into matter. That "breakthrough" cannot be logically explained, but only compared to, say, an illumination—that is, a light occurring everywhere at once, that became a medium for life as you define it. It had nothing to do with the propensity of certain kinds of cells to reproduce—[all cells are] imbued with the "drive" for value fulfillment—but with an overall illumination that set the conditions in which life was possible as you think of it; and at that imaginary, hypothetical point, all species became latent. The inner pulsations of the invisible universe reached certain intensities that "impregnated" the entire physical system simultaneously. That illumination was everywhere then at every point aware of itself, and of the conditions formed by its presence.

At the same time, EE units *(see Note 3)* became manifest. I have said, for example, that the universe expands as an idea does, and so the visible universe sprang into being in the same manner. The same energy that gave birth to the universe is, in those terms, still being created. The EE units contain within themselves the latent knowledge of all of the various species that can emerge under those conditions. It is according to your relative position. You can say that it took untold centuries for the EE units to "initially" combine, forming classifications of matter and various species, or you can say that this process happened at once. In your terms, each species is aware of the condition of each other species, and of the entire environment. In those terms the environment forms the species and the species form the environment. There were fully developed men—that is, of full intellect, emotion, and will—living at the same time, in your terms, as those creatures supposed to be man's evolutionary ancestors.

[However, as] you begin to question the nature of time itself, then the "when" of the universe is beside the point. The motion and energy of the universe still comes from within. I certainly realize that this is hardly a scientific statement—yet the moment that All That Is conceived of a physical system it was invisibly created, endowed with creativity, and bound to emerge [into physical reality].

There is a design and a designer, but they are so combined, the one within the other, the one within and the one without, that it is impossible to separate them. The creator is within its creations, and the creations themselves are gifted with creativity. The world comes to know itself, to discover itself, for the planner left room for divine surprise, and the plan was nowhere foreordained. Nor is there anywhere within it anything that corresponds to your "survival of the fittest" theories.

(Seth's statement just given, that fully developed men coexisted with their supposed ancestors, led to our request that he follow through with more information on the subject. He's done so to some extent, and here we're presenting material from one of those later sessions to show his thinking. He continues to confound accepted evolutionary theory. As usual, however, Seth's new data obviously imply new questions that we haven't gone into yet. But at least, I told Jane, he's said certain things that we can ask questions about, whether from the viewpoint of evolution, time, language, civilization, or whatever. The excerpts to follow, incidentally, are those I referred to earlier in this appendix, when I wrote that just as Jane had supplemented Seth's material on early man with some of her own [as given in Appendix 6 in Volume 1], he in turn added to hers:)

In your terms of history, man appeared in several different ages—not from an animal ancestor in the way generally supposed. There <u>were</u> men-animals, but they were not your stock. They did not "lead" to anything. They were species in their own right.[23]

There were animal-men. The terms are for your convenience. In some species the animal-like tendencies predominated, in others the manlike tendencies did so: Some were more like men, some more like animals. The Russan steppes had a particular giant-sized species. Some also I believe in Spain—that area.

There is considerable confusion, for that matter, as to the geological ages as they are understood.[24] Such species existed in many of these ages. Man, as you think of him, shared the earth with the other creatures just mentioned. In those terms so-called modern man, with your skull structure and so forth, existed alongside of the creatures now supposed to be his ancestors.

There was some rivalry among these groups, as well as some cooperation. Several species, say, of modern man died out. There was some mating among these groups—that is, among the groups in existence at any given time.

The brain capacities of your particular species have always been the same . . . Many of the man-animal groups had their own communities. To you they may seem to have been limited, yet they combined animal and human characteristics beautifully, and they used tools quite well. In a manner of speaking they had the earth to themselves for many centuries, in that modern man did not compete with them.

Both the man-animals and the animal-men were born with stronger instincts. They did not need long periods of protection as infants, but in an animal fashion were physically more agile at younger ages than, say, the human infant.

The earth has gone through entire cycles unsuspected by your scientists. Modern man, then, existed with other manlike species, and appeared in many different places on the earth, and at different ages.

There were then also animal-man and man-animal civilizations of their kinds, and there were complete civilizations of modern man, existing [long] before the ages now given for, say, the birth of writing (in 3100 B.C.)

My position after writing this appendix is that in scientific and religious terms we know little about our world [and universe], its origins, and its amazing variety of forms, both "living" and "nonliving." Our own limitations may have something to do with our attitudes here, yet Jane and I have become very careful about believing science or religion when either one tells us it can explain our world, for each of those disciplines ignores too much. No matter what the source of this camouflage reality may be, our conscious lack of knowledge and understanding as we manipulate within it, through naive realism or any other system of belief or perception, ought to make us humble indeed; all arrogance should be transcended as we become more and more aware of the limitless beauty, complexity, and mystery that surrounds us, and of which we are part. Jane and I just don't think it all came about through chance! The mind can ask too many questions to be satisfied with mechanistic explanations, and nurturing that characteristic of dissatisfaction alone may be one of the most valuable contributions the Seth material can make.

(To us, even "ordinary" linear knowledge as it accumulates through the next century or two, not to mention over longer spans of time, is certain to severely modify or make obsolete many concepts about origins and evolution that today are dispensed by those in authority—and which most people accept unthinkingly.

(For some years now, organized religion as a whole has been suffering from a loss of faith and members, stripped of its

*mysteries by science, which, with the best of intentions, offers in
religion's place a secular humanism—the belief that one doesn't
need blind faith in a god in order to be morally concerned for
the common welfare; paradoxically, however, this concern is
most of the time expressed in religious terms, or with religious
feeling. Yet science too has experienced many failures in theory
and technology, and knows a new humility; at least partly because of these failures, anti-intellectualism has grown noticeably
in recent years.*

*(Now we read late surveys that show increase in religious
faith, and statements to the effect that science does not claim to
reveal absolute truth, that any scientific theory is valid only until
a variance is shown. Jane and I certainly aren't turned on to
realize that a major religion, for instance, teaches the "facts" of
man's basically corrupt and sinful nature; surely a religion in
the best sense can offer beliefs superior to those! At the same
time, we take note of the latest efforts of biological researchers
to explain how, millions of years ago, a primitive DNA molecule
could begin to manufacture the protein upon which life "rides,"
and thus get around the contradiction posed in Note 8: What
made the protein that sustains the processes of life, before that
life was present to make the protein? The scientists involved
hope the new hypothesis will survive further tests and become
"fact," thus giving clues to the riddles of origins and evolution.
But to briefly paraphrase material Jane came through with not
long ago [and which, again, will eventually be published]: "How
does one deal with new facts that undermine old facts, in whatever field of endeavor? Do you say that reality has changed?
Upon examination, facts give."*

*(And as I work on this appendix, Seth has already remarked in
the 709th session, just before break at 10:35:)*

You are well acquainted with the exterior method, that involves studying the objective universe and collecting facts upon
which certain deductions are made. In this book [Volume 2],
therefore, we will be stressing interior ways of attaining, not
necessarily facts, but knowledge and wisdom. Now facts may or
may not give you wisdom. They can, if they are slavishly
followed, lead you away from true knowledge. Wisdom shows
you the insides of facts, so to speak, and the realities from which
facts emerge.

(The search, then, is on for new unities and meanings; a

convergence, one might say of the realities of science, nature, religion—and, of course, mysticism. By mysticism I mean simply the intuitional penetration of our camouflage reality to achieve deeper understandings relative to our physical and mental environments—and such comprehensions are what Jane seeks to accomplish through her expression of the Seth material.[25] In that sense, it isn't necessary here to discuss attaining "ultimate" knowledge—it will be enough to note that as one person Jane can use her abilities to help unify a number of viewponits. She can also bring to consciousness the idea that no matter what our individual orientations may be, collectively we do have overall purposes in the world we've created. This realization alone can be a transforming one; as I show in the Introductory Notes for Volume I of "Unknown" Reality, it can be a most useful one in practical, everyday life as well. Within that sort of framework, the evolution referred to by Seth—in whatever way it may concern the developments of ideas, planets, creatures, or anything else—makes sense.)

NOTES: Appendix 1

1. Over the years, my outside reading on evolution has covered many often conflicting viewpoints. Whether their beliefs are rooted in the tenets of conventional biology (Darwinism), for instance, or allied with those of the creationists (who hold that God made the earth and all of its creatures, just as described in the Book of Genesis), the advocates of rival theories have impressed me as having at least one thing in common: No matter how violently they may disagree, their arguments lack all sense of *humor*. This is serious stuff, world! Whatever happened to the spontaneity and joy in life? For surely, I found myself thinking as I read all of those antagonistic ideas, spontaneity and joy were the very ingredients that Seth would place uppermost in any theory or scheme of life's "beginnings," regardless of its philosophical stance.

2. As I wrote in the Introductory Notes for Volume 1 of *"Unknown" Reality*, I think it important to periodically remind the reader of certain of Seth's basic ideas throughout both volumes. . . ." His simultaneous time, or spacious present, is certainly such a concept. Yet in the next paragraph I added that in my opinion, "Seth's concept of simultaneous time will always elude us to some extent as long as we're physical creatures. . . ." To me the challenge of confronting that idea is well worthwhile, however, for to grasp it even partially is bound to enlarge one's view of reality.

A close analogy to this material can be found in remarks Seth made in the 682nd session for that first volume: "The idea of one universe alone is basically nonsensical. Your reality must be seen in its relationship to others. Otherwise you are always caught in questions like 'How did the universe begin?' or 'When will it end?' All systems are constantly being created."

Then see the 688th session for Seth's discussion of closed systems and the backward and forward, inward and outward motions of time.

In light of the excerpts to come in this appendix from the 44th session, it should be noted that when Seth used the term "camouflage," he referred not only to our physical world as one of the forms (or camouflages) taken by basic reality, but to another kind of time as well—the medium of successive moments the outer ego is used to, and in which our ordinary world exists.

Seth's first mention of "camouflage" is described in Volume 1; see Note 3 for Appendix 11.

3. In this 1964 session, Seth was several years away from any attempt to elaborate upon the vitality that "composes from itself all other phenomena." In October 1969 he began his material on EE (electromagnetic energy) units. These, he declared, exist just below the range of physical matter, and accrete in response to emotional intensity; eventually, they form physical objects. See session 504–6 in the Appendix of *The Seth Material*, and the 581st session (held in April 1971) in Chapter 21 of *Seth Speaks*.

In Volume 1, Seth carried this material a step further through his description of his CU's, or "units" of consciousness. "I do not want you to think of these units as particles," he said in the 682nd session (given in February 1974). "There is a basic unit of consciousness that, expressed, will not be broken down. . . ." Also see sessions 683–84.

4. This paragraph and the preceding one were used as a footnote for the 637th session in Chapter 9 of *Personal Reality*. That session, held 18 months ago, contains material appropriate to this appendix: As an analogy, Seth compares the "evolution" of souls in terms of value fulfillment to cellular growth in our physical reality.

5. According to my interpretation of this sentence, Seth stops short of telling us that in our reality all species—man, animals, and plant life (and viruses and bacteria too, for that matter)—developed from a single primordial living source. Evolutionary theory maintains that such a source spontaneously came into being, riding upon various protein molecules (or certain other kinds of molecules) that had themselves chemically—and miraculously—evolved out of nonliving matter, then demonstrated the ability to duplicate themselves. (When Seth came through with this 44th session, neither Jane nor I had enough background information about theories of evolution to ask him to be more specific. Proteins, for instance, are very complex chains of amino acids, and consist of nitrogen, oxygen, hydrogen, carbon, and/or certain other elements. They

exist in great variety in all animal and vegetable matter; in the body each protein supports a very definite function.) But the view that all life had a common origin, that by pure chance it originated on the earth—*just once*—without the aid of God, or any sort of designer, is today accepted by most scientists in biology and related disciplines. Such thinking stems from the work done in the 19th century by the English naturalists Charles Darwin and Alfred Wallace.

However, Jane and I believe that at most the "facts of evolution" make up a working hypothesis—or unproven proposition—only, for many of evolution's tenets, especially those involving energy/entropy (see Note 6), are open to serious challenge. There's plenty of evidence around for changes occuring *within* species, but the "upward" transmutation of one species into another has not been scientifically proven from the index fossil record, nor has it been experimentally verified. The arguments about evolution can get very technical, so in my notes I'm referring to those aspects of the subject in the barest terms possible.

In Volume 1, see Appendix 6 for Session 687, and Session 689 with its notes.

6. Ever since Seth came through with the material in this (44th) session 10 years ago, I've been interested in comparing his second law of the inner universe with the second law of thermodynamics of our "camouflage" physical sciences. Both deal with energy, yet to me they're opposites. At the same time I see them as linked through our distorted perception of that inner reality, thus pointing up Seth's statement just given, that "the so-called laws of your camouflage universe do not apply to the inner universe." (When this session was held Jane knew nothing of the three laws of thermodynamics, or how they define energy/heat relationships in our universe. Nor is she concerned with them now, *per se;* they're simply outside of her interests.)

Seth has always maintained that there are no closed systems, that energy is constantly exchanged between them, regardless of whether such transfers can be detected. (In Volume 1, see Session 688, plus Note 2 for the same session.) The second law of thermodynamics, on the other hand, tell us that our universe *is* a closed system—and that it's fated to eventually run down because the amount of energy available for useful work is always decreasing, even though the supply of that energy is constant. A measure of this unavailable energy is called entropy.

I think it obvious that by "energy transformation" Seth doesn't mean that the energy (or consciousness, to my way of thinking) in our system is inevitably decreasing. I can best express it intuitively: In physics, that well-known second law of thermodynamics may usually be so reliable for us, distorted as it is, just *because* of our limited physical interpretation as mediated by the central nervous system.

At the same time, it's worth noting that the second law of thermodynamics is still questioned by some theoreticians—the idea being that it's impossible to prove a scientific "truth" in each of an unlimited number of instances.

7. Charles Darwin (1809–1881) published *On the Origin of Species* in 1859. In his book Darwin presented his ideas of natural selection—that all species evolve from earlier versions by inheriting slight (genetic) variations through the generations. (See Note 5.) Thus, in a process called gradualism, there has been over many millions of years the slow development of flora and fauna from the simple to the complex, with those structures surviving that are best suited to their environments—the "survival of the fittest," in popular terms.

Any biologist who is a true Darwinist would find these statements of Seth's to be anathema: "Psychic and religious ideas, then, despite many drawbacks . . . are far more important in terms of 'evolution' than is recognized." And: "I am telling you that so-called evolution and religion are closely connected." (From the 690th session, in Volume 1.) Such a scientist would have the same reaction to Seth's statement that "Consciousness always creates form, and not the other way around." (From the 513th session, in Chapter 2 of *Seth Speaks*.)

It's often been claimed that Darwin's natural selection, while ruling out any question of design or a planner—God, say—behind living matter, leaves unexplained the same question relative to the structure of *non*living matter, which in those terms obviously preceded life. I'd rather approach that argument through another statement Seth made in Chapter 20 of *Seth Speaks* (in the 582nd session): "You are biologically connected, chemically connected with the Earth that you know. . . ." How is it that as living creatures we're made-up of ingredients—atoms of iron, molecules of water, for instance—from a supposedly dead world? In the scientific view we're utterly dependent upon that contradictory situation. No one denies the amazing structure or design of our physical universe, from the scale of subatomic particles on "up" (regardless of what cosmological theory is used to explain the universe's beginning). The study of design as one of the links between "living" and "nonliving" systems would certainly be a difficult challenge—but a most rewarding one, I think—for science. I have little idea of how the work would be carried out. Evidently it would lead from biology through microbiology to physics with, ultimately, a search that at least approached Seth's electromagnetic energy (EE) units and units of consciousness (CU's). Yet according to Seth, both classes of "particles" are in actuality nonphysical; as best words can note, they have their realities on scales so minute that we cannot hope to detect them through our present technology. . . .

Yet here we run into irony and paradox: Any scientist who considered the existence of Seth's EE units and CU's would be called a heretic by his more conventional colleagues, for he would be acknowledging the possibility that *all* matter, being made up of such conscious entities, was living. From that viewpoint, at least, there would be no link through design to be discovered.

In connection with material in this note, I think it quite interesting and revealing that several millennia before Darwin, man *himself* began playing the role of a designer within the framework of nature, through his selective breeding of animals and his hybridization of plants. These activities certainly represent evolution through conscious intent, guided by the same creature who insists that no sort of consciousness could have been responsible for the origin or development of "life," let alone the "dead" matter of his planet. Not only that: We read that even now in his laboratories man is trying hard to *create* some of that life itself. This is always done, of course, with the idea that the right combination of simple ingredients (water, methane, ammonia, et al.) in the test tube, stimulated by the right kind of energy under just the right conditions, will automatically produce life. It's confidently predicted that eventually at least one such experiment will succeed. I have yet to see in those accounts anything about the role consciousness will play in this truly miraculous conversion of dead matter into that of the living. Perhaps those involved in the experiments fear that the idea of consciousness will impugn the scientific "purity" of their work.

Finally, in this appendix I haven't used the term "Neo-Darwinism" in order to avoid confusion with the familiar Darwinism that most people—including scientists—will employ. Neo-Darwinism is simply the original idea of natural selection in plants and animals updated to take present-day genetics into account.

8. Very briefly, for those who are interested: It's often been shown mathematically that contrary to Darwinistic belief, enormous time spans (in the millions of years, say) will not aid in the chance formation of even the chemical precursors to life—the protein or nucleic acid molecules—but will instead make their creation even less likely. For with time, the even distribution or equilibrium of matter increases, moving it away from the ordered sequences necessary to support life. Scientifically, in the closed system of our universe, the second law of thermodynamics and entropy eventually conquer all. (See Note 6.)

Nor can solar energy be thought of as the agent that directly turned nonliving matter into its living counterpart; in those terms, life required its intermediate molecules, which sunlight is not able to construct. Life needs protein in order to "be," and to sustain it through metabolism— *then* it can use solar energy! Darwin's theory that life arose by chance poses a basic contradiction: What made the protein that sustains the processes of life, before that life was present to make the protein?

Many times in laboratory studies, substances called proteinoids (often misleadingly defined in dictionaries as "primitive proteins") have been observed forming from amino acids, which are subunits of proteins. Some researchers think of proteinoids as the forerunners of the protein that life needs to ride upon, but for quite complex scientific reasons, proteinoids are far from being true biological proteins and do not lead to life. Jane and I strongly object to being told that dead matter turns itself into living matter. Just how does this transformation come about?

Evolutionary thinking is challenged not only by questions of protein synthesis, and energy/entropy (see Note 5), however. Equally insistent are the puzzles posed by the missing intermediate forms in the fossil record: Where *are* all the remnants of those creatures that linked birds, reptiles, cats, monkeys, and human beings? The hypothetical evolutionary tree of life demands that such in-between forms existed; it seems that by now paleontologists should have unearthed enough signs of them to make at least a modest case for their belief systems; the lack of scientific evidence is embarrassing. Since my mind works that way, I could make minutely detailed drawings of a graduated series of such entities (gradualism being a basic premise in Charles Darwin's theory), but would the creatures shown have been viable? Could they actually have existed for the necessary millennia while evolving into the species where fossil remains *have* been discovered, or that live today? As indicated in Note 5, evolutionists are serving goodly portions of speculation along with inadequate theory—or, really, hypothesis.

9. Seth prepared the way for these statements by declaring in the 684th session, in Volume 1: "It is <u>truer</u> to say that heredity operates from the future backward into the past, then it is to say that it operates from the past into the present. Neither statement would be precisely correct in any case, because your present is a poised balance affected as much by the probable future as the probable past."

10. See Note 2 for this appendix. Then, in Volume 1 see the material on time reversal and symmetry in Note 6 for Session 702.

11. Both of these references originate in the first volume of this work. Seth, in Session 681: "In your terms—the phrase is necessary—the moment point, the present, is the point of interaction between all existences and reality. All probabilities flow through it, though one of your moment points may be experiences as <u>centuries, or as a breath,</u> in other probable realities of which you are a part." Also see notes 1 and 5 for the same session.

And Seth, in Session 683: "All kinds of time—backward and forward—emerge from the basic unpredictable nature of consciousness, and are due to 'series' of significances."

12. I'm not sure how something like naive realism fits in with out-of-body travel (or "projection"), however. I've read nothing about the two together, nor have I yet asked Seth for what will surely be some very interesting material on such a possible relationship. Paradoxically, our perceptions while out-of-body can be more tenuously connected to temporal reality than usual, yet more acute at the same time. I was aware of the accustomed physical world during a projection that's

described in *Seth Speaks* (see the 583rd session in Chapter 20), and in some other dream-connected out-of-body situations. However, our use of naive realism must often govern what we allow ourselves to experience while consciousness is separated from the body. I also think that some out-of-body travels, apparently to "alien" nonphysical realities, may actually be based instead upon interior bodily states or events. But there are times when the projecting consciousness, free of frameworks like naive realism, at least approaches truly different realities, or probabilities. Jane has had some success here; in Chapter 6 of *Adventures*, see her projection experience involving "Dr. Sam's house."

13. A note added much later: Sometimes things develop in unexpected ways: One might say that several years later Seth continued the material just presented. By the time he did so he'd been through with *"Unknown" Reality* for quite a while, but I was still working on the notes and appendixes for Volume 2. As I wrote Appendix 1 of Volume 2 Part I in particular I discussed with Jane the passages on naive realism; soon afterward Seth began to refer to the subject during scheduled sessions, and one of them contained the excellent information below. (Only one part of that session is quoted, but eventually it will be published in its entirety as part of a Seth book.) Very evocative, to consider how consciousness *chooses* to manifest itself physically, in direct contradiction to the mechanistic beliefs held so tightly—and with so little humor—by those adhering to Charles Darwin's theory of evolution. From Session 803:)

"You perceive your body as solid. Again, the very senses that make such a deduction are the result of the behavior of atoms and molecules literally coming together to form the organs, filling a <u>pattern</u> of flesh. All other objects that you perceive are formed <u>in their own way</u> in the same fashion.

"The physical world that you recognize is made up of invisible patterns. These patterns are 'plastic' in that while they exist, their final form is a matter of probabilties directed by consciousness. Your senses perceive these patterns in their own way. The patterns themselves can be 'activiated' in innumerable fashions. (*Humorously:*) There is <u>something out there</u> to observe.

"Your sense apparatus determines what form that something will take, however. The mass world rises up before your eyes, but your eyes are part of that mass world. You cannot <u>see</u> your thoughts, so you do not realize that they have shape and form, even as, say, clouds do. There are currents of thought as their are currents of air, and the mental patterns of man's feelings and thoughts rise up like flames from a fire, or steam from hot water, to fall like ashes or like rain.

". . . these patterns of probabilities themselves are not inactive. They are possessed by the desire to be-actualized (with a hyphen). Behind all realities there are mental states. These always seek form, though again there are other forms than those <u>you</u> recognize."

14. Deoxyribonucleic acid, or DNA, is often referred to as the "master molecule," or the "basic building block" of life. DNA is an essential component of the protoplasmic substance of which genes and chromosomes are formed in the cell nucleus, and governs the heredity of all living things.

15. In microbiology, the first stages of the exciting and controversial "genetic engineering" are at hand. This long-sought goal of science involves the very sophisticated recombination of DNA from such different life forms as plants and mammals, say, into new forms not seen on earth before. Such work has been called vital for the understanding of many things—the genetic of all species, the control of at least some diseases, great improvements in the quality of food plants, and so forth. It's also been called outright interference with the evolutionary constraints that prevent the interbreeding of species. Although risks may be present in DNA research, such as the unforeseen creation of new diseases, it seems that within strict safeguards recombinant techniques are here to say.

Once again, however, it's obvious that as a whole, science is far removed from Seth's idea that each of us—whether that "us" is a human being or a molecule of DNA—creates our own reality. And what if we *can* learn to assemble sections of DNA from various life forms into new forms? To at least some extent such basic genetic substances *would* cooperate in the efforts at recombination: for no matter what kind of life developed, it would represent a gestalt of myriad consciousness, embarking upon unique explorations.

In Note 7 (also see Note 5), I wrote that for centuries now—most of them obviously preceding Darwin—man himself has been playing the role of a designer through his creation of certain breeds of animals and hybrid plants. But we see now that man is no longer content to bring about changes *within* species, as in cattle, for instance: With vast excitement he faces the challenge of "engineering" new kinds of life. Those urges are creative even when, as a designer, he goes against his own Darwinian concepts that there is no conscious plan involved in the design of his world.

16. In this appendix I've consistently thought of probabilities and reincarnation as being nearly synonymous, while hardly mentioning the latter to avoid making the material unnecessarily complicated. As Seth himself told us in the 683rd session for Volume 1 of this work: "Reincarnation simply represents probabilities in a time context (underlined)—portions of the self that are materialized in historical contexts."

17. These excerpts from Seth's material in the 690th session, for Volume 1, furnish a close analogy to the sort of "time" available to molecular consciousness: ". . . biological precognition is firmly based in the chromosomes and genes, and reflected in the cells . . . The cells' practically felt 'Now' includes, then, what you think of as past and

future, as simple conditions of Nowness. They maintain the body's structure in <u>your</u> poised time only by manipulating themselves in a rich medium of probabilites. There is a constant give-and-take of communication between the cell as you know it in present time, and the cell as it 'was' in the past, or 'will be.' ''

18. See the information on ''the true mental physicist'' in Session 701 for Volume 1. Seth discussed how in our future such a scientist will be able to allow ''his consciousness to flow into the many open doors (*or inner realities*) that can be found with no instruments, but with the mind.'' And Seth commented in the same session: ''Ruburt has at times been able to throw his consciousness into small physical instruments (*computer components, for instance*), and to perceive their inner activity at the level of, say, electrons.''

19. Jane described one of her adventures with probable realities in Appendix 4 for Volume 1: She tuned in to her own ''sidepools of consciousness,'' her own ''probable neurological materializations. . . .'' (My personal opinion is that although many may think it difficult reading, Appendix 4 contains some of the most important information in Volume 1.)

20. I remind the reader that an agnostic (as I think Charles Darwin was) is one who believes the mind can know only physical phenomena, and not whether there are final realities, causes, or gods. An atheist believes there is no God.

I should add that the passages on science and scientists in Appendix 12 aren't intended to add up to any general indictment of what are very powerful cultural forces, but to give insights into ''where we're at'' at this time in linear history. Many scientists *are* agnostic or atheistic. However, Jane and I feel that if science represents the ''search for truth,'' as it so often reminds us, then eventually it will contend with the kind of gifts she demonstrates. Subjective and objective abilities, working together, can create a whole greater than the sum of its parts. A number of scientists, representing various disciplines, have written Jane about the Seth material, and many of them have expressed such views.

The material in Volume 1 on the dream-art scientists, the true mental physicist, and the complete physician (as well as on science in general), applies here. See sessions 700–4.

21. Earlier in this appendix, see Seth as quoted from Chapter 20 of *Seth Speaks* and Chapter 8 of *Personal Reality*.

22. A note added later: I inserted ''counterparts'' here because in Section 5 of this volume Seth devotes portions of several sessions to his counterpart concept: ''<u>Quite literally, you live more than one life at a time</u>'' (his emphasis). Among others, see Session 721, here quoted, with its Appendix 10. As the reader studies those particular sessions, he or she will quickly see how counterpart ideas fit in with the subject matter of Appendix 1.

23. I suggest that sessions 562–63, in Chapter 11 of *Seth Speaks*, be reviewed in connection with all of this material. In Volume 1, see Note 4 for Session 689.

24. Without going into detail yet—nor have we asked him to—Seth has insisted more than once that the earth is ''much much'' older than its currently estimated age of 4.6 billion years.

25. In Volume 1, Jane and mysticism are discussed in the Introductory Notes, Session 679, and Appendix 1 for that session.

APPENDIX 2
(For Session 708)

(Seth's phrase, ". . . you cannot see before or after what you think of as your birth or death. . . ." triggered a set of associations for me, but they proved to have their complications. I thought I remembered a statement he'd made long ago, but now I couldn't locate it within the body of its material. One by one my mental connections fell into place as I searched for it, yet for a time I was quite frustrated while I tried to physically verify my unconscious knowledge of its location.

(First I thought of Seth's assertion in the 92nd session for September 28, 1964, that "trees have their dreams"; [in Volume 1, see the quotations in Note 1 for Session 698]. Then I remembered that he'd come through with extensive material on tree consciousness in a much earlier session. With Jane's help the next day I found that information in the 18th session, which had been held on January 22, 1964. Most of that session is unpublished, although someday we'd like to print it in full. It contains many intriguing ideas—as, for example: "A tree knows a human being also . . . [yet it] does not even build up an image of a man, which is why this is so difficult to explain . . . And the same tree will recognize the same man who passes it by each day."

(Next, the subject matter of the 18th session led me to recall that Seth had also discussed trees several years later. But this time, in spite of my system of indexing each session in at least a fairly adequate fashion, several days passed before I found the passage I wanted. Discovering it involved a patient combing of many sessions and notes. [If the indexes listed everything in detail, they'd end up being almost as long as the sessions themselves.] The search was worth it, though; now I had the key phrase I'd associated with Seth's remark in Session 708. It's underlined below for easy reference.

(Seth, then, in the 453rd session for December 4, 1968:)

212

To your way of thinking some lives are lived in a twinkling, and others last for centuries, as some huge trees. The perception of consciousness is not limited . . . I have told you, for example, that the consciousness of the tree is not as specifically focused as your own. To all intents and purposes, however, <u>the tree is conscious of 50 years before and too years hence.</u>

Its sense of identity spontaneously goes beyond the change of its own form. It has no ego to cut the "I" identification short. Creatures without the compartment of the ego can easily follow their own identities beyond any changes of form. The inner self <u>is</u> aware of this integrity of identity, but the ego focused so securely in physical reality cannot afford this luxury.

APPENDIX 3
(For Session 708)

(The morning after the above session had been held [on September 30, 1974], I asked Jane to write down what she'd told me at about 1:15 A.M. I remembered her description of it at the time, even though I'd been pretty bleary by then, but I wanted her own version for use here. She wrote:)

"As I was getting ready for bed after our last Seth session, I suddenly wondered about Atlantis. Then from Seth, mentally, I thought, I got the information that Atlantis, as it's come down to us in myth and story, was actually a composite of three civilizations. Atlantis is a myth in response to a truth, then, I suppose. Next I got that Plato picked up the Atlantic material himself, physically—he didn't get in the way he said he did. I never ask Seth about Atlantis; I'm afraid the cultish ideas connected with it turned me off long ago."

(In his dialogues Timaeus *and* Critias, *the Greek philosopher Plato [427?–347? B.C.] described now the fabled island continent of Atlantis sank beneath the ocean west of the Pillars of Hercules—the Strait of Gibraltar—some 12,000 years previously. Looking backward in time, Plato heard the story of Atlantis from his maternal uncle, Critias the Younger, who was told about it by his father, Critias and Elder, who heard about it through the works of the Athenian statesman and lawgiver, Solon, who had lived two centuries earlier (c. 640–559 B.C.]; and Solon got the story of Atlantis from Egyptian priests, who got it from—? Whether Atlantis actually existed in historic terms, its location, the time of its suggested demise, and so forth, are of course points strongly contested by scholars, scientists, and others.*

(Any specific associations that might have brought the Atlantis information to mind were hidden from Jane, though. Neither of us had been reading or talking about it. We were left thinking that the general tone of Seth's material early in the session,

*especially in his references to such ideas as "historical se-
quences" and "alternate realities," might have served as a
trigger.*

*(A note added later: Seth himself had some things to say about
Atlantis in the 742nd session for Section 6; the session also
contains excerpts from the Atlantis material he delivered a month
or so after finishing Volume 2 of "Unknown" Reality. Without
giving away any "secrets," I can write that on both occasions
Seth discussed the subject in conjunction with his postulates
about ideals, myths, religion, probabilities, and the simultaneous nature of time.)*

APPENDIX 4
(For Session 710)

(Today we read a long treatise on the "truths" advocated by "holy men" associated with various Eastern religious philosophies—Hinduism, Buddhism, Taiosm, and so forth. Jane's quick and impassioned response through her own writing, as prevented below, reflects feelings deeply rooted within her mystical nature, and also illuminates important aspects of the body and direction of the Seth material as a whole. Given those points, she's bound to have differences of belief with other views of reality.

(Yet I think more is involved than choosing among the belief systems offered by Eastern or Western cultures, for instance— that is, in more basic terms each personality would make that kind of choice before *physical birth, with the full understanding of the vast influence such a decision would have upon a life's work. Obviously, in those terms of linear time, Jane and I each feel that we chose our present environments.*

(Being individualists, then, as I wrote in the Introduction Notes for Volume 1, we don't concentrate upon whatever parallels exist between Seth's concepts on the one hand and those of Eastern religious, philosophical, and mystical doctrines on the other; while we know of such similarities, we're just as aware of how different from them Seth's viewpoint can be, too. I added that even though we have no interest in putting down other approaches to inner reality, still we're firm believers in the "inviolate nature of the individual consciousness, before, during, and after physical existence, in ordinary terms."[1] So, here, we leave it up to the reader to make the intuitive and overt connections between Seth's philosophy and the material Jane wrote today. The interested reader will also be able to compare her composition with certain passages in her long poem, Dialogues of the Soul and Mortal Self in Time, when that work is published in book form in September 1975.

216

(Thus Jane demanded in her composition of this afternoon, October 7, 1974:)

"What is this passion for nonbeing, this denial of sensual life, that drives so many gurus and self-proclaimed prophets? They speak out against desire while propelled by the overwhelming desire to lose themselves. They luxuriate in a kind of cosmic masturbation, titillating their psychic organisms into pitches of mindless excitement; cavorting in orgasms of self-surrender. They bask in a sort of universal steam bath that drives all impurities of individuality or creativity from their souls, leaving them immersed, supposedly forever, in a bliss beyond description; in which, indeed, their own experience disappears.

"Thank God that some god managed to disentangle itself from such physic oneness, if that's what it's supposed to be. Thank God that some god loved itself enough to diversity, to create itself in a million different forms; to multiply, to explode its being inward and outward. Thank God that some god loved its own individuality enough to endow the least and the most, the greatest and the smallest, with its own unique being.

"The gurus say: 'Give it all up.' One of those we read about today counsels: 'When you want to do one thing, do another instead. Do not do what you want to do, but what you should do.' Never trust the self that you are, the gurus say, but the self that you should be. And that self is supposed to be dead to desire, beyond wanting or caring; yet paradoxically, this nonfeeling leads to bliss. The gurus say that All That Is is within you, yet tell you not to trustst yourself. If All That Is didn't want appearances, we wouldn't experience any! Yet appearances, the gurus say, are untruths, changing and therefore false.[2]

"Is my body an appearance, hence an untruth amid the truth which is changeless? Ah dear body, then, how lovely and blessed your untruth, which is senate and feels desire through the hollowest of bones. How blessed, bodies, leaping alive from the microscopic molecules that combine to walk down the autumn streets; assemble to form the sweet senses' discrimination that perceives, for a time, the precise joy and unity of even one passing afternoon. The body's untruth, then, is holier than all truths, and if the body is an untruth then I hereby proclaim untruth, and truth and all the gurus' truths as lies.

"God knows itself through the flesh. God may know itself through a million or a thousand million other worlds, as so may

I—but because this world *is,* and because I am alive in it, it is more than appearance, more than a shackle to be thrown aside. It is a privilege to be here, to look out with this unique focus, with these individual eyes; no to be blinded by cosmic vision, but to see this corner of reality which I form through the miraculous connections of soul and flesh.

"Cherish the gifts of the gods. Don't be so anxious to throw your individuality back into their faces, saying, 'I'm sick to death of myself and of my individuality; it burdens me.' Even one squirrel's consciousness, suddenly thrown into the body of another of its kind, would feel a sense of loss, encounter a strangeness, and know in the sacredness of its being that something was wrong. Wear your individuality proudly. It is the badge of your godhood. You are a god living a life—being, desiring, creating. Through honoring yourself, you honor whatever it is God is, and become a conscious co-creator."

NOTES: Appendix 4

1. In Volume 1 of *"Unknown" Reality,* see the material on Jane, mysticism, and religion in the Introductory Notes, the 679th session, and Appendix 1 for that session. In that first appendix, the notes on Jane as an "independent mystic" (despite her denial that she even thinks of herself as a mystic), are especially appropriate here.

2. From any of Seth's books—let alone Jane's—I could cite a number of comments that question much of the thinking behind different Eastern systems of religious thought. Seth, for example, in the 642nd session in Chapter 11 of *Personal Reality:* You will **not** attain spirituality or even a happy life by denying the wisdom and experience of the flesh. You can learn more from watching the animals that you can from a guru or a minister—or from reading my book. But first you must divest yourself of the idea that your creaturehood is suspect. Your humanness did not emerge by refusing your animal heritage, but upon an extension of it."

For ourselves, and even considering Seth's concept of "camouflage" (in Volume 1, see Note 3 for Appendix 11), Jane and I certainly believe that our physical existences and mental experiences are quite "real" in themselves. We could easily take a book to present the reasons for our particular beliefs, examining them in connection with both Eastern and Western religious philosphies. A good general question, we think, and one we'd like to see discussed with our own ideas of the inviolate nature of the individual in mind, has to do with the prevalence of ordinary, daily, conscious-mind thinking and perception throughout much of the world. In historical terms this situation has always existed for the human species; and we think it applies almost equally in Eastern lands, especially among the political leaders and ruling classes within them.

Yet Buddhist belief, for instance, maintains that our perception of the world is not fundamental, but an illusion; our "ignorance" of this basic undifferentiated "suchness' then results in the division of reality into objects and ideas. But why call our generalized awareness an illusion, instead of regarding it as one of the innumerable manifestations that reality takes? No one is free of certain minimum physical needs or of self-oriented thought, I remarked to Jane recently, and each nation strives to expand its technological base no matter what its philosophy may be. Would a widespread use of Eastern religious doctrines be more practical on our earth today, or the kind of self-knowledge Seth advocates? Even given their undeniable accomplishments, why didn't the Eastern countries create ages ago the immortal societies that could have served as models for those of the West to emulate—cultures and/or nations in which all the mundane human vicissitudes (in those terms) had been long understood and abolished: war, crime, poverty, ignorance, and disease?

Certainly the species must be putting its conscious activities to long-term use, however, even with the endless conflicts and questions that grow out of such behavior. During the many centuries of our remembered history, those conflicts in themselves have been—and are—surely serving at least one of consciousness's overall purposes, within our limits of understanding: to know itself more fully in those particular, differentiated ways.

APPENDIX 5
(For Session 711)

(In the opening notes for the 711th session, I referred to Seth's deliveries in ESP class on the previous evening, October 8, 1974. When Jane and I received the transcript of his material at next week's class, we saw that it ran to five single-spaced typewritten pages. Seth talked about many things, but his remarks here, as I've put them together, mainly concerned a subject he'd first discussed with members of class just a week ago [on October 1][1]—the "city" they could start building in their individual and collective dream states;)

There is much I have not told you about your city, for you will have to discover it for yourselves. I am merely encouraging you to focus your joint energies in that direction . . . You will be dealing with symbols, yet you will learn that symbols are reality, for you are symbols of yourselves that live and speak. You do not think of yourselves as symbols [but] there is no symbol that does not have its individual life.

I speak to you of other theoretical realities. I challenge you now to be as creative in another reality as you are in this one. And if it seems to you, because of your beliefs, that you are limited here, then I joyfully challenge each of you to create a city, an environment, and perhaps a world, in which no such limitations occur. What kind of world would you create?

I speak to you from the known and unknown desire that gives you your own birth, and that speaks to you from the tiniest, least-acknowledged thought that flies like a pigeon within your skull . . . And in this moment of your reality, and in the desire of your being, do you even create All That Is. Bow down before no man, no woman, and no belief—but know you are indeed the creators.

For some of you the city will have a theater. For some of you it will not. For those of you who like theater, it will be like none you have ever seen. In it the actors and actresses will take the parts of beliefs—of fleshed beliefs—and the morality play, so to speak, will deal with the nature of beliefs and how they are enacted through the centuries as well as through the hours. That theater then will serve many purposes, even as each of you are exquisite performers, and have chosen the roles and beliefs that you have taken . . .

Now there are books programming out-of-body activity; millions of you are told that when you leave your body you will meet this demon or that demon, or this or that angry god. So, instead, we will form a free city to which those travelers can come, and where those who enter can read books about Buddhism if they prefer, or play at being Catholic. There will also be certain beloved traps set about the city, that will be of an enlightening nature . . . Now listen: You think there is nothing intrinsically impossible about building a platform in [your] space . . . I am suggesting, then, a platform in inner reality. It is as valid . . . I am suggesting, then, a platform in inner reality. It is as valid— far more valid—as an orbiting city in the sky, in physical terms, and it challenges your creative abilities much more. You need a good challenge—it is fun! Not because you *should* do it, but because you *desire* it . . . It is a great creative challenge that you can throw down to yourselves from your future selves.

(In answer to a question from a student:) A beloved trap is one that you set for yourself. And so our city will be full of them. When you are tired of playing a Catholic priest, for example, you will fall into your own trap—in which your beliefs [as such a one] are suddenly worked out to their logical perfection, and you see what they mean.

Now when children walk down streets, they count the cracks in the sidewalks. And so our city will have its own kind of tricky walks! There will be sidewalks within, and above and below sidewalks. But it is for each individual to decide which one he or she will follow. When Ruburt *(as Seth calls Jane)* was a young girl he wrote a poem in which he declares:

> *You make your own sidewalk,*
> *And I make my own sidewalk.*[2]

And so our city will simply have alternate sidewalks, and they will be beloved traps, set by each self.

I feel no great responsibility for any of your beings. [If I did] then I would be denying you your own power, and therefore seemingly building my own . . . I am here because I enjoy it. I am a teacher, and because I am a teacher I love to teach. A person who loves to teach needs people who love to learn. That is why I am here and why you are here . .. My view of reality is different from your own, and that is fine, and so I can teach. A true teacher allows you to learn from yourself. I enjoy the great vitality and exuberance of your reality, and our city will have joy and exuberance. Now joy sounds quite acceptable, but *(with amusement)* our city will also have fun—which in many spiritual circles is <u>not</u> so acceptable!

(In that class session Seth had much more to say about the dream city. Because of the individual freedom of creation implied in the city's very existence, and in Jane's early poem in Note 2, I'll close this appendix with another of her verses. This one is from an even earlier poem, Lorrylo, *written when she was but 15 years old:)*

> *I am the daughter of the wind,*
> *I am the vagabond of time.*
> *I am a spirit, unleashed and free,*
> *Foster child of infinity.*

NOTES: Appendix 5

1. "You can colonize an entire inner level of reality," Seth told that October 1st class. "to do so, you must give your best with dedication and joyful creativity. This will not be an imaginary city. It will have a greater reality than any physical city that you know, and it can, in its own way, shine with brighter lights in inner reality than any nighttime city displays. There, I hope, you will work at developing skills, in terms of the dream-art scientist *(for instance; see Session 700 in Volume 1 of* 'Unknown' Reality), and learn other professions than the ones you now know."

2. Seth didn't quote Jane's little poem exactly from 26 years ago, but paraphrased it. It's called *Echo,* and Jane wrote it in 1948, when she was 19 years old. Once again in an early work we see clear signs of the Seth material to come (in 1963). *Echo* begins:

> *I stand upon a block*
> *of stillness.*
> *It is more secure*
> *than any sidewalk.*
> *I bring with me*
> *My own sidewalk . . .*

APPENDIX 6
(For Session 711)

(I started this appendix 13 months after the 711th session was held. Jane and I have seldom been concerned with trying for strict definitions of qualities like "altered states of consciousness." All of us experience such altered states of consciousness often throughout each day, so the phrase itself should hardly mean anything mysterious—even though others usually look at Jane or me questioningly if either of us uses it in conversation.

(Jane, for instance, hasn't had her brain waves formally recorded by an EEG, or electroencephalograph. It's not that she's against that procedure—just that she's much more interested in what she feels and does than she is in the mechanical records offered by the machine.

(There are four recognized [electrical] brain waves, and in speed they range upward from 0 to 26 and more Hertz units, or cycles per second. These rhythms can vary somewhat, and are best thought of as areas of activity. Brain wave overlap. Very simply, delta brain waves are connected with dreamless sleep, theta with creativity and dreams, alpha with a relaxed alertness and changing consciousness; beta—the fastest—with concentration, and with an intense focus upon all of the challenges [and anxieties and stresses, many would say] faced in the ordinary daily world.

(Even if beta waves, then, seem to be the "official pulses" of our civilization [to use Seth's phrase from a session that will be quoted in part below], still Jane and I wonder. When aren't we actually in a state of altered consciousness? For no matter which brain rhythm may predominate at any time, that state is certainly an altered one in relation to the other three. But more than this, why not call all actions of the brain "altered" when compared to Seth's concept of the individual personality's whole self, or entity?[1]

223

(We read that in ordinary terms highly creative people [like Jane] usually generate large amounts of theta and low-alpha waves pretty constantly while doing their thing. Measuring and recording brain waves is a complicated task, however; not only is it important which areas or lobes of the brain are monitored—if not all of them—but because of the mechanical limitations of the EEG itself much that goes on in the brain is necessarily missed. In addition, the two hemispheres of the individual brain often show variations in electrical energy states. But most importantly, we think, while the EEG can indicate broad categories of brain activity, it can hardly probe the participant's very individual and subjective content of mind *within this camouflage [physical] reality. Nor at this time, given the minimum premise that Jane's speaking for Seth constitutes any indication of "paranormal" activity, do we think that her performance could be identified as such* per se *on the graphs of her brain waves. The state of "EEG art" isn't that advanced yet [if it ever will be]. Presumably, however, when speaking for Seth, Jane would show definite changes in all frequency areas in both hemispheres, with the theta and delta ranges altered the most. We also think that her EEG readings would vary once again when she spoke or sang in Sumari, her trance "language."*

(Our curiosity about such speculations led me to plan this appendix shortly after the 711th session was hold, and I asked Jane if Seth could eventually offer some insights about the brain's electrical reality. He finished dictating Volume 2 of "Unknown" Reality in April 1975, and we finally got around to the session I wanted six and a half months later.

(Seth did give much unexpected material about the brain—and about his own reality, incidentaly—but the session turned out to be so long and closely interrelated that I found it very difficult to excerpt; most of the portions I picked out were left hanging, or were too incomplete. Naturally, Seth said what he said from his own viewpoint. I ended up choosing the few quotations gathered together here just to indicate the direction of the information, while hoping that the entire session, with others promised on the subject by Seth, will be published some day.

(From the 760th session for November 10, 1975:)

The beta waves quicken. They seem to be the official pulses of your civilization, giving precedence to official reality, but you have little idea that the psyche is <u>inherently</u> able to seek its conscious experience from all of the known ranges, according to the kind of experience chosen at any given "time."

Beta was not meant to carry the full weight of conscious activity, however, although its accelerating qualities can lead to initiations into "higher" realms of consciousnes, where indeed the brain waves quicken. The other patterns *(delta, theta, and alpha)* are highly important to physical and mental stability, being very interwound with cellular consciousness. In cases usually called schizophrenic, the beta acceleration is not supported by the stabilizing attributes of the other known frequencies.

It is possible, then, for a brain to register all of the known patterns at once, though your machines would note only the predominating rhythm.

A kind of inverted beta pattern, difficult to describe, often appears suddenly in the midst of the other ranges, <u>driving through</u> them, accelerating consciousness to a high degree of creativity. The brian waves as they are known are separately registered segments of a greater "whole" kind of consciousness, and your machines are just as segmented, perceiving only those patterns [they were designed to recognize]. Other activity escapes them. They cannot note the rapidity with which you move through all of the known patterns constantly. This behavior can be learned by anyone willing to take the time and effort. Some courage would also help.

I told you that you flashed in and out of the reality that you know.[2] In between one moment and the next of the waking day, there are, in your terms, long delta and theta waves that you cannot recognize. They are not recorded by your machines because quite literally they go in a different, "unofficial" direction. Each official waking brain wave is a peak <u>in your world</u> of a far deeper "wave" of other experience, and represents your points of continuity.

Each beta wave rides atop the other patterns. In normal sleep, the "conscious" wave rides beneath the others, <u>with the face of consciousness turned inward</u>, so to speak. All the recognized characteristics of consciousness are "inverted," probing other realities than the one you know. They are quite effective and lightning fast. In sleep the beta waves are not turned off—the "conscious" part of you, with its beta rhythms, is elsewhere.

In these sessions the full range of brain waves is utilized as you understand them. Here, in a highly creative, disciplined, <u>and</u>

<u>yet</u> spontaneous performance, a situation is set up in which knowledge is obtained from the known frequencies, combined so that consciousness can use itself more fully, reaching into many areas closed to <u>one</u> range of consciousness alone. The various diverse, unique characteristics of each level of awareness are given play. In a way this is like an accelerated, chosen, well-organized "conscious" dream venture, in which Rubert travels through mediums of consciousness until finally he, still being himself, is nevertheless <u>no longer himself</u> *(humorously),* but me.

He is combining and alternating frequencies so that he literally brings forth a different creature of consciousness—one that in your terms is not alive, yet one whose very reality straddles the life that you know. The most elemental portions of my reality begin at the furthest reaches of your own.

In sleep your ordinary brain waves <u>as you understand them</u> register a chaotic jungle of experience not normally processed. Biologically or physically, there is little need for such disorientation. The normal waking consciousness, with its characteristic patterns, can indeed follow [into sleep]. A mixture of brian waves would result. Consciousness as you think of it expands tremendously under such conditions. You would follow your own pattern of continuity and understanding, weaving this into the sleep and dream states, forming a "new" pattern that triumphantly combines all, as to some extent this occurs in our sessions.

In an ideal society, each brain wave would be utilized purposefully. You would go to sleep to solve certain problems . . . There <u>is</u> an overall general difference, nationally speaking—that is, people of various nations do differ to some extent in their prevalent brain frequencies . . . All in all, however, the beta has predominated, and been expected to solve many problems unsuited to its own characteristics.

Despite your reliance upon one range only, your world of consciousness draws heavily upon all of the known wave patterns, and from others of which you are unaware. For now that is the end of this material, though I will continue it at any time at your request.

NOTES: Appendix 6

1. See Seth's definition of the entity as given in Chapter 5 of *The Seth Material*.

2. In Volume 1 of *"Unknown" Reality*, see Session 684 after 10:07, as well as Note 3.

APPENDIX 7
(For Session 711)

(I'll open this appendix by referring to a pair of short notes I wrote for Volume 1 of "Unknown" Reality. First, Note 6 for Session 686: "We're still acquiring information about the psychic connections between Jane and Seth, of course. Even now, more than 10 years after Jane began speaking for Seth, one might say that each session we hold represents another step in this learning process; we fully expect it to continue as long as the sessions do." Then, Note 3 for the 688th session contains my statement that in an appendix for Session 711, "I assemble from various sessions information on the complex relationships involving Jane-Ruburt-Seth [and also Rob–Joseph]).")

(Sometimes, though, I find it quite a challenge to excerpt a number of sessions to illuminate a particular one. I want the passages chosen to make sense on their own, out of context, and to focus clearly on the subject; at the same time, I don't want to include too many or too few of my own notes. But in this appendix, at least, I discovered that it wasn't always possible to achieve both of those goals just as I wanted to—not in connection with each point mentioned. It also became inevitable that at least some elements of Seth's own "separate-but-connected" reality would have to be considered. In addition to those concerns, on occasion I found myself rearranging the quoted discussions a bit—although really to a minor degree—for even greater brevity and clarity. So here's how it all worked out:)

(This appendix was inspired by two blocks of material Seth covered in the 711th session: Jane's hearing his voice recently in the sleep state [see her own notes at the start of the 710th session], and the bridge personality she and Seth have created "between dimensions," or between themselves.)

(I finally decided that the best way to present the variety of material desired, whether from Seth, Jane, or myself, was in

chronological order, letting a composite picture emerge as the work progresses. This system automatically makes room for any references in Volume 1. In actuality the chronology begins long before "Unknown" Reality was started, and continues well beyond the date of its ending, in April 1975. Since the excerpts are still more representative than complete, however, due to the accumulated mass of information available, my own choices enter in: ESP class data are quoted a number of times; included is material summarizing Jane's own theories about the Seth phenomena, as she worked them out in her recently completed Adventures in Consciousness; *but reincarnation, while mentioned often, isn't stressed in terms of particulars—that is, I refer to Seth's statements that he, Jane and I led closely involved lives in Denmark in the 1600's, but those lives aren't studied per se. Within our ordinary context of linear time I think of reincarnation, even though in Seth's terms it's really a simultaneous phenomenon, as being further away, or more removed, from us physical creatures than the more "immediate" psychic connections and mechanics I want to show as linking Seth, Jane, and myself. And also because of that sense of removal, Seth Two[1] is hardly mentioned at all.*

(Perhaps I put this appendix together as I did partly because Jane herself isn't much turned on by reincarnational concepts, although she does like the way Seth insists upon the unlimited attributes of each personality; and within such a "simultaneous" framework there's plenty of room for probable selves, reincarnational selves, and [added later] counterpart selves.[2]

(Seth began talking about his connections with Ruburt-Jane— and, therefore, himself and his own reality—almost from the time these sessions began on December 2, 1963. Such relationships were of great interest to us as we sought to understand the blossoming of Jane's psychic abilities. They still are. Every bit of information helped, although often in the beginning I didn't know enough to follow up answers with more questions. As the sessions multiplied, however, this became more and more difficult to do: There was a steadily widening pool of material to ask questions about!

(I'll begin our chronology by reminding the reader that Note 6 for Session 711 contains a description of how, through the Quija board, Seth announced himself by that name in the 4th session

*for December 8. [Note 6 also includes his reasoning about
names, as given a decade later.]*

*(Then, in the 6th session Seth's answer to my question: "Do
you have a last name?" couldn't have been more precise: "No."
I still think his reply has its own kind of wit, even though it came
to us through the board.[3]*

*(Speaking of names, this is the time to remind all that Seth
calls both Jane and me by* male *names: Ruburt and Joseph. Why
does he speak of Jane as a male—and so as "he" and "him?"
In Note 6 for Session 679, in Volume 1, I quoted Seth from the
12th session for January 2, 1964:)* Sex, regardless of all your
fleshy tales, is a psychic phenomenon, merely certain qualities
which you call male and female. The qualities are real, however,
and permeate other planes as well as your own. They are opposites which are nevertheless complementary, and which merge
into one. When I say as I have that the overall entity [or whole
self] is neither male nor female, and yet refer to [some] entities
by definite male names such as "Ruburt" and "Joseph," I
merely mean that in the overall essence, the [given] entity identifies itself more with the so-called male characteristics than with
the female.

*(Sessions 12 through 15 are briefly quoted in Note 4 for the
680th session, in Volume 1; Seth remarked upon the impossibility of closed systems, his own senses [including something of
their limits], his ability to visit other "planes" of reality, and his
"incipient" man's form.*

*(However, from Session 14 [for January 8, 1964], there's
other material that can be given here, as well as some that
makes an interesting note at the end of this appendix.[4] First,
from my own note at 11:05: "Jane said that Seth was quite
pleased with the new voice, and that she now knows what he's
thinking sometimes, even though he doesn't relay it to or through
her as part of a message."*

(Then from Seth himself:) In one sense meeting with you costs
me little energy, it is true. On the other hand the effort to
communicate explanations does involve a very real endeavor on
my part. And so you are not the only ones who grow weary in
this respect. As I have said, feeling is action, and in my communications to you feeling plays a strong part.

*(Nor did Seth agree with Jane's assessment of her reactions to
her Seth voice. He was very outspoken—yet his materials came*

*through with a much lighter touch than these printed words
alone can indicate:)* . . . Ruburt's voice sounds rather dreary in
this transitional phase, [yet] the one thing that pleases me im-
mensely is the way he can translate at least a few of my
humorous remarks and the inflections of my natural speech . . .
As a man's voice I fear he will sound rather unmelodious. I do
not have the voice of an angel by any means, but neither do I
sound like an asexual eunuch, which is all I've been able to
make him sound like all night. And incidentally, Ruburt, you
were a good brother at one time. The so-called male aspect of
your personality has always been strong, but by this I mean
powerful. Without the loyalty that you are learning as a woman,
your character had many defects—and there, I said I would not
get into anything serious.

(Then to me, later yet in the session:) . . . and as a woman
[when I knew you], you certainly put your present wife to shame
as far as vanity was concerned!

(From the 22nd session for February 4, 1964:) I have never
trusted the written word half as much as I trust the spoken word,
and on your plane it is difficult to trust either. But I do not feel
that I could be myself as easily by means of automatic writing,
for example. I do not mind speaking through Ruburt's mouth—
somehow the sound of the words is rather pleasant. But seeing
myself transformed more or less into plain black and white
words on a sheet of paper seems dull and uninteresting. And I
have always enjoyed conversation, which is the liveliest of all
arts . . .

Because Ruburt deals in words [as a writer], it is easy for me
to communicate in this manner. That is, he automatically translates inner data given by me into coherent, valid, and faithful
camouflage[5] patterns —into words. My information is not actually given as sound. Its transference is instantaneous on Ruburt's
part, and his performed through the workings of the mind, the
inner senses,[6] and the brain.

*(In Note 3 for the 688th session, in Volume 1, I quoted my
own note from the 24th session for February 10, 1964: I described how Jane could sense the whole of whatever concept
Seth was discussing—and how, since such a structure was too
much for her to handle at once, she could feel Seth "withdraw-
ing it, to release it to her a little at a time in the form of
connected words."*

(Then Seth himself continued in that 24th session:) Concepts fit together in patterns. In order for there to be communication between us I must disentangle a concept from its pattern, which is somewhat difficult. It is somewhat like having to free a particular word from a strong emotional association. I experience patterns made up of concepts, and you use words in associations.

When I speak through Ruburt I must disentangle the concept. This sometimes leaves me with short ends, because it is natural for me to experience the concepts in their entirety; and yet I must drop very important data by the wayside because you are not capable of handling it, except in consecutive form. I feel concept patterns.[7]

(From the 27th session for February 19, 1964:) There is so much I want to say. When your training is further advanced, much further advanced, we may be able to take certain shortcuts. It is difficult for me to have a strong out this material in words, and for you to record it. You see, it is possible in theory for you to experience directly a concept-essence of the material in any given night's session.[8]

As for another advancement made, besides dispensing with the material [Ouija] board, Ruburt has achieved a state in which he can receive inner data from me more readily. But beyond this, he is now able in some small way to contact me . . .

One reason for the success of our communications is the peculiar abilities in you both and the interaction between them, and the use that you allow me to make of them. Ruburt's intellect had to be of high quality. His conscious and unconscious mind had to be acquainted with certain ideas to begin with, in order for the complexity of this material to come through.

In the beginning, for example, there is always a distortion of material by the person who receives it, at least on the topmost subconscious level. So an individual whose personal prejudices are at a minimum is excellent. If, for example, Ruburt's prejudices happen to lie along lines which do not contradict what I know to be true, then all the better, and there is much less resistance.

Information like this is sifted through many layers of subconscious conception, and is subsequently colored. People believing in your organized religions color it in a manner that is highly disadvantageous, and that unfortunately adds to existing superstitions. Ruburt's mind, believe it or not, is much like my own—

though, if you'll forgive me, in a very limited fashion. Therefore the distortions are much less distortive, much less harmful, and more easily discovered and cleared . . . Others less perfectionist than myself are content with more distortion. I am not. Ruburt's *Idea Construction*[9] was rather amazing. The inner senses provided him with much, but nevertheless the ideas contained in it represented an achievement of the conscious mind. I was drawn by this to realize that he was ready for me.

(To me, later in the session and with much humor:) You had no problems with parents in the part—and, my dear Yo-Yo, you were an excellent father to me at one time, and if I may say so, at one time I was an excellent father to you. As a son you were helpful, considerate, and kind.

To me this [reincarnational and family material] is all so obvious that I almost hesitate to mention it, but this is because I tend to forget what human existence on your plane actually involves . . .

And now, most devoted friends, a fond good evening. I will always help you to the best of my ability, and as far as I know I will be accessible for your present lifetimes.[10] And my dear Joseph, if you whacked me many times, I got my blows in too. And I made Ruburt one lovely wife—so there, my lovelies.

(From the 28th session for February 24, 1964:) As far as Ruburt is concerned, there is no danger [to him in these sessions]. For one thing, I am an extremely sensitive but disciplined, and sensible if somewhat irascible, gentleman, if you will forgive the term. None of the communcations from me have been in any way conducive to a development toward mental or emotional instability. *(Smiling:)* I may make bold to remark that I am more stable than you or Ruburt, or your fine psychologist [who just wrote to you].[11]

I also do not take my responsibility lightly, and to a great degree I feel responsible for you, and for any results coming from your communications with me. If anything, the personal advice I have given you both should add to your mental and emotional balance, and result in a stronger relationship with the outside world.

I do depend upon Ruburt's willingness to dissociate.[12] There is no doubt that at times he is unaware of his surroundings during a session. However, this is no more binding upon him than autosuggestion. It is a phenomenon in which he gives consent, and he could, at any time and in a split second, return his conscious attention upon his physical environment.

There is no danger, and I will repeat this: There is no danger of dissociation grabbing ahold of him like some black, vague and furry monster, carrying him away to the netherlands of hysteria, schizophrenia, or insanity . . . Withdrawal into dissociation as a hiding place from the world could, of course, have dire consequences. Certain personalities could, and have, fallen prey here, but with you, with Ruburt, this is not the case.

Also, Ruburt has experienced and used dissociation, though to a lesser degree, before our communications—that is, in his work—and knows how to handle it.

We have gone into this before, and I have no doubt that we will on endless occasions. And if I succeed in convincing you of my reality as a personality, I will have done extremely well . . . Ruburt's subconscious has enough camouflage pattern to enable me to make contact, but not so much as to distort me out of all recognition. I am not his subconscious, though I speak through it. It is the atmosphere through which I can come to you, as the air is the atmosphere through which the bird flies. A certain reassembly of myself is necessary when I enter your plane, and this is done partially by myself, and by the combined subconscious efforts of you, Joseph, and Ruburt. Will this satisfy you for now?

("Sure, Seth," I said, agreeing with the implication that Jane and I would want the same material discussed again—and again.[13])

. . . *and Ruburt did get a rather embarrassing flash from me before the session. I blush to admit the fact, but at one time I did call you Yo-Yo (see the excerpts for the 27th session.*

("When did you call me that, Seth?")

I called you Yo-Yo when you were my father, and I am not going into any reincarnational material tonight.

(From the 33rd session for March 9, 1964:) I do not bring about the trance state in the manner of which you [Joseph] are speaking. Ruburt switches on another channel, through which my essence can enter more readily. This certainly does involve a looking inward on his part, but it is not self-hypnosis in usual terms—merely a focusing upon an objective inner stimulus . . . Any such signs *(as the powerful, deeper Seth voice)* involve camouflage patterns, and do not actually represent direct experience. This is not my voice, for example. It is a representation or

approximation of my voice for your edification. Furthermore, in your terms I do not have a voice. But it is a valid representation, and if I say so myself—that's a pun—the voice is much like the one I would use. . . .

(From the 49th session for April 29, 1964:) It is much better in the long run to quietly and cautiously advance [in these sessions]. I am not the Holy Ghost. I do not require or demand the vows of poverty, obedience, and certainly not chastity. I will at all times demand integrity, and perhaps when all is said and done that is my only requirement. *(Then to a friend of a friend of ours—both were present, and among the few to witness a session up to that time:)* Excess enthusiasm can lead to fanaticism, and this at all costs must be avoided.

(From the 54th session for May 18, 1964:) Your Ruburt was, indeed, Seth . . . I have provided to give you more material dealing with the psychic construction of the entity, and its relationship with its various [physical] personalities. In the beginning, I could not tell you in so many words that Ruburt is myself, because you would have leaped to the conclusion that I was Ruburt's subconscious mind, and this is not so.

Ruburt is not myself now, in his present life. He is nevertheless an extension and materializtion of the Seth that I—was at one time. Nothing remains unchanging, entities and personalities least of all. You cannot stop them in time . . . I am Seth today. I keep my continuity but I change, and offshoots like currents explode into being. Ruburt was myself, Seth, any centuries ago, but he grew, evolved, and expanded in terms of a particular personal set of value fulfillments. He is now a personality that was one of the probable personalities[14] into which Seth could grow. I represent another. I am another.

To make it simpler, we split—this being necessary always so that various possibilities can be brought into action . . . Yet we are bound together, and no invasion [of Ruburt] occurs because in one way of speaking our psychic territory is the same.

(From the 58th session for June 1, 1964:) Ruburt and myself are offshoots of the same entity. The difference in time is but a camouflage distortion. The entity was a particularly strong one, and many of its egos have made the decision to turn into entities . . . And now, my dear patient Joseph, may I tell you that you are also part of that same entity—and this is one of the reasons why I am able to communicate with you both.

(From the 82nd session for August 27, 1964:) When man realizes that he creates his own image <u>now,</u> he will not find it so
startling to believe that he creates other images in other times.
Only after such a basis [is established] will the idea of reincarnation achieve its natural validity, and only when it is understood
that the subconscious, certain layers of it, in a link between the
present personality and past ones, will the theory of reincarnation
be accepted as fact.

(From the 83rd session for August 31, 1964:) Man sees not
even half of the whole entity which is himself. It is true that on
this journey [with the sessions] discipline, some caution and
understanding, and much courage, is demanded. This is as it
should be. I am helping you in this . . . You are both *(meaning
Jane and me)* peculiarly suited for such a pursuit, with a combination of intuitiveness, basic psychic facility, and yet integrated
inner identies . . . I also want to add that I am <u>not</u> a control, as
mediums speak of controls. I am not, as I believe I have mentioned, a secondary or split personality of Ruburt's. For example, I am not a conglomeration of male tendencies that have
collected themselves into a subsidiary personality that struggles
for recognition or release. I say that I am an energy personality
essence, since that is what I am . . . My name for him is
Ruburt,[15] which happens to be a male name simply because it is
the closest translation, in your terms, for the name of the whole
self or entity of which he is now a self-conscious part.

(From the 119th session for January 6, 1965:) Ruburt should
learn much of advantage from the book by Jung[16] which he is
reading. And I would like to mention here that I am not <u>Jane's</u>
animus . . . Nor could I possibly live up to Jane's animus. I use
the name "Jane" here rather than "Ruburt" because the animus
belongs to Jane and to the present personality. Talk about
reflections—because <u>Ruburt</u> has an anima![17]

Scientists have glimpsed the complications of the human body.
They have scarcely glimpsed the complicated realities of the
mind.

*(Jane's account of "a year of testing" Seth's [and her own]
psychic abilities is given in chapter 6 through 8 of* The Seth
Material. *The tests began with the 179th session for August 18,
1965, and finally ended with the 310th session for January 9,
1967, although actually most of them were held during the year
following their inception. All that work can't be described here,*

but we accomplished our main goal: exploring from new angles the relationships involving Jane, Seth, and our physical [camouflage] reality.

(The tests concerned two main approaches. The first, for our own study, was for Seth to describe objects thoroughly sealed in double envelopes; the envelopes were prepared [unknown to Jane, of course] by myself and by others. The second was for Seth to give long-distance impressions on a regular basis about the reality of an eminent, elderly psychologist at an Eastern university. We met "Dr. Instream," as Jane called him in The Seth Material, *but once, a few weeks after I'd written him in the spring of 1965 about Jane's growing psychic abilities. Seth conducted 83 envelope tests for Jane and me, and within a concentrated period of nine months during that "year of testing," gave impressions for Dr. Instream on 75 occasions; those I mailed to the doctor as they came through.*[18] *Often both tests were held during each of our twice-weekly sessions.*

(Here's what Seth said after that first, only moderately successful envelope test had taken place in the 179th session:)

We are dealing here with something rather unusual *(the tests)*, in that we are attempting to permit two personalities to exist side by side, so to speak. Ruburt is not in a deep trance state. I do not supersede his own personality. He <u>allows</u> me, in our sessions, to coexist with himself.

A deeper trance state would allow us to get less distorted information on such a test as this, initially, but our results will improve, and such experiments will be helpful in that the various layers of the two personalities, Ruburt's and my own, will be seen in their operating procedures.

Ruburt will learn very quickly through such practice . . . The distortions that appeared are most helpful, in that they allow Ruburt to differentiate between my own communications and his own thoughts.

(From the 180th session for August 23, 1964:) Tonight's *(second envelope)* test dealt with clairvoyance—I happened to pick up my information that way, although it could just as easily have been obtained through telepathic communication.[19] In the future, tests will be worked out in whatever manner is needed.

I myself operate well clairvoyantly . . . for my own reasons and peculiarities, and usually obtain such information [in that manner]. We will have much to say concerning the ways in which that kind of material is received and interpreted, as this is very important.

(From the 211th session for November 24, 1965:) First of all, as far as the hands are concerned, to be left- or right-handed has to do with inner mechanisms and brain patterns that come first, before the motions of the hands. Characteristically I operated in certain manners that resulted in the primary use of my left hand, when I was focused within physical matter.

Now and then with Ruburt, when I am allowed to manifest myself to a smaller or lesser degree, my own habits therefore show through, for I manipulate his muscles in a different way than he does. But, scientifically, this would not be proof of my existence as an independent personality who has survived physical death. Not that this concerns me, for it does not . . . Or, if you are thinking in terms of secondary personalities,[20] you can prove nothing one way or another. A secondary personality could indeed use gestures that are different [from Ruburt's]. Either way, this would be no proof as to my independent nature. *(With humor:)* I am glad to see that it has been bothering you. You have had a good think session!

(Seth came through with this material, including his jocular closing remarks, because a good friend of ours had asked many questions as he witnessed the session—one of them being why the right-handed Jane gestured mainly with her left hand while speaking in trance. I hadn't noticed this mannerism.

(It's of interest to add that as far as she knows Jane was born right-handed, yet does recall her mother saying that she [Jane] was originally left-handed and had been taught to switch handedness. Jane is sure she wasn't compelled to do so in school, say. At the same time, she laughed, in early grades she had much trouble learning to salute the flag with her right hand; she repeatedly used her left hand until she "learned better."

(Incidentally, it's been many years since she showed any signs of favoring either hand in trance.

(From the 242nd session for March 16, 1966:) The ego is not the most powerful or the most knowledgeable portion of the self. It is simply a well-specialized part of the personality, fully equipped to operate under certain circumstances[21] . . . When those conditions no longer exist [after "death"], then other layers of the self take over the dominant position, and the personality realigns its psychological components. The ego does not <u>disappear</u>, however; it merely takes a back seat in some respects, as your own subconscious does during physical existence. The ego is under the control of what may loosely be called "the inner self." The survival or nonphysical personality has somewhat the same relationship to the ego as the dreaming personality has to it in physical life.

When communication takes place between a survival personality and one who exists within the physical system, this involves a reshuffling on the part of the survival personality, where the ego is momentarily given greater reign . . . If this was not done, then in most cases communication would not be possible, just because the survival personality would have such difficulty <u>impressing</u> the personality who was still ego-oriented within the physical system.

The nonphysical personality does not think in terms of words, but experiences concepts in a much more direct manner. This sort of thing simply could not be understood by the physically focused individual . . . The survival personality's inner self gives this reassembled ego ideas in the same way that, often, the subconscious gives the ego concepts in physical existence. This reassembled ego then attempts to perceive these insights in terms of <u>sense</u> perceptions, which are sent to the physical individual at the other end. Sometimes the communications are made directly, though they must be sifted through the subconscious of the one who is physical. When that person is trained along these lines, however [as Ruburt is], he or she helps in this process, and a <u>psychological framework, like a bridge</u>,[22] is erected that serves to connect the two personalities.

I speak as my whole self to you . . . since my personality structure is more advanced than is usual for communications from other systems. Therefore, I do not need to adopt a past ego [of my own]. Perhaps because this is not necessary, the psychological bridge <u>is</u> required to make my messages comprehensible to Ruburt. This connected framework does some of the translating for me that a reassembled ego would do. It delivers information to Ruburt in a way that he can understand. Occasionally [in your tests] I do impress him <u>directly</u>, telepathically *(see Note 19)*, with a concept. When he receives data in the form of images the framework is operating. With <u>my</u> direction, this framework uses Ruburt's personal associations to direct his impressions toward the correct point. Then when we are successful I insert the right information.[23]

I am a communicator. In our case the control personality, so-called, the psychological framework to which I have referred, is entirely passive, and shall remain so.

(In the 263rd session for May 29, 1966, Seth stated that eventually Jane would be able to entirely dispense with the psychological bridge linking the two of them, but he hasn't attained that situation at this writing.

(From the 398th session for March 11, 1968): Personalities are not static things. Entities are eternal. They are not as nicely nor as neatly packaged out, one to a body, as your psychologists believe. They constantly change. They grow. They make decisions. They use the physical body fully, or they partially depart according to their own inner needs and development.

When psychic gestalts are formed they are not static. They make different alliances until they find their place in a whole identity that serves their purposes, or are strong enough to become indestructable. They are always <u>becoming</u>. They are not closed units.

(To me [Rob]:) Now I hope you will understand me intuitively, for what I have said [tonight] confounds the intellect to some considerable degree. But I speak through Ruburt, and Ruburt is himself and I am myself, yet without your support of Ruburt I could not speak. This in no way minimizes my reality, or Ruburt's.

(The Seth Two phenomenon began to manifest itself through Jane in the 406th session for April 22, 1968. Seth Two exists in relation to Seth in somewhat the same manner that Seth does to Jane, although that analogy should be carried very far. Even though deep connections endure among the three, then, at the same time, as I wrote early in this study, Seth Two is too far "away" from Jane [and the subject matter of this appendix] to go into here. See Note 1.

(Now I'll refer the reader to Chapter 20 of Jane's The Seth Material. *She called the chapter "Personal Evaluations—Who or What is Seth?" In it she made a number of excellent points concerning her relationship with Seth and Seth Two; for example: "If physical life evolves [in ordinary terms], why not consciousness itself?" The questions we have at the time can be found throughout the chapter. Indeed, we still have many of them—or, I should note, we're still intrigued by the latest versions of those "old" questions, for like consciousness itself they're*

endless in their ramifactions. But here I want to call attention mainly to the excerpts in Chapter 20 that Jane presented from the 458th session for January 20, 1969. Seth discussed the psychological bridge Jane and he have created between themselves for purposes of communication; yet most of his material came through in response to my question about his availability to us. "We [Rob and I] both know that some sessions seem more 'immediate' than others, and now as Seth continued we say why," Jane wrote in Chapter 20. Seth, briefly, from the 458th session:)

I am, however, automatically a part of the message that I bring to you. At times I am "here" more completely than in other sessions. These reasons often have to do with circumstances usually beyond normal control: electromagnetic conditions, psychological circumstances. These could be considered as atmospheric conditions through which I must travel.

As I have told you, projection is involved to some extent, both on my part and Ruburt's. Your *(Rob's)* own presence is also important, whether or not you are present at any given session . . . Now when you watch, say, educational television, you see the teacher, and he speaks. [Actually] you may be watching a film. But the teacher exists whether or not he is speaking at that time, and his message is legitimate . . . It makes no difference whether or not I am myself speaking through Ruburt now, or whether I did this last night in his sleep, and tonight is a film or playback. Again *(with a smile):* the medium is the message . . .

This does not mean that I use Ruburt as a puppet, and stuff his mouth with tapes as a recorder, that you are always listening to replays, or that emotionally I am not always with you in sessions. It means that in such multidimensional communications more is involved than you suppose.

(Now here's an excerpt from the 458th session that wasn't given in Chapter 20. It concerns witnesses asking questions of Seth during a session:)

It is unfortunate that I must use terms of time to explain all of this to you, but as I told you many sessions ago, my time is not your time *(humorously)* . . . Because you ask specific questions at a specific session, it does not necessarily mean that the program has not been prepared, in your terms, earlier. For on many occasions I will see the questions within your mind, or the

minds of your witnesses, and [again in your terms] will therefore answer them ahead of time.

Even on such occasions, however, I look in on you closely . . .
to see whether or not my message is coming across clearly,
and I also learn.

(Later in Chapter 20 of The Seth Material, *Jane quotes Seth
from the 463rd session for February 3, 1969. While discussing
the impossibility of any medium being an absolutely clear channel for paranormal knowledge, even when "in a trance as deep
as the Atlantic Ocean," Seth had some extremely interesting
things to say about the nature of perception in general. Presenting a few sentences from that session here serves two purposes: I
can remind the reader of important material, and in Note 24 I
can offer some unpublished extensions of it from the next session.)*

Information must be sifted through the layers of the medium's
personality. Any perception instantly alters the electromagnetic
and neurological systems of the perceiver . . . It is a logistic
contradiction to imagine, with your physical systems, that any
perception can be received without the perceiver's inner situation
being altered. I am trying to make it as clear as possible:
Information automatically blends with, is intermingled with, and
enmeshed with, the entire physically valid structure of the
personality.

Any perception is action; it changes that upon which it acts,
and in so doing it is itself changed. The slightest perception
alters every atom within your body.[24] This, in turn, sends out its
ripples, so that as you know, the most minute action is felt
everywhere.

*(From here on I'll start occasionally presenting excerpts from a
few of the sessions Jane has delivered in her ESP class.[25] I've saved
some of this material for a considerable time. More often than
not I wasn't present when Seth produced his material, and in all
cases it was recorded by students; Jane meets with them on Tuesday
evening, when I'm usually occupied typing Monday night's
private session [or book material, often] from my own notes.*

*(Class offers an extremely rich learning environment, for Jane
as well as her students. Since in this appendix the focus is
primarily upon the relationship involving Jane-Ruburt-Seth, however, I can only write here that many other developments of
great interest to us [Jane's Sumari songs and poetry, for in-
stance], had their origins within the class framework.*

(From the ESP class session for February 26, 1971:) I [come through so forcefully] for several reasons: because that is the way I am, in the guise that I choose to use in my communications, and to get everyone over the idea that so-called spirits must be sweet-faced, quiet, sober, and dignified. That, for example, is one of my main concerns. I also want each of you to understand that energy is being used—and that the <u>same</u> energy Ruburt uses is available to <u>each of you</u>.

(With much good humor:) For all of those who have in their deepest, most sacred thoughts, imagined that to be quite was good and to be dignified was pious, then such a performance as mine should certainly make them think!

The voice mechanism, unfortunately, is something that we must work with, and to get my own personality across through the female image and vocal chords, certain adjustments must be made. Beyond this, however, as I have mentioned before in class, it is not out of the inner sense of my invisible heart, but out of the depths of your own psychologies that you make me into a wise old man, and project upon me the authority images that lurk in your own minds. I have always tried to keep you from making this error, and sought to release from within yourselves your own abilities.

(To a particular student:) I remain spontaneous and alive, and do not allow myself to be deadened by your projections upon me. I have a cosmopolitan accent—not sophisticated, but cosmopolitan. <u>You have an accent to me</u>, *(Amused:)* I have spoken many tongues, and in translation this [voice] is what it ends up as, and so we are all stuck with it. Now continue . . .

(From the ESP class session for April 20, 1971:) I am very afraid to tell [all of] you that I have forgotten what I considered to be secrets through the lives I have lived. I certainly know that like any of you I have not always been charitable in the past. I know that I have hated one parent or another. I know, certainly, that once I plundered in the wages of war. I do not come to you as someone who does not know what it is like to be human,[26] and in those personality characteristics that I use when I speak to you, I show you that the emotional life continues . . .

Now my relationship with you [and Ruburt] is indeed a strange one, since you do no relate to me as you do to each other. The—I hope—delightfully human egotistical characteristics that I show help calm your fears and show you that the self as you think of it continues to exist [after physical death]. I have a reservoir of personality bank upon which I can draw, and as a teacher I use the one that is most effective in any given system of reality; this is the one I use here. It is a portion of myself that is the most closely connected with earthly existence, and it is a self that I liked very well, indeed.

I very seldom speak symbolically to you. I speak as literally as possible, but in order that any information may appear within your three-dimensional system, translations of it [through Ruburt] are automatically necessary or you would not perceive it.

(In July 1971 Jane began a book to be called Adventures in Consciousness, *based on the experiences of her students in ESP class. Within a few days Seth mentioned it while dictating Chapter 21 of* Seth Speaks: *See the 587th session. Class was now providing a wealth of material on reincarnation, various states of consciousness, and out-of-body travel. It was also bombarding Jane with questions for which she found no acceptable answers. Her own intuitive experiences were accelerating, and these, she felt, were more and more outgrowing the ordinary concepts of psychology.*

(Jane was particulary bothered by people's attitudes about Seth, for they often considered him as a "spirit guide" in conventional spiritualistic terms. Though almost eight years had passed since Seth had first come through, she'd known for some time that she wanted to explore the whole phenomenon more deeply. Jane believed Seth when he told us he was an "energy personality essence, no longer focused in physical reality"—she just wanted to know more about what he meant by that statement. She was certain, she wrote, that far more than Seth's being a spirit guide was involved, that "in larger terms of abilities of living personality are connected with . . . other facets of creative consciousness."

(Now I'll refer the reader to Note 6 for Session 711, which is the session for which I'm assembling this chronology to begin with. In that note I presented some material on ancient connections with the name, Seth, then quoted Seth on the subject of names from the ESP class session for April 17, 1973. For instance:)

I told Ruburt from our earliest sessions that he could call me Seth. I never said, 'My name is Seth,' . . . for I am nameless. I have had too many identities to cling to one name!

(At the end of Note 6 are a few references to some of Seth's reincarnational names as he gave them while dictating Seth Speaks. *A reference not given there is the 541st session for Chapter 11 of* Seth Speaks. *That session contains information and notes relevant to the concurrent lives that Jane, Seth, and I lived in Denmark in the 1600's. As mentioned at the beginning of this appendix, even though I'm considering the Jane-Ruburt-Seth relationship, I want to avoid becoming too enmeshed within the intertwining connections several personalities would experience in any one set of lives; such particulars would lead too far away from the focus chosen her.*

(Jane and I would rather explore specific reincarnational information in an outright book on the subject, and then only after we'd acquired much more personal [and theoretical] material. We do think that in detail, reincarnation, whether it's seen in ordinary terms or within the "simultaneous" framework espoused by Seth, can be an endless subject.[27]

(From my notes at the close of the 700th session for May 29, 1974, in Volume 1: "In our case," Seth said a bit later, "Ruburt almost 'becomes' the material he receives from me. If certain other beneficial alterations occur, and further understanding on Ruburt's part, we may be able to meet at other *levels of consciousness—in the dream state, when he is not cooperating in the production of our book material." For Jane has never met Seth, face to face, you might say, in a dream. The closest she's come to this situation is in giving a session for him in the dream state, as she does in waking life.*

(From the ESP class session for July 16, 1974:) In certain terms, then, you cannot separate yourselves from me [as Ruburt cannot], nor can I seperate myself from you. For we are all portions of an event that is taking place within the universe, and the universe is acquainted with all of its parts. When one part of the universe speaks, then all parts speak. When one portion of the universe dies, all portions die—but in your terms, to get into the kind of life you know again, you must exit from space and time so that you can re-enter it.

Now, I can be playful became I am not as serious and mystical as the rest of you. I am yourself, and if you were yourselves,[28] you would not be so self-consciously profound about your beliefs and the nature of your reality. *(Humorously, to a certain student:)* You would trust your mustache!

(In the opening notes for the 708th session, in this Volume 2, I write that Jane finished Adventures *in August 1974. She'd started it in July 1971 [as noted a few paragraphs ago], but there was never any straight line of activity for her on the book from beginning to end. She finished* Seth Speaks. *Then during a class in November 1971, she first gave voice to her trance language, Sumari; so besides the other class material she had several more stages of consciousness—if very dependable ones—to deal with in* Adventures. *At the same time she worked on her autobiography,* From This Rich Bed *[which still isn't done]. At times the creative pace grew even more complicated: From March to July 1972, she put* Adventures *aside completely to write her novel,* The Education of Oversoul Seven, *when that idea spontaneously came to her. But overall, Jane discovered that she was frustrated in dealing with class experiments and records for* Adventures *while she still had so much to learn about her own connections with Seth. More than ever, she needed larger concepts of reality to explain her experiences, those of her students, and of some who wrote.*

(Shortly after Jane finished Seven, *the entire idea for what she calls "Aspect Psychology" came to her—an "intuitive construct" that she thought was large enough to contain her experience. At one sitting she wrote 20 or so pages of material in which she understood her relationship with Seth, Seth Two, the Sumari, the characters in* Seven, *and other psychic concepts—all as aspects of a larger self that was independent of space and time. The aspects represented the dynamics of personality. As Jane wrote, she realized that the questions she had been struggling with in* Adventures *had triggered a new psychology, a new way of approaching the creative portions of human personality.*

(The material itself, of course, came from another state of consciousness, and this Jane called her "aspects channel." More on aspects came to her spontaneously at intervals during the next two years. Throughout this period she did a great deal of other work. Besides holding class and continuing Rich Bed, *she produced in their entirety* Dialogues, Personal Reality, *Volume 1 of* "Unknown" Reality, *and started Volume 2. Toward the end of this period the aspects channel began opening up regularly, providing further refinements on her original inspirations. And Jane put it all together; the class experiments she'd started out with in 1971, and all of the later material, became*

Adventures in Consciousness: An Introduction to Aspect Psychology. *For Part Two of that book I drew 16 diagrams to illustrate her theories.*

(As she probed the Jane-Ruburt-Seth relationship in Adventures, Jane found herself developing her own nomenclature, separate from Seth's, for many of the concepts she and Seth had experienced over the years. "But I didn't plan it that way," she said. "That's just the way it all came out." She calls the conscious self the "focus personality," for instance, since it's focused in this physical [camouflage] reality. The focus personality is composed of aspects of the "source self" [or entity]. Each aspect exists independently, in its own dimension of actuality, but the aspects' combined attributes form the basic components of the selves that we know. To Jane, Seth is a "personagram"—an actual personality formed in the psyche at the intersection point of the focus personality with another aspect.

(Seth then, would be a message from the source self, except that in this case the messenger is the message, formed into a richly "worded" psychological structure instead of into dry words on, say, a telegram. Seth in sessions would stand for Jane's Seth Aspect, who does indeed exist in a different kind of reality than ours. But that "invisible" Seth would send out an actual psychological structure that takes over in place of Jane's, as her own structure voluntarily steps aside during sessions. Earlier in this appendix, see the excerpts on the psychological bridge from the 242nd session.

(From the ESP class session for September 24, 1974:) The excitement [of living] must come from each of you, and not for me. You come here to know yourselves, and that should always be your purpose. I can help you—I can help you—but I am not the person you search for. You are the person you search for. The dimensions of your reality are the important points . . .

In certain terms, and in certain terms only, and speaking now as the psychological bridge personality, then what you perceive in me and these abilities represents a portion of Ruburt that is utterly free in those directions—a portion of the human mind, as you understand it, goes beyond the threshold of itself into other dimensions of actuality; then, as best it can, it translates what it learns, sees, and experiences. It goes out of itself—it launches itself on paths that it does not understand, taking journeys that even Ruburt does not understand; and yet, that one portion of

Ruburt's human personality is <u>that</u> free. And so you can see what happens!

(The following excerpt is from an ESP class session that Seth delivered three months after the 711th session [which inspired this appendix] was held on October 9, 1974. As noted much earlier, the chronology for our study of the Jane-Ruburt-Seth relationship "begins long before 'Unknown Realty *was started, and continues well beyond the date of its ending in April 1974." Very soon, then, the quotations to come reach beyond that date: They're usually short, and are from a mixture of class, regular, and private [or "deleted"] session. With an exception or two they contain material that ordinarily might not have been published for several years—if ever. But all of them contribute insights into the subject under consideration.*

(From the ESP class session for January 7, 1975:) Ruburt can do many things that surprise me—that I did not do in my past, for remember that fresh creativity emerges from the past also, as in Ruburt's novel, Oversoul Seven.[29]

My memory does not include a predetermined past in which Ruburt exists. He can do things that did not happen in my memory of that existence, and did not, in fact, occur. Now that is a "mind-blowing" statement, and it applies to each of you. It is important in terms of your own understanding of yourself and the nature of time.

(The following exchange between Seth and a student—Bill, say—took place in the ESP class for February 18, 1975. Seth had been discussing certain psychic aspects of a rather complicated experience involving Jane, myself, and a house. Then he said:) We all learn, as each of us experiences. In certain terms, again, and <u>only</u> in my relationship to Ruburt and Joseph *(as Seth calls Jane and me),* I am a future Ruburt. But only in terms of that relationship—as I may be an uncle to someone here, and an aunt to someone there, an ancestor to someone else, and a descendent of still another person. Or, as <u>you</u> might be.

(Bill: "So, in other words you had this [house] information and you're somehow being reminded of it again through the experience of Ruburt? Because you had it through another life?")

Not in that way at all. That experience of Ruburt's and Joseph's was completely new. I was, in those terms, <u>not</u> the Ruburt that Ruburt <u>is</u>. My experiences as Ruburt were different, and Ruburt's experiences as Seth, in those terms, will be different. Ruburt will be a different Seth than I am.[30]

(Bill: "But you did experience this house event, in order to say it through Ruburt—")

I did not experience it. Ruburt experienced it. I commented on Ruburt's experience . . . In his experience, Ruburt is also free enough so that he can open up certain channels of his mind that then comment upon his activity. Some of those channels lead to <u>my</u> reality. But, I am not some spooky Big Brother experiencing his reality for him!

(The 768th session was held on March 22, 1976, 11 months after Seth had finished dictating "Unknown" Reality. Originally Jane and I deleted the following rather personal material from the session—yet we present it here because in it Seth explores further the connections involving the three of us. My notes at the time show that I was also distinctly surprised by Seth's comments on his emotional behavior at his own "level of activity," but I soon understood my reaction as a sign that we still had things to learn about him, as well as ourselves. In one passage Seth referred to some health difficulties, now resolved, that had bothered me just before our sessions with him began.

(To me:) You have often said that the [Seth] books were Ruburt's. That is true. Yet to a certain degree it is also a simplication.

Ruburt's experience is obviously intertwined with yours. My characteristics as they are displayed through the Seth personality, therefore, come from you as well as Ruburt . . . Triggers were needed also to initiate my emergence into your world through that personality I display. Ruburt's own background and questions were highly vital as such initiating principles. Your questions merged with his. It was the practical impetus <u>of your need</u> at the time, however, that operated as the final emotional trigger—you recall the circumstances.[31]

Ruburt provided himself with a background in which a parent (Jane's mother) was steadily, chronically ill,[32] and in which the medical profession with its beliefs was in constant sight. His mother was not medically neglected. His background included far more than sickness and the medical profession, however, but Ruburt knew that the conventional medical framework was not the answer to human ills. As you became more and more incapacitated, the trigger was set to find another solution. Psychic structures interweave, and realities do, one through the other *(as Jane had written a few hours before the session.)*

(With a smile:) My personality, as it so richly presents itself, is *(louder)* to some extent a joint creation of the two of you. This does not mean that I do not have my own reality, for I do, but in my relationship with you and Ruburt, and with your world, I do take certain characteristics that come from each of your realities.

You two do not understand how alike you are. Ruburt is as "detailed" about his own working habits as you both admit you are in yours. He seems to be in awe, relatively speaking, of your simplified "perfectionist" detailed ways, while to a certain extent you seem to be equally awed by his inspired, undetailed ways—a game each of you plays.

In your terms, I am relatively unemotional at my own level of activity. Rather, my emotional behavior does not follow your patterns—that is closer to "the truth." I have long delegated your kind of emotional activity to what you would call unconscious behavior. Our focuses are different, yet the overall coloration of your experiences does come through to me, and through this delightful personality *(Jane indicated herself)*, I can to some extent relate to it.

You set upon this adventure, the two of you. It is meaningless to say that the books are Ruburt's. Your ideas of "perfection" and love of detail, or if you prefer, your feeling for the significance of detail that appears exteriorized in your notes, is as present in the inner consistency of the material itself as given by me.

Ruburt keeps track of intuitive details that neither of you are even conscious of, and so there shows an integrity that at least sometimes he is not aware of. You yourselves adopt personalities, though usually you are not aware of doing so. So I adopt a personality that can communicate with your own.[33] In one manner of speaking mine is heroic, larger, and multidimentional. On the other hand, I can operate only mentally in your world. It is Ruburt who must walk down the street.

(From the 775th session for May 10, 1976:) Bits of your consciousness,[34] Joseph and Ruburt, go out through these books. I am not speaking symbolically. Those portions will mix with the consciousness of others. Portions of your intent and purpose become theirs. My own psychological reality is not particleized. My identity includes the idenities of many others, and they each

operate in their own fashion. In those terms I am a wave formation. More specifically, however, and to a lesser degree, each physical person operates partially as a particleized being, and partially in terms of a wave.[35] But identity, being itself inviolate, is on the other hand everchanging—and there is, in the larger framework of reality, no contradiction.

(Jane stopped holding ESP class on a regular basis early in 1975; the rhythm of those weekly gatherings was broken when we gave up apartment living to move into our own house in March of that year. In spite of our good intentions class in the old sense was never resumed, as we became more and more involved with producing Seth's and Jane's books, painting, correspondence, and all of the other events that make up our daily lives. The following material came through during a session on March 11, 1977, when a group of former students assembled to hear Seth speak "for old time's sake":)

Now I do not mind being nonscientific, and neither do any of you mind, because if all of your realities were confined to scientific theories you would have no realities at all, and neither would your fine scientists.[36] And in my time, I was also quite a dogmatic scientist. The times were different, however, and then I was even more intolerant in my beliefs than your scientists generally—underline—are today!

In the terms of my book *("Unknown" Reality)*, I was a dream-art scientist,[37] but I was very dogmatic, and I demanded that others follow <u>my</u> symbols and not their own. And that is why I now so carefully tell you to follow your own ways.

(Finally, I'll close this appendix with a couple of quotations from Seth that I return to again and again. [These in turn lead to a last note.] In Chapter 3 of Seth Speaks, see the 519th session for March 23, 1970:) When I enter your system, I move through a series of mental and psychic events. You would interpret these events as space and time, and so often I must use the terms, for I must use your language rather than my own . . . In one way, I translate what I am into an event that you can understand to some extent.[38]

NOTES: Appendix 7

1. Jane discussed Seth Two rather often in *Adventures*. I do plan to write at least briefly about Seth Two in another appendix for this Volume 2 of *"Unknown" Reality*, however, the idea being that such material can be taken as an extension of the Jane-Ruburt-Seth study presented here.

And added later: The opportunity to do so developed much sooner than I thought it would—only a week after the 711th session was held. See Appendix 8 in Volume 2 Part I for Session 712.

2. Seth began his material on counterpart selves late next month, in the 721st session. Out of that session grew Appendix 21. The material in Appendix 7 in Volume 2 Part I, then, is intended to further enrich the counterpart information in Session 721, as well as in its appendix.

3. In Chapter 3 of *The Seth Material* Jane describes our use of the Ouija board in the early sessions. In the 8th session for December 15, 1963, she began dictating portions of each session; by the 14th session, she was delivering verbally all of Seth's material except for an opening remark or two obtained through the board. A month after that we dispensed with the board entirely.

4. In the 14th session Seth came through with some very valuable remarks about his concepts of time—"It is therefore still a reality of some kind to me," for instance. Because I've always thought those insights well worth repeating, I quoted them in the Introduction for Volume 1 (and, added later, following Session 724 in Volume 2). Now let me further excerpt Seth from that 14th session: "You mentioned earlier, Joseph, that you had the feeling I could refer back to myself almost as if I could turn a later page of a book to an earlier one, and of course this is the case." With a smile: "Viewing a historical moment through your marvelous television, you can refer to much that has passed, [but] one minute of such a referral costs you one minute of present time. Also you end up shortchanged: You give up your precious moment in the present, but you do not have a complete *(my emphasis)* moment in the past to show for it . . When I refer back to myself, I do not expend an identical moment of time in doing so."

5. See Note 2 for Appendix 1 in Volume 2 Part I.

6. By the time the 22nd session was held Seth had mentioned the inner senses upon occasion, but had given up a breakdown on just the first one: Inner Vibrational Touch. Consciously, then, we had no way of appreciating what important and interesting parts those "senses leading to an inner reality" were to play in the material over the years. In Chapters 19 of *The Seth Material* Jane quoted Seth on the nine inner senses he'd described so far.

(I should note that Jane's own use of that first inner sense, demonstrated in the example she gives in Chapter 19, reflects a very strong facet of her psychic ability that she seldom indulges. Her reluctance here is closely connected to her deep feelings about personal privacy.)

7. For some related material on patterns and probabilities, see Note 13 for Appendix 1 in Volume 2 Part I.

8. Even 11 years later, I'm certainly far away from experiencing the concept-essence of any given session, as Seth suggests may be possible. I'm expressing contradictory beliefs, obviously, but it seems unlikely that I can use my abilities in such a fashion, even though I tell myself I'd like to.

I *do* believe, however, that on occasion Jane has known a stepped-up awareness that almost equates with Seth's concept-essence. One such instance is described in Appendix 7 for Volume 1: her reception of the material for a book called *The Way Toward Health*. At that time she turned in to a different "neurological speed," a faster one, so that much of the book was available to her at once. Jane's pleasure at having the ability was strongly tempered, though—for while she "could feel the bulk and immediacy of the book," as I quoted her in Appendix 7, she was "also frustrated that what I've got down is so little and sketchy—WHEN IT'S ALREADY HERE . . . If I could have immediately *spoken* the whole thing, it would have been done at once . . . I can't tell you how frustrated—how blocked—this made me feel at the time."

(In Volume 1, see the material on neurological speeds in Session 686. In Appendix 5 for the same session, see Jane's own notes on that subject.)

9. Jane produced her manuscript, *The Physical Universe as Idea Construction*, three months before the sessions began. That key event is briefly described in Volume 1. See Note 7 for Session 679.

10. Well, obviously, it's true so far at least that Seth will be "accessible" for the present lifetimes of Jane and me . . .

11. In this appendix, I'm quoting certain portions of the 28th session to make certain points. In Chapter 5 of *The Seth Material*, however, Jane presented much longer experts from the same session in order to explain her own views.

12. When Jane began speaking for Seth we checked out the definitions for concepts like dissociation, trance, and so forth, without being particularly influenced by what we found. We merely thought the meanings given were quite incomplete, so we decided to go our own collective way. As the sessions progressed we came to understand that for Jane dissociation simply meant her ability to direct an intense concentration toward certain highly creative goals—Seth and the sessions—so that we could learn from them.

Her "psychic" accomplishments grew outside the session framework too, of course, as can be seen in much of the appendix material in Volume 1 (to mention those examples only); and so to varying degrees, dissociation, or that strong power of concentration, entered into those activities.

13. Following his comments about his reassembly in our reality, Seth went into some analogous material (in that 28th session) that I've always wanted to see published. In part, then: "Condensed time is the time felt or experienced by the enity, while any of its given personalities 'live' —and you had better put that in quotes—on a plane of physical materializations. To go into this a bit further, many men have said that life was a dream. They were true to the facts in one strong regard, and yet far afield as far as the main issue is concerned.

"Individual life, or the life of the present individual, could be legitimately compared to the dream of an entity. While the individual suffers and enjoys his [Or her] given number of years, these are but a flash to the entity. The entity is concerned with such years in the same manner that you are concerned with your own dreams . . . And as your dreams originate with you, arise from you, attain a seeming independence and have their ending with you, so an entity's personalities arise from it, attain various degrees of independence, and return to it <u>while never leaving it for an instant</u>.

"The entity organizes its personalities and to some extent directs their activities while still allowing them what you would call free will. Their exist infinites of diversity and opportunity for the personalities.

"The entity itself does not have to keep constant check on its personalities, because in each one there is an inner self-conscious part that knows its origin. I have mentioned before that some part of you knows exactly how much oxygen the lungs breathe, and how much energy it takes to pace a floor, and that is the part of you of which I spoke. It is the self-conscious part that receives all inner data.

". . . the part that translates inner data sifts it down through the subconscious, which is a barrier and also a threshold to the present camouflage personality. I have said that the topmost part of the subconscious contains personal memories, that beneath these are racial memories, and so forth. Things are simply not layered in the way I speak of them, but continuing with the necessary analogy, on the other side of (or beneath, to you) the racial memories, you no longer exist within your plane; you look out upon another with the face of this other self-conscious part of you. This part receives inner data, is in contact with the entity to some greater degree than you are in contact with your dreams, and actually directs all of the important functions that you think are either automatically or unconsciously controlled.

"When such abilities as telepathy occur, this telepathic function is carried on continually by this other self-conscious part of you; but as a rule you act upon those data without the knowledge of the conscious self with which you are familiar.

(With a laugh:) "There is of course an apparent contradiction here, but it is only apparent—your dilemma being this: If you have another self-conscious self, <u>then why aren't you aware of it</u>?

"Pretend that you are some weird creature with two faces. One face looks out upon one world and one looks out upon another. Imagine, further, this poor creature having a brain to go with each face, and that each brain interprets reality in terms of the world it looks upon. Yet the worlds are different, and more, the creatures are Siamese twins.

"At the same time imagine that these creatures are really one creature, but with definite parts equipped to handle two entirely different worlds. The subconscious, therefore, in this ludicrous analogy, would exist between the two brains, and would enable the creature to operate as a single unit.

"At the same time—and this is the difficult part to explain—neither of the two faces would ever see the other world. They would not [usually] be aware of each other, and yet each would be fully self-conscious."

14. Seth discussed many facets of his concept of probabilities in Volume 1, of course. In Volume 2, see Note 16 for Appendix 1 in Volume 2 Part I.

15. In Volume 1, see Note 3 for Session 679.

16. *Memories, Dreams, Reflections* by C. G. Jung, © 1961 by Random House, Inc., New York, N.Y.

17. For many readers Seth's remarks about the anima and the animus will require a bit of explaining. Carl Jung (1876–1961), the Swiss psychologist and psychiatrist, postulated that the unconscious of the male contains a female, archetypal (or typical, instinctive) figure called the "anima"; the correlative male form in the unconscious of the female Jung called the 'animus." In Session 119, then, Seth comments on how Jane herself has an animus—the hidden male within—and on how Ruburt, that larger "male" entity of which she is a self-conscious part," contains an anima, or hidden female. (See the excerpts in this appendix from the 83rd session.) The contrasts are most interesting. From this information I infer that the entity or whole self of each of us, regardless of our current, individual sexual orientation, contains its own counter-balancing male or female quality, whichever the case may be. Seth hasn't said so yet—nor have we asked him—but I suspect that an energy gestalt like the entity is much more aware than we can of its "hidden" opposite-sex form—or forms; for there may be many of them.

Below, I'll quote very short passages from sessions 555–56 in Chapter 13 of *Seth Speaks*, while referring the reader to them at the same time, then present some additional material from the 83rd session that I saved for this note—since in it Seth discussed the theories of both Jung and Jung's famous teacher, Sigmund Freud (1856–1939).

In *Seth Speaks*, Seth developed Jung's ideas about the anima and animus by stating that such other-sex qualities or personifications within each of us actually represent memories of past lives. (Jung himself thought the questions of reincarnation, and of karma [or, roughly, destiny or fate], to be "obscure"—he couldn't be sure of the exis-

tence of such phenomena.) From Session 555 for October 21, 1970:
"The anima and the animus . . . are highly charged psychically, and
also appear in the dream state. They operate as compensations and
reminders to prevent you from overidentifying yourself with your present physical body." And from Session 556: "The reality of the anima
and the animus is far deeper than Jung supposed. Symbolically speaking, the two together represent the whole self with its diverse abilities,
desires, and characteristics . . . Personality as you know it cannot be
understood unless the true meanings of the anima and the animus is
taken into consideration."

Two notes in connection with the excerpts from the 83rd session: 1.
The famous professional break between Freud and the younger Jung
occured in 1931: Seth's material touches upon the divergent pyschological
paths taken by each of them. 2. The libido is regarded as the sexual urge
or instinct—postive, loving, psychic energy that shows itself in changing
ways as the individual matures. Seth:

"There are a few points of a general nature that I would like to make.
Ruburt has been reading Jung, though not consistently. The libido does
not originate in the subconscious of the present personality. It begins
instead in the energy of the enity and inner self, and is directed by
means of the inner senses—outward, so to speak, through the deeper
layers of the individual subconscious mind, then through the outer or
personal areas.

"Your Freud and Jung have probed into the personal subconscious.
Jung saw glimpses of other depths, but that is all. There are rather
unfortunate distortions occurring in his writings, as well as in Freud's,
since they did not understand the primary, cooperative nature of the
libido . . .

"We have spoken of the biological interdependence and cooperation
among organisms in your physical universe. The apperance of an individual into the physical realm is aided by the psychic collaboration of
individuals on your plane. Almost at once the new libido takes up its
adopted duty of maintaining the physical universe, along with all others.
If it did not do so it would not exist for long. Cooperation on all levels is
the necessity on all planes.

"I was somewhat concerned with Ruburt's reading of Jung, simply
because while Jung seems to offer more than Freud, in some aspects he
has attempted much and his distortions are fairly important: Seeing to
delve further and offering many significant results, June nevertheless
causes conclusions . . . all the more hampering because of his scope.

"It is true that the outward manifestations of the libido are directed
toward the physical world, but until its source is seen, not in the
topmost subconscious layers of the individual, and not even in the racial
subconscious, but within the entity itself, then man will not know
himself.

"Basically, Jung feared such a journey because he felt that it led only to the racial source . . . that anyone involved in such a study would end up in the bottleneck of a first womb—but there, there is an opening up into other realism, through which the libido also passed. Figuratively speaking, it squeezed itself through the bottleneck, and there is a lack of limitation on the other side.

"Freud courageously probed into the individual topmost layers of the subconscious, and found them deeper than even he suspected. These levels are indeed filled with what may be termed life-giving differentiated and undifferentiated impulses acquired in the present life of an individual, but when these have been passed there are many discoveries still to be made. After that passage of the diligent, consistent, intuitive, and flexible seeker-after-knowledge will find horizons of which Freud never dreamed. Freud merely touched the outer boundaries. Jung, with his eyes clouded by the turmoil set up by Freud, glimpsed some further regions, but poorly."

18. As Jane wrote in Chapter 8 of *The Seth Material*, the Instream tests were very unsatisfactory for us. Since we were never imformed as to their results, we were left with no way to judge what proportions of Seth's impressions could be considered hits, near-misses, or failures. Our nine-month involvement under those conditions revealed both our naiveté at the time and our stubborness in trying to learn. But learn we did, if not always as we'd expected to; for besides gaining valuable insights into Seth-Jane's abilities through her own envelope tests, we discovered much through our dealings with at least some kinds of "authority." Overall, the affair of the tests was most instructive.

19. Seth commented upon some of his own "psychic" abilities when I asked him if he'd telepathically acquired any information about the test object form me, since I was the one who had chosen it, rather than from the object itself. The results of the second envelope test were obviously more precise than for the first one. At break I told Jane that she'd done well. We were very encouraged.

Two quick reminders: 1. Clairvoyance ("clear-seeing") is the paranormal perception of events or objects regardless of distance, and without help from another mind. 2. Telepathy is the communication of thoughts or emotions between minds, regardless of distance. In actuality, it's often difficult to tell whether clairvoyance, telepathy, or both operated in a given instance. Nor am I noting here how the use of these phenomena may be connected to the perception of the past or future.

20. In this appendix, the presentations from sessions 28 and 83 contain Seth's comments as to whether he's "a secondary or split personality of Ruburt's" (to quote him from the latter). On her own, Jane expressed concern about secondary personalities in Chapter 6 of *The Seth Material;* see her account of our meetings with Dr. Instream. Additional, related material can be found in Chapter 2 of *The Coming of*

Seth, and in the sessions dealing with "Augustus" in Chapter 6 of *Personal Reality*.

21. In Volume 1, see Seth's material on man's emerging ego consciousness in sessions 686 (after 10:37), 687, 689, and Appendix 6.

22. I noted at the beginning of this appendix that it was inspired, at least in part, by the material Seth had given in the 711th session on the psychological bridge, or framework, linking Jane and himself. I refer the reader to those passages now; they start at 11:40. Also see the last two paragraphs of the opening notes for Session 705 (in this volume), with Note 2 for that session.

Seth actually initiated his material on the psychological bridge in the last (241st) session. However, I chose to excerpt the 242nd session on the subject because of the information it also contains on the ego and survival personalities in general.

23. The 241st session, mentioned in Note 22, is one of those we hope to publish in full, for in it Seth discussed how the psychological bridge helps Jane "translate" his telepathic material. The information came through in connection with our envelope tests and those for Dr. Instream, both sets of which were in mid-course then, in March 1966. (See the account of Jane's "year of testing" and the excerpts from sessions 179–80.)

Here are a few insights from Seth's material in the 241st session: "This psychological framework is in itself capable of growth. It represents on Ruburt's part an expansion, and indeed on my own part also. It is formed partially by abilities inherent within all personalities—psychic abilities—and it is composed of energy. It is not a secondary personality, for it exists in quite a different dimension than do secondary personalities . . .

"The psychological bridge can transmit, you see, and to some extent translate, but not interpret. I am dependent in a large measure upon Ruburt's own knowledge, and lack of it, that I cannot force from him, from his speech mechanism, concepts with which he is _entirely_ unfamiliar. I must introduce them step by step . . . as I explained moment points *(see Note 11 for Appendix 1 in Volume 2 Part I)* to you . . . It is not as simple a thing as it might seem, for there is no coercion involved, Ruburt always consenting to let me push concepts at him, which he interprets speechwise with my assistance.

"In our experiments, often, I will give him an impression, and he will automatically translate it into visual terms . . . There is sometimes at his end a last tug and pull, so that the vocal mechanism will finally speak the correct interpretation. Of course Ruburt's own association are used by me, up to a certain point, to lead him to the proper subject or image . . . When we are successful there is a divergence from his associations so that he says the _correct_ word, even though for him personally it may be the _wrong_ word.

"On Ruburt's part this can sometimes be disconcerting. We must always work with psychological organizations, however. The emotions always follow associative lines in this regard.

"The trick is to allow Ruburt's associations free reign to a certain point, and then expertly insert the correct data. This is sometimes difficult. His associations may go, for example, from C, D, E, and F, but precisely where he would say 'G,' we must insert X or Y, and do it so smoothly that he is quite unaware.

"He consents for me; he consents to let me <u>use</u> his associations in such a manner."

24. In the 464th session I made sure that I asked Seth to elaborate upon his statement in the last session: "The slightest perception alters every atom within your body." He came through with his answer just before first break:

"Returning to the material on perception, there are changes in the positive and negative atomic charges, alterations of movement inside the atoms in the smaller particles, a change in pulsation rate. The activity of atoms is actually caused by perceptive qualities. To begin with, atoms do not just move within themselves because they are atoms. The constant motion within them is caused by the unending perceptive nature of any consciousness, however minute in your terms. Does that answer your question?"

"Yes," I said, "but I could ask a lot more of them."

Seth continued: "Each of the particles within the atom is perceptively aware of all of the other particles within that same atom. They move in response to stimuli received from each other, and to stimuli that come from other atoms . . . Each atom within a cell, for example, is aware of the activity of each of the other atoms there, and to some extent of the stimuli that come to the cell itself from outside.

"Perceptions in general physical terms usually seem to involve information picked up from an arbitrarily designated structure, of an event seemingly occurring in another structure outside of itself. In the entire act of perception, however, there is a oneness and a unity between the seeingly objectively perceived event and the perceiver.

"The entire act has its own electromagnetic reality, and the event is actually electromagnetic motion. The movement within the atoms, mentioned earlier, is therefore basically a part of the entire perceived event. Does this make the issue plainer for you?"

"Yes . . ."

"Egotistically, you make arbitrary designations of necessity, perceiving only portions of any given action: again, the ego attempting to separate itself from overall action, and to see itself as an entirely independent structure." (See the excerpts from the 242nd session.)

"You may take your break."

(To go into modern knowledge of the components of the atom can be a very complicated task, so I'll note only that such particles are regarded as actually being packets of energy, or "probability patterns," that can also manifest themselves as waves; both the particle and the wave aspects are legitimate in space-time. An atom, then, is composed of a "heavy" positively charged nucleus orbited by "lighter" negatively charged electrons. Generally speaking, these positive and negative qualities could be those Seth referred to in the 464th session.

The electron is the lightest particle known to have mass and charge, and its internal structure—whatever it may be—is unknown. The atomic nucleus is largely made up of more massive protons and neutrons, but investigation within the nucleus has either uncovered or produced many other subatomic particles as well—over 200 of these, some of them very unstable, are presently known. According to Seth, of course, all of the particles or probability patterns discussed here would be composed of the much, much smaller CU's, or units of consciousness.

(In Volume 1, see Note 4 for Session 682; in Session 702, see the material on electron spin, and Note 6. Note 5 for that session also contains applicable references.)

25. Jane held her first ESP class on the evening of September 12, 1967, although she didn't let Seth come through within that format until the following December, so cautious was she in taking that psychic step. She had no personal experience or other precedent to go by: her *How to Develop your ESP Power* had been published in 1966, but she was still experimenting with her own abilities (even as she is now). It could also be said that at issue was the whole question of firsthand public interaction with, and acceptance or rejection of, Seth and his material. Classes were quite small for some time, although they'd grown considerably by the end of 1969. After *The Seth Material* was published in 1970, class became well-known enough to start attracting visitors from various parts of the country. It still does so.

Class Seth material and other events can be found in all of the books by Jane and/or Seth, of course. See, for example, Chapter 13 of *The Seth Material*, the Appendix of *Seth Speaks*, and several chapters in Part One of *Adventures in Consciousness*.

(A note added later: Jane's *ESP Power* was originally issued by Frederick Fell Publishers, Inc. Pocket Books reprinted it in 1976 as a paperback and with a new title: *The Coming of Seth*. In Volume 1, see Note 2 of the *Preface by Seth*.)

26. Although in that 1971 class Seth stressed his experiences with the human condition through reincarnation, in 1964 he'd had this to say: "To me this [reincarnational and family material] is all so obvious that I almost hesitate to mention it, but this is because I tend to forget what human experience on your plane actually involves." (See the excerpts from the 27th session in this appendix.) In that early session Seth spoke to me alone; in class he faced a large group. I'd say that from his

position or focus as an "energy personality essence" both attitudes are true, rather than contradictory—and that one or the other predominated according to the circumstances and subject matter of the session involved. I don't think the time gap between the two sessions—seven years—was a factor.

27. Concerning reincarnation, as well as books on the subject, here's Seth the 588th session in Chapter 22 of *Seth Speaks:* "Now when I began contacting Ruburt and Joseph, I hid from them the fact of my numerous lives. *(Smile:)* Ruburt, in particular, did not accept reincarnation, and the idea of such multiple life experiences would have been highly scandalous to him.

"The times and names and dates are not nearly as important as the experiences, and they are too numerous to list here. However, I will see to it at some time that these are made fully available . . . In a book on reincarnation, I hope to have each of my previous personalities speak for themselves, for they should tell their own stories."

Seth said a lot in that last sentence, of course, but that just means that more questions than usual come to mind. Although Jane and I think his idea for such a book is unique, we haven't done anything to implement it, nor have we asked him to explain further. Just how would Seth purpose to have his "previous personalities speak for themselves . . ."? Since Seth presumably wouldn't simply relay such messages, would Jane find herself giving voice for a host of others, male and female, young and old, from many time periods and of the most diverse nationalities? A long project, and one for which she would use her abilities in new ways.

28. Seth's remarks here are actually an extension of a long discussion on individual beliefs and spontaneity that he'd initiated in a class session two weeks ago: "Now, my words will not, I hope, be used to begin a new dogma. My dogma is the freedom of the individual *(my emphasis)*. My dogma is the sacrilegious one—that each of you is a good individual. There is nothing wrong with your emotions, or feelings, or being. When you know yourself then you are joyfully—joyfully—responsive, and, being joyfully responsive, you can carry your society to the furthest reaches of its creativity."

29. See chapter 17 of *Oversoul Seven*, for instance. In *Personal Reality*, Seth discussed "a sort of reprogramming" of the past; see sessions 653–54 in Chapter 14.

(A note added later: That January 1975 class session is an excellent one in many respects, and Jane presented much of it in Chapter 15 of her *Psychic Politics.* although Seth finished his work on both volumes of *"Unknown" Reality* well before Jane was through with *Politics*, the latter was published first—and *that* chronology is treated in my Introductory Notes for Volume 1.

30. In this appendix, see the excerpts from sessions 54 and 58.

31. "In late 1963," Jane wrote in Chapter 2 of *The Seth Material*, "some months before our sessions began, we'd taken a vacation in York Beach, Maine, hoping that a change of environment would improve Rob's health. The doctor didn't know what was wrong with his back and suggested that he spend some time under traction in the hospital. Instead we decided that his reaction to stress was at least partially responsible, hence this trip."

By then I'd lost many months from my job as a commercial artist, which was work I'd returned to several years earlier to help ease our financial pressures. I was 44 years old—and, as I recognized after the sessions began, at a point in life where I greatly needed more penetrating insights into the meaning of existence. So did Jane, even though she was almost 10 years younger. As the sessions became part of our joint reality, we gradually came to understand that the illness I struggled with was a disguised expression of rebellion for both of us. We were very dissatisfied with our status quo: After years of work, Jane had managed to publish but a few poems and a few pieces of science fantasy (several short stories and two brief novels), and in my own view I wasn't making it as the kind of artist I wanted to be. We were driven to know more—about art, about writing, about the human condition, about everything. My own need, as well as Jane's, struck deep responses within her psyche.

For an account of what happened to us at York Beach on that trip, see more of Chapter 2 in *The Seth Material*. Also see Note 6 for Session 680, in Volume 1.

32. In Volume 1, see Session 679 (with its Note 4, among others) for material on Jane's early years with her mother. I often remind myself that from her earliest years Jane lived in an atmosphere permeated by the fact of illness, while by contrast my background in that respect was much more ordinary. Growing up, she was "frightened most of the time," Jane told me as I prepared this note: She often lived alone with her bedridden mother, such periods being punctuated by a succession of itinerant housekeepers appointed by the welfare department. She soon became strongly imprinted by human frailty and vulnerability.

Yet, we fully agree with Seth—that like any other personality Jane chose her physical environment before birth, planning to meet certain challenges within that setting.

33. See Seth in the excerpts from the ESP class session for April 20, 1971: "I have a reservoir of personality banks upon which I can draw. . . ."

34. Since Jane and I equate the "bits" of consciousness mentioned in this excerpt with Seth's EE (electromagnetic energy) units and his CU's (units of consciousness), see the references listed in Note 3 for appendix 12.

35. Seth's material in this excerpt reminded me strongly of certain

passages of his (and mine) in the 702nd session in Volume 1: "As long as you think in terms of [subatomic] particles, you are basically off the track—or even when you think in terms of waves. The idea of interrelated <u>fields</u> comes closer, of course, yet even here you are simply changing one kind of term for one like it, only slightly different. In all of these cases you are ignoring the reality of consciousness, and its gestalt formation and manifestations. Until you perceive the innate consciousness behind any 'visible' or 'invisible' manifestations, then, you put a definite barrier to your own knowledge."

Then in my note at 10:20 I wrote: "I thought it very interesting that Seth had talked about subatomic waves and particles in the last paragraph of his delivery tonight. Such ideas involve the physicists' ongoing conception of the duality of nature. For instance: Is light made up of waves or particles? A contemporary accomodation, called complementarity, leads experimenters to accept results that show *either* aspect to be true."

Since Seth obviously sees little real difference between the concept of fields and wave/particles, I'd say that in the 775th session he cast his material in accord with the latter so as to make it as clear as possible to us, who are so bound by ideas of space and time: "In those terms . . ." But overall the physicists discuss *energy* and Seth talks about *consciousness*—and therein, as I see it, lies the basic contrast between the two approaches to reality.

Apropos of that "reality of consciousness" quoted above (from the 702nd session), Seth also came through with the following more generalized material in Session 775: "You are actually 'reincarnated' many times during one accepted lifetime. There are often great challenges to which you respond. You pick these for your own reasons. In doing so you often change affiliations.

"Consciousness forms patterns of identities. They move faster than the speed of light. They can be in more than one place at one time. *(See notes 5 and 6 for Session 702.)* They can operate in a freewheeling fashion as identities in themselves, or as 'psychological particles.' They can also operate in a wavelike fashion, flowing through other such particles. They can form together into endless, infinite combinations, forming psychological gestalts. Certain portions of these gestalts can then operate as 'psychological particles' in time and space, while other portions operate in a wavelike manner outside of time and space. These represent the unconscious elements of the species, which become 'particleized' in physical existence."

Although these final paragraphs from the 775th session contain many ideas, I want to stress two of them that I find especially evocative: Seth's reference to many reincarnations in one accepted lifetime, and the unconscious elements of the species being represented by its wavelike characteristics.

Since this session was held almost 13 months after *"Unknown" Reality* was completed, I can look back and note that Seth developed the statement on reincarnation in his material on counterparts; this begins with Session 721 in Section 5. Appendix 10 in Volume 2 Part I grew out of that session. In that same section, the 725th session (with Note 4) contains additional information on particles, identities, and psychological gestalts.

36. Many passages in Appendix 1 in Volume 2 Part I, and in its notes, could be quoted to illuminate Seth's comments here. Notes 13 and 20 are examples, and their superscription numbers can be used as references to the appropriate paragraphs in the appendix itself. In general, I suggest reviewing the last few pages of Appendix 1, beginning with my own material: "My position after wiring this appendix is . . ."

37. In Volume 1, see Session 700. Seth at 9:53: "The true art of dreaming is a <u>science</u> long forgotten by your world. Such an art, pursued, trains the mind in a new kind of consciousness—one that is equally at home in either [exterior or interior] existence, well grounded and secure in each."

And from Session 704: "The dream-art scientist, the true mental physicist, the complete physician—such designations represent the kinds of training that could allow you to understand the unknown, and therefore the known reality, and so become aware of the blueprints that exist beyond the physical universe."

38. Apropos of his quotations from *Seth Speaks,* here's what Seth had to say in a later personal session: "There are rhythms that exist over a period of time, as I have mentioned before, and had you the leisure to check your records you would see that overall we have about the same number of sessions each year. There are many cycles involved—some connected with the two of you, with myself, or with other conditions quite apart.

"Some of these conditions could be called the result of psychological atmospheres that surround the earth, say. I do not travel physically in a UFO *(with amusement),* and yet my mental or psychic journeys must occur in a medium of some kind. There are rhythmic activities in that atmosphere that I count upon and use, as for example a sea captain might use the rhythm of the waves for his voyages. Those inner atmospheric 'waves' have a certain regularity. They are more intense at certain times than others."

APPENDIX 8
(For Session 712)

(I'll preface the abbreviated version to follow of Jane's first slow, or "long sound" session, the 612th for September 6, 1972, with these notes about Seth Two, since this is the ideal place for them.

(Seth Two wasn't dealt with in Volume 1 of "Unknown" Reality. In Note 1 for Appendix 18, I wrote that I wanted to at least briefly discuss Seth Two in another appendix for this Volume 2, "the idea being that that material can be taken as an extention of the Jane-Ruburt-Seth study presented here." The few references to Seth Two in Appendix 18 were all meant to be resolved below, including my note that "Seth Two exists in relation to Seth in somewhat the same manner that Seth does to Jane, although that analogy shouldn't be carried very far."

(With Seth's help, Jane first encountered the idea of Seth Two in the 406th session for April 22, 1968. That important development in her abilities took place four and a half years after she began to speak for Seth, and once it opened up Seth Two came through in the next seven twice-weekly sessions. Most of that material hasn't been published, although in Chapter 17 of The Seth Material *Jane described Seth Two to some extent, including "his, hers, or its" intimate connections with Seth: the subjective pyramid or cone effects she experiences just above her head when contacting Seth Two; and the great energy she feels at such times. In Chapter 17 she quoted Seth Two from sessions 406–7, and from couple of others that were held later in the year. The excerpts show not only something of Seth's connections on the "other side" of Jane, but in one case her violent reactions of surprise and panic when she attempted to translate something of Seth Two's reality in terms of our own camouflage world: She found herself deeply involved in an unexpected experience with "massiveness"—one of the subjects I want to refer to in these*

265

preliminary notes. And Seth Two—or our imperfect grasp of what such an energy gestalt can mean or represent—comprises at least one of the sources of the Seth material itself.

(Unlike Seth, Seth Two has never been physical in our terms, and only partially comprehends our reality even while helping to form it. Very quickly, and perhaps simplifying too much, here's Seth Two from the 407th session, speaking in Jane's high, distant, deliberate and asexual interpretation of what such an energy gestalt's "voice" might sound like:)

Seth is what I am, and yet I am more than Seth is. Seth is, however, independent, and continues to develop as I do . . . Simply as an analogy, and <u>only</u> as an analogy, I am what you would refer to as a future Seth, as Seth in a "higher" stage of development. This is not to be taken literally, however, since both of us are fully independent and exist simultaneously.

(Following those introductory sessions, Seth Two has spoken at widely spaced intervals. At this writing I think it's been well over a year since I've heard that very complicated personality. Occasionally Jane will speak for Seth Two in class. I do think that she could contact Seth Two at my request. Yet she has to get into a "certain mental climate" in order to reach Seth Two, Jane said, and all of her other trance phenomena—Sumari, and so forth—are also related to that state.[1]

(I've already cited Jane's experience, as given in Chapter 17 of The Seth Material, *showing that on rare occasions Seth Two and her feelings of massiveness can go together; but she can also be in an altered, massive state of consciousness without having a session, or she can be speaking for* Seth. *Seth or Seth Two— obviously, when either of those qualities combine with her massive perceptions, then Jane knows a multifaceted trance state. In Volume 1, Seth devoted much of 681st session to a discussion of probabilities, or, in sum, All That Is, and interwound Jane's psychic and physical experiences with that material: "The cellular consciousness experiences itself as eternal . . . Part of Ruburt's feeling of massiveness[2] comes from the mass [Life-to-death] experience of the body, existing all at once. Therefore to him the body feels* <u>larger</u>.*" Beginning at 11:10 in that session, see also Jane's own comments on her massive responses.*

(These two ideas from Seth, which came through in connection with his data on moment points, are to me very suggestive of the concept of long sound. From 681st session:) In your

terms—the phrase is necessary—the moment point, the present, is the point of intersection between all existences and reality. All probabilities flow through it, though one of your moments may be experienced as <u>centuries, or as a breath</u>, in other probable realities of which you are a part. *(From session 682:)* There are systems in which a moment, from your standpoint, is made to endure for the life of a universe. . . .[3]

(Jane's expressions of long sound and her sensations of massiveness are of course directly related to the multidimensional neurological activity, the "sidepools" of consciousness, that she described in Appendix 4 of Volume 1. Seth also mentioned neurological pulses and/or speeds in various sessions in Volume 1. In the opening delivery for Session 686, for example, see his information on our species' selection of one "official" series of neurological pulses for physical reality, and, at 12:19 A.M., his remarks on prejudiced perception. Appendix 5 for the same session contains more of Jane's own material on neurological speeds.

(Finally, the excerpt to follow from the 612th session is presented just as received, but I've updated some of the notes for it [beginning with Note 4] in order to take advantage of later material, including some published in Volume 1.)

Session 612
September 6, 1972
9:19 P.M. Wednesday

(The first delivery for this session,[4] running until break at 9:47, is deleted here since it contains much personal material. During it Jane spoke for Seth as usual. His last sentence before break was: "I will have something to say concerning Ruburt's experience the other evening. . . ." With that statement he referred to Monday night's session, which had been an entirely personal one. Just before its start, Jane had had the self-conscious idea that she should rub between her eyes with a circular motion—"You know, where the third eye[5] would be. . . ." In the session itself, she came through with material about herself on her "own," without Seth, but in an altered state of consciousness in which she experienced many vivid subjective images, coupled with strong feelings of massiveness. Some of the

images reflected internal states of her own body. I thought her very interesting way of acquiring the information represented another step in the development of her abilities.

(Now to recap the situation leading up to tonight's [612th] session: At supper time Jane encountered some relaxation effects[6]—so much so, in fact, that she had to lay down briefly in the midst of preparing the meal. Then not long before the session was due she became aware to some extent of her pyramid sensation, meaning that Seth Two, or possibly a variation of that personalities way behind my head were open; she was very relaxed; she smoked a cigarette as we waited for Seth to return. Then after a Many things, it seemed, were developing at once; we expected that after first break tonight Seth would comment upon them, as well as upon Monday evening's session. But events didn't work out that way at all; Seth did not return. Jane carried the rest of the session herself—and a unique one it turned out to be. . . .

(10:09. "I'm getting the feeling of a whole lot of beings or per-sonalities way behind me heas were open; she was very relaxed; she smoked a cigarette as we waited for Seth to return. Then after a pause: "I'm getting stuff but I don't know how I'm supposed to give it—through Seth Two, or what. So I'm just waiting. . . ."

(10:06. Jane's head was lowered, but I could still see various expressions of puzzlement and inquiry move across her face. "I've got that massive feeling again," she said finally, referring to Monday night's session. Her massiveness, among other ef-fects, had been very pronounced for her then; she'd felt herself to be truly giant-sized. Now her eyes slit open. Two minutes later she spoke through lips that hardly moved: "Like in my head this enormous body is out through space—all space as we think of it—"

(10:20. "I can't do it," she said quietly. "I don't think I can do it. . . ." She repeated variations of this idea several times; some of them were less intelligible than others. "I don't under-stand what I'm getting, and I don't know what to do with it. It . . . doesn't sound logical." Pause. "I don't now . . . but I'll try. . . ."

(10:22. In a voice quite a bit deeper and stronger than usual, but not as overpowering as I've heard it be on occasion, Jane began to express a series of very "long," drawn-out syllables. I'd expected anything from a whisper to a scream. What follows at first are my phonetic interpretations of the sounds she uttered.

Her eyes were closed, her head still down. [When Jane reads these typed notes she may not agree with some of my approximations. Now in a heavy voice, almost grating:)

Aaaaaaahhhhhhhhhhaaaaaa. . . . Thhhhhhheeeeeeuuuuuu. . . . Mmmmmmmaaaaaahhhhhhnnnnnnnssss. . . . Eeeeeeehhhhhhrrrr uuuuuu. . . . Aaaaaaahhhhhhhmmmmmmmmmm. . . . Wwwww whhhhheeeeeuuuuu. . . . Jaaaaaahhhhhhuuuuuu. . . . Wwwww hhhhhheeeeeeuuuuuuuuuu.''

(Pause at 10:26. I couldn't distinguish words or meanings here. I concentrated merely on trying to convert the sounds into letters:)

''Wwwwhhhheeeeeeuuuuuuuunnnnn . . . . . . Aaaahhhhhhmmmmmmnnn . . . . . . Wwwwhhhheeeeeee . . . . . . Baaaayyyyyyeeeeeeuuuuu. . . . . . Sssseeeeeeuuuuuuuugggghhhheeeee.''

(Pause at 10:27. Now I began to make out very drawn-out ::long'' or slow words. Jane's voice remained on the same deep, even keel) ''Wwwwhhhhhheeeeeeennnnnnn . . . . . . Wwwweeeeeeeeee . . . . . . Sssspeeeeeeeaaaaakkkkk . . . . . . Wwwwooooorrrrrlllllldsssssss . . . . . Ffffoooooorrrrrmmmmmmm.''

(My interpretation: "When we speak worlds form."

(10:28. Jane's head vibrated quickly from side to side on a small scale, not at all disruptive, as she continued:) ''Wwwweeeeeeee . . . . . . Cooooooommmmmmmmeeeee . . . . . . Wwwweeeeeeeeee . . . . . . Aaaahhhrrrrrrr . . . . . . Thhhheeeeeeee . . . . . . Iiiiinnnnneeeeerrrrr . . . . . . Mmmmooooossssshhhhhiiiiioooooonnnnnnnn . . . . . . Sssssooooooooooot.''

("We come. We are the inner motion—" I couldn't decipher the last syllable or word.)

(10:30.) ''Wwwweeeeeeee . . . . . . Aaaaaarrrrrreeeee . . . . . . Thhhhheeeeee . . . . . . Sssssstrrrreeeeeennnnnngthhhhh . . . . . .Iiiiinnnnnnn . . . . . . Mmmmmaaaaaaaeeeeeeeerrrrrr.''

("We are the strength in matter.")

(10:32.) ''Wwwwwiiiiilllliiiiinnnnnggllyyyyy . . . . . . Fffffoooooorrrrmmmmmmiiinnngggggg . . . . . . Ssssslllloooowwwwweeeerrrrrr . . . . . . Thhhhaaaaannnnnnnn . . . . . . Llllliiiiiiighhhhhhhtt . . . . . . Paaaaaaarrrrrrtiiiiiclllleeeeeessssss . . . . . . Thhhhhiiiiissssss . . . . . Iiiiiiisssssssss . . . . Oooooonnnnnneeeee . . . . . . Aaaaasssssspeeeeect . . . . . . Ooooooffffff . . . . . . Oooooooooouuuuuurrrrrrr . . . . . . Aaaaaaactiiiiivvvvviiiiiitiiiiieeeeeessssss . . . . . . ''(Willingly forming slower-thanlight particles. This is one aspect of our activities).''*

(10:35. Jane paused briefly, her eyes closed. Suddenly her

voice became high-pitched and, at first, quite imcomprehensible to me because of the rapidity of her speech. The effect was remarkably like that of a tape recording played too fast: Her voice went way up the scale, issuing from stiffly held lips. After a few moments I began to understand her;) "—on another level this is completely unintelligible—at another level the pieces are completely unintelligible—"

(She repeated variations of this idea again and again, which gave me time to write down some of them. Her speech was as fast as it could be while remaining at all explicit. Then at a bit slower rate:) "All of these are aspects of one reality . . . Atoms are sound. You do not hear them. . . ."

(10:36. Now Jane's place slowed considerably. In the same high voice she began stressing as separate units many of the syllables of the words she spoke. This was reminiscent of Seth Two's method of delivery, yet subjectively I felt differences. Also, Seth Two had usually expressed "itself" in the singular, whereas tonight's material was coming through under the plural "we":) "All con-scious-ness has as-pects that are act-i-va-ted and ex-pressed in all idi-oms or real-i-ties. This is all we can clear-ly com-mun-i-cate with you now."

(10:38. Jane slumped in her rocker, eyes closed. She had trouble getting them open. She remembered giving the variations on the sounds and methods of speech. She told me that "some-thing" wanted to manifest through her so slowly that it was almost inexpressible; she'd felt deep rolling sounds going through her, yearning to be translated, yearning to make sense in our terms. "It would have taken me three hours to do it right." The slow material simply came out that way when she tried to express it. She couldn't really understand what "they" wanted her to do, if anything.

(Jane said the high-voiced, rapid delivery reminded her of Seth Two, then mentioned a point I'd forgotten: She'd experienced a similar effect once before—last month, while writing poetry, and only mentally. At that time, as now, she hadn't been able to comprehend what was happening well enough to trans-late it, let alone write down anything.[7]

(10:48. After we'd rested for a few minutes, Jane began to speak in her regular voice. I've purposely refrained from men-tioning earlier the rather extensive material that follows; per-haps the reader, coming upon it unexpectedly, will feel something

of my own surprise as Jane started to develop it out of both the slow and rapid effects she'd already demonstrated:)

"I'm getting something, Rob. Something to do with atoms. The slow thing, represented by those drawn-out sounds, is in the center of the atom. Then that's surrounded by faster-than-light particles, represented by the real fast sounds. So the center of this thing—whatever it is—is massive in terms of mass.[8] I don't know whether this means it's <u>heavy</u> or not, but it's tremendous in terms of mass—though it <u>may</u>, underlined, be very small in size.

"Everything is conscious, of course. Atoms and molecules, the whole thing. The massive part is the core. This core is, I believe, not discovered yet [by physicists], and it's so slow to us that no motion is apparent. I don't know whether this is an atom or not. You can call it a dead hole" *(Pause.)* "It's motion is our terms is so slow as not to be observable, but in terms of time it's a backward motion."[9]

(Pause at 10:50.) ". . . [this core is] always surrounded by these faster-than-light particles. this is a structure . . . but it does cause a pulling-in or wrinkling effect where it appears. There are many of these, I think, in our galaxy as well as others. Nothing can be drawn <u>through</u> the dead hole, though, as things can be drawn through the black hole, because of [The dead hole's] literally impenetrable mass. Now as with atoms alone, and all other such structures, these also exist as sound.[10] Black holes and white holes do also.*[11] The sounds are actually characteristics that act as cohesives, characteristics automatically given off. The slower center por ions of the dead holes themselves move backward into beginnings becoming heavier and heavier."

(11:00.) "In a way of speaking you could say these centers fall through space, but they really fall through the space of themselves. *(Jane shook her head, her eyes closed.)* As they fall backward through themselves—I'm getting this—I don't know how to say it—the faster-than-light particles collapse in on top. The dead hole seems to swallow itself, with the real fast particles like a lid that gradually diminishes . . . From our point of view the hole is closed, say, once the faster-than-light particles follow the slower core backward into beginnings."

(11:05.) "As the core goes backward—in quotes—'in time,' however, it begins to accelerate. I don't know how to put this. When it emerges in another universe, the faster-than-light parti-

cles have slowed down, and the core becomes faster than light. The dead hole is repeated in microscopic size—that's small, isn't it? Before the emergence of the atom . . oh, dear . . . as an analogy, you could say that the dead hole we've been talking about emerges as an atom in another universe. But it's the stage <u>before</u> the appearance, or the stage <u>from which</u> an atom comes.

"Speaking of the dead hole in a galaxy, say ours, it emerges in what would be to us an atom of fantastic size, but the same thing happens on a different scale as far as the creation of matter is concerned within our own system."[12]

(11:12.) "As mentioned, sound is connected here also, and each one of these phenomena has consciousness that does express itself, and is aware of the stages through which is passes. In certain terms, dead holes connect past and present; also future. In practical terms, they have to do with the seeming permanence of an object. They are the invisible portions of the atom. There are giant-sized atoms, as well as the ones you're familiar with."

(11:17.) I—I know there's more there . . . I want to find out more. I don't get their [the 'consciousnesses' behind tonight's material] purpose. *(Jane looked tired and disheveled now, and I suggested she end the session. She sat with her eyes closed. She had trouble enunciating the next sentence, and had to repeat it:)* Dead holes turn into live holes . . . where the motion and impetus, in your terms, would be toward the future . . . I can't get any more. . . . *(Once again I urged her to quit.)* I'm almost finished. In this case, the core appears as matter-to-be. I guess I'll stop. I can't follow it. This whole thing has to do with those voice effects earlier. . . ."

(11:19.) "I was getting images through the whole thing. *(Jane rested briefly.)* I was trying to explain what *they* meant. It's something when you don't know what you're trying to say. . . . *(She described the images to some extent—delineating stars, a series of circles, condensing matter, imploding galaxies and other such effects—but they didn't mean as much to me as her material in the session itself.)* I just got tired receiving the stuff. That was really a workout. There's a lot more there to be had, too. . . ." *(She likened her dissertation to the way she often gets impressions concerning people; the information "just comes," and she recites it.*

(I'd maintain that Jane has been on a creative upsurge for a

year now. During that time she finished Seth Speaks *and helped me proofread it, wrote her novel,* Oversoul Seven, *and worked on another* Seven *book [still unfinished], as well as* Personal Reality *and* Adventures. *These activities meant keeping to her schedule of two regular sessions a week for the most part, although I do the work of transcribing her trance material. Jane also held her weekly ESP classes and writing classes, and continued her work on poetry and an autobiography [also unfinished]. With all of this, we also went through the flood caused by Tropical Storm Agnes in June 1972. Jane's daily predictions have been working out exceptionally well. Recently she was informed that impressions she gave for certain people as long as two years ago have been proving correct in large measure—a very heartening development. . . .*

(The day after this session, Jane greatly enlarged upon her original estimate—three hours—of the time she'd need to interpret the long or slow sounds. Now she felt that "to do proper justice to them would take years—centuries perhaps." Because of our ordinary time sense the sounds were actually so slow to us that they appeared to be motionless, or "dead" she told me, leading us to speculate that this may be one of the reasons why in usual terms we call inanimate matter—rocks, for instance—"dead." But Jane couldn't really define any sources behind last night's material, beyond calling them "consciousnesses, or beings—but maybe not personalities as we think of that term." Then, again increasing her estimate, she said that if "they" tried to communicate with us through sound, through our sensual equipment, "it would take forever."

(After reading my typed interpretations of the long sounds she'd started to deliver at 10:22, Jane wrote: "I knew what the drawn-out words were at the beginning, and thought Rob had understood them. Now I haven't the slightest idea of what they said."

(I want to conclude this appendix with a poem Jane wrote during the summer of 1963, a few months before she began the sessions. To me her long-sound material, given nine years later in the 612th session, simply represented her psychic way of "catching up" with, and developing, deeply intuitive knowledge that she'd possessed all along:)

Long is the Light

Long is the light
Of the moth and the willow.
Long is the journey
Of the root and the stem.
Deep is the cry
Of the tree bark and blossom.
The leaf hears its growing,
And life sings its truth.

Sweet is the depth
Of air to the swallow.
Long is the still breath
Of the stone and the pebble.
Deep is the trance
Of the mountain and meadow.
The leaf hears its growing,
And stones speak their truth.

NOTES: Appendix 8

1. In Appendix 3 of *Adventures* Jane listed and described the altered states of consciousness that she's attained so far in her psychic development. She also considered Seth Two in various other parts of *Adventures*. In Chapter 2, for instance, the Seth Two quotations are cast in the editorial "we," the guise in which that energy gestalt often comes through: "We are trying to appreciate the nature of your present existence . . . For you there may seem to be an unbearable loneliness, because you are so used to relating to the warm victory of the flesh, and [here] there is no physical being . . . Yet beyond and within that isolation is a point of light that is consciousness. It pulses with the power behind all the emotions that you know . . . This is the warmth that . . . is born from the very devotion of our isolation . . . that creates the reality that you know, without itself experiencing it."

Seth Two is mentioned but a few times in *Personal Reality*. Those who are interested can also refer to the Seth Two descriptions and excerpts in Chapter 22 of *Seth Speaks;* see Session 588 from 11:35 P.M., and Session 589.

2. Jane's earliest experiences with the phenomenon of massiveness are described in the 39th session for March 30, 1964; in Volume 1, see the excerpts in Appendix 3 (for Session 681).

(I remind the reader that Appendix 3 also contains a reference to

Jane's extraordinary adventure with—and in—massiveness on April 4, 1973. She described it herself in the 653rd session for Chapter 13 of *Personal Reality*.

3. In Note 9 for the 712th session, see the two analogies to long sound that I drew from the 514th session in *Seth Speaks*.

4. By the time the 612th session was held we were finally getting back into our old rhythms of work; they'd been seriously disrupted by the flood caused by Tropical Storm Agnes in June 1972. Just before the flood materialized (over two months ago), Seth-Jane had completed the Preface and the first session for Chapter 1 of *Personal Reality;* see the opening notes for Session 613 in that work.

5. I was surprised to hear Jane's somewhat embarrassed references to the third eye, since I couldn't remember her mentioning it before in the sessions. The third eye (sometimes called the "back eye") is the legendary organ of psychic perception, supposedly located behind the forehead. In occult science it's been connected with the pineal body, or gland; that mysterious member of the endocrine system is buried deep within the brain, and through the centuries has been considered by many—including the French philospher and mathematician, René Descartes (1596–1650)—to be the seat of the soul.

Many are familiar with the Hindu discipline of Yoga. In that ascetic system of breathing, meditation, and postures, the third eye corresponds to the sixth chakra, as one starts counting the positions of those seven nonphysical wheels of psychic energy from the base of the spine to the brian's cerebrum.

Consciously Jane knows very little about the history of the third eye, so-called. I wouldn't say that either of us believes in it particularly, so it's interesting, then, to consider what intuitive knowledge she might possess that led her to talk about it now.

6. In Chapter 6 of *Adventures,* Jane described who we rented a second apartment across the hall from our first one in order to have more living and working space. (The apartments are on the second floor.) Jane's psychic identification with the leaves of the great oak tree, growing so close beside the second apartment's kitchen windows, marked the beginning of a different kind of relaxation for her; the kitchen became her evocative "tree house." Several years later, I asked her to write for this note her own account of the relaxation effects that grew out of the hours she spent in contemplation with that massive tree:

"That particular kind of relaxation seems to repeatedly come upon me over a period of several months or even a year, then to vanish for the same amount of time. I first felt it right after we moved into the new apartment in June 1971, and when it started I knew it was a different kind of feeling. It's a sort of superrelaxation; almost profound, and mental and physical at once. A completely different thing than just yawning, even though I might *be* yawning.

...ation involves a curious sense of dropping down inwardly, ...owly beneath the realities we usually recognize. It's a smooth ...n in which perception is slowed down topwise, but deepened so ...usually unperceived stimuli seem to rise from an underside of consciousness and bodily sensation. In that kind of relaxation the body itself perceives differently; *that's* what I'm trying to emphasize. Looking at a leaf while in that state, I easily feel myself as part of the leaf, and I think this is a biological as well as a psychic perception. At certain levels the body feels that way itself, although ordinarily we aren't aware of it. Such a relaxation, then, is almost an extension of biological insight.''

7. From Jane's notebook: "I was writing poetry one day early in August 1971, when suddenly I mentally heard the oddest sounds— incredibly fast, too quick to follow. Instantly I 'knew' that these faster sounds were objects coming into material focus. They slowed down to become physical. I sensed this neurologically, though how that was possible, I don't know. . . .''

Perhaps this mental event was Jane's way of "practicing" for the physical one that was to follow a month latter, in the 612th session. In my opinion, she offers a most important insight here toward understanding the formation of our mundane physical reality. Besides Jane's material in appendix 4 and 5 for Volume 1 of *"Unknown" Reality*, see Seth's deliveries on inner sound, light, and electromagnetic patterns in the four sessions (623–26) making up Chapter 5 of *Personal Reality*.

8. Since Jane has just referred to them, in this note I'll touch upon atoms (and, incidentally, molecules), faster-than-light particles, and mass. The reader can use the definitions below to make his or her own associations with Jane's material. (The other sources given will also add extra dimensions to this 612th session.)

In conventional terms, atoms are regarded as the submicroscopic entities making up all objects and substances in our world. Each atom consists of a nucleus of protons, neutrons, and other subatomic particles, around all of which move a complicated system of much lighter electrons. (An atom of hydrogen, however, is made up of but one proton and one electron.) All is in balance: The number of positive charges on the nucleus equals the number of negatively charged electrons. Note 24 for Appendix 18 contains a short discussion of the particle-wave duality involving the components of the atom. In Note 35 for the same appendix, I quoted Seth from the 702nd session in Volume 1; he advanced his own idea of interrelated fields versus particle-wave theory.

Atoms combine to form molecules. If the assembled atoms are all alike, an element results; if two or more different kinds of atoms combine into molecules, a compound is created.

In Note 1 for Session 709 I wrote that ''Tachyons . . . are supposed faster-than-light particles that are thought to be possible within Ein-

of its nuclear fires. Such an object is very small and unimaginably dense; within it, time and space are interchangable. It's also quite invisible, because its surface gravity is so enormous that not even light can escape from it. (Yet, in Volume 1, see the comments in Note 4 for Session 688, on the possibility of light radrition from the "event horizon" of the black hole.) So far just two black holes have been tentatively located, although many of them are believed to exist.

Since the matter surrounding a black hole would also be drawn into it, some astrophysicists have suggested that this might emerge into another universe through its opposite—a white hole—where it would be seen as an extremely brilliant quasar, or quasi-stellar radio source. So there would be an exchange of matter-energy between universes or realities.

Interestingly enough, several very distant quasars have been linked to certain observed faster-than-light effects, thus contradicting current physical theory that nothing can exceed the speed of light. For science this is a very uncomfortable situation that has yet to be resolved. But I'm sure that in scientific terms (quite aside from Seth's material in Note 1 for the 712th session) there are many discoveries to be made in this area. The faster-than-light effects may be the results of observations that are simply not understood in some as-yet-unexplained way. . . .

In trance or out, Jane likes to "take off" in her own creative ways from concepts like that of the tachyon, or the black hole or the white hole—so in this Session she came up with the "dead hole." Then, from another angle, she explored related ideas in *Adventures;* see Chapter 19, "Earth Experience as a White Hole," in which she wrote, "What kind of structured universe could explain both the inner and exterior worlds? If we consider the universe as a white hole—our exterior universe of sense—we at least have a theoretical framework that reconciles our inner and outer activity, our physical and spiritual or psychic experience; and the apparent dilemma between a simultaneous present in which all events happen at once, and our daily experience in which we seem to progress through time from birth to death."

In closing: See the 593rd session in the Appendix of *Seth Speaks* for Seth's material on black holes, white holes, and coordination points: "A black hole is a white hole turned inside out . . . The holes, therefore, or coordination points [points of double reality, or where realities merge], are actually great accelerators that reenergize energy itself." In the 688th session for Volume 1, Seth presents an analogy in which his basic units of consciousness, or CU's, operate as minute but very powerful black holes and white holes.

12. A note added over a year later: For some time I've untuitively felt connections between Jane's material in this paragraph and ideas we first read about some six months after this 612th session was held in Septem-

ber 1972: that for various reasons (having to do with gravitational waves, mass, et cetera) many galaxies, including our own, could have been formed out of matter accumulating around black holes at their centers.

APPENDIX 9
(For Session 713)

(Seth hasn't often talked about UFO's—unidentified flying objects—in the sessions. He thinks they have various states of origin. Occasionally he'll mention them in connection with another subject; as an example, see the two paragraphs about "saucers" and the pulsating nature of atoms and molecules in the ESP class session for January 12, 1971, in the Appendix of Seth Speaks.

(That material actually flows from a session held seven years earlier: the 16th for January 15, 1964, which still contains Seth-Jane's longest delivery on such craft. We found the information in the session quite intriguing because we thought it offered a fresh approach to a very controversial puzzle. We still think so. [In the early sessions, incidentally, Seth used the word "plane" often, but not long afterward began the general change-over to "reality," which for the most part we like better. However, note at the end of these excerpts from the 16th session the meanings and delineations he found within that word "plane"— even though he regarded it as our term.])

The strange thing about your flying saucers is not that they appear, but that you can see them. As science advances on various planes the inhabitants learn to travel between planes occasionally, while carrying with them the [camouflage] manifestations of their home stations . . .

I am quite sure—I know for a fact—that beings from other planes have appeared among you, sometimes on purpose and sometimes completely by accident. As in some cases humans have quite accidentally blundered through the apparent curtain between your present and your past, so have beings blundered into the apparent division between one plane and another. Usually when they have done so they were invisible on your plane, as the few of you who fell into the past, or the apparent past, were invisible to the people of the past.

281

This sort of experience involves a sudden psychic awareness, straight from the entity, that all boundaries are for practical purposes only. However, there are indeed many kinds of science. There are a number of sciences dealing just with locomotion. Had the human species gone into certain mental disciplines as thoroughly as it has explored technological disciplines, its practical transportation system would be vastly different, and yet by this time even more practical than it is now. *(With amusement:)* I am making this point because I want it made plain—this, dear Joseph, is a pun—that when I speak of science on another plane I may not speak of the plain old science that you know.

Now back to the point. When sciences progress on various planes, then visitations become less accidental and more planned. Once the inhabitants of a plane have learned mental-science patterns, then they are to a great degree freed from the more regular camouflage [physical] patterns. This applies to "higher" planes than mine, generally speaking, although mine is further along in these sciences than your own.

[Many of] the flying saucer appearances come from [such] a plane, [one] that is much more advanced in technological sciences than earth at this time. However, this is still not a mental-science plane. Therefore, the camouflage paraphernalia appears, more or less visible to your own astonishment. Now, so strong is this tendency for vitality to change from one apparent form to another, that what you have here in your flying object is something that is actually, as you view it, not of your plane or of [whatever] plane of its origin . . . The atoms and molecules that structurally compose the UFO, and which are themselves formed by vitality, are more or less aligned according to the pattern of its own territory. Now as the craft enters your plane a distortion occurs. Its actual structure is caught in a dilemma of form . . . between transforming itself completely into earth's particular camouflage pattern, and retaining its original pattern. The earthly viewer attempts to correlate what he sees with what he supposedly knows or imagines possible in the universe.

What he sees is something between a horse and a dog, that resembles neither. The flying saucer retains what is can of its original structure and changes what it must. This accounts for many of the conflicting reports as to shape, size, and color. The few times the craft shoots off at right angles, it has managed to retain functions ordinary to it in its particular habitat.

I do not believe you will have any saucer landings for quite a while, not physical landings in the usual sense of the word. These vehicles cannot stay on your plane for any length of time at all. The pressures that push against the saucer itself are tremendous . . . The struggle to be one thing or another is very great on any plane. To conform to the laws of a particular plane is a practical necessity, and at this time the flying saucer craft simply cannot afford to stay betwixt and between for any indefinite period.

What they do is take quick glimpses of your plane—and hold in mind that the saucer or cigar shape [often] seen on your planet is a bastard from having little relation to the structure as it is at home base.

At a later date I may go into the inhabitants of [those planes] more thoroughly, but as it is I am not very much acquainted with them myself.[1]

There are so many things you do not understand that I hope to explain to you. There are other things you do not understand that I cannot explain to you, simply because they would be too alien now for your regular mode of thought . . .

One note along these lines. A plane—and I am using your term; I will try to think of a better one—is not necessarily a planet. A plane may be one planet, but a plane may also exist where no planet is. One planet may have several planes. Planes may also involve various aspects of apparent time—this particular matter being too difficult to go into right now, although I will continue it later.

Planes can and do intermix without the knowledge of the inhabitants of the particular planes involved. I want to get away from the idea of a plane being a place. It may be in some cases but is not always. A plane may be a time. A plane, believe it or not, may be only one iota of vitality that seems to exist by itself. A plane is something apparently divided from the rest of the universe for a time and for a reason. A plane may cease to be. A plane may spring up where there was none. A plane is formed for entities as patterns for fulfillment on various levels. A plane is a climate conducive to the development of unique and particular capacities and achievements. A plane is an isolation of elements where each one is given the most possible space in which to function.

Planets have been used as planes and used again as other

planes. A plane is not a cosmic location. It is oftentimes practical that entities or their various personalities visit one plane before another. This does not necessarily mean that one plane <u>must</u> be visited before another. A certain succession is merely more useful for the entity as a whole.

In other terms, you could say that an entity visits all planes simultaneously, as it is possible for you to visit a certain state, county, and city at one time. You might also visit the states of sorrow and joy almost simultaneously, and experience both emotions in heightened form because of the almost immediate contrast between them.

In fact, the analogy of a plane with an emotional state is much more valid than that between a plane and a geographical state—particularly since emotional states take up no room.

NOTES: Appendix 9

1. A note added a decade later: So far, Seth has failed to volunteer information on the inhabitants of any of the "saucer" planes—but neither have we asked him to do so.

APPENDIX 10
(For Session 721)

(Jane and I consider Seth's concept of counterparts to be an intriguing psychological framework, spacious enough to serve as a workable thematic structure in which the social and nationalistic characteristics of our species can be studied, as well as the components of the individual psyche. That is, the private person is here seen as interacting with others because there is, beneath our awareness, an inner "person-to-person" relationship connecting each individual with his or her physical counterparts, though they may well be living in other parts of the globe while sharing the same historical period. It follows, then, that one may or may not ever meet a counterpart "in the flesh"—may or may not even suspect the existence of such relationships.

(The material on counterparts emerged from Seth's treatment of reincarnation. Along with his addition of simultaneous time, I'd say that the concept of counterparts provides reincarnation with a novel approach indeed; and that our awareness of both has always been latent within the reincarnational framework, whether in simultaneous or linear terms.

(Now I'd like to present a batch of notes, ideas, and excerpts from sessions about reincarnation, counterparts, and related data, pulling them together into a coherent picture. Although reincarnation and its variations has been discussed by Seth almost from the very beginning of our sessions, the subject didn't represent one of our own main concerns. For that matter, Jane almost actively resisted such information in the past. She still says comparatively little about reincarnation on her own, although Seth shows no such reservations.

(Actually, we've had two recent indications that Seth was going to initiate something like the counterpart thesis, even though he hadn't used the term itself. The first clue came in a private, or deleted, session held a week ago on Monday night

285

[November 18, 1974]; the second hint was given in ESP class on the following evening.

(In our private session, Seth commented on my "quite legitimate" reincarnational data involving the black woman, Maumee or Mawmee, who'd lived on the Caribbean island of Jamaica early in the 19th century. He went on to say:) You helped that woman. Your present sense of security and relative detachment gave her strength. She knew she would survive, because she was aware of your knowledge. I will say more about it, but for now that is the end of the session. Ruburt has had enough for a night.

(Jane was tired by the session's end. Without thinking, I casually remarked that currently I had three things going reincarnationally[1]—involving the Roman soldier, the black woman, and Nebene—and that if I could untangle their time sequences, I could use them as part of a chronological list of my "past" lives.

("I wish you hadn't said that, Rob," Jane answered, somewhat ruefully. "Now I've got a whole bunch of stuff on reincarnation and time. So let's get it down."

(I humorously protested, knowing that she was really tired, and told her not to say anything that later she'd wish we had recorded. I refused to get out my notebook and pen again. It was obvious that Jane wanted only to sleep, even though she was willing to continue the session after trying to wake up by drinking a cup of coffee.

("All right," she said finally. "I'll just tell you this: The whole idea of reincarnation is all screwed up. To unscramble it would really be confusing. What I'm getting is that the idea of just one life in any given time is bullshit—the psyche is so rich that it can have more than one life in one time period, like your Nebene and Roman soldier living together in the first century. But if you tell people that, you'll just get them all mixed up."

("Well, assuming that my intuitions were reasonably accurate when I picked up on those two personalities," I said, "there have to be explanations."

("Sure," Jane replied. "There's a whole lot there I could give you right now—"

("Okay. I really want to know all about it. But at some other time."

(After that, we gave up and went to bed. In ESP class the following night, Seth indicated that he was ready to expand his

concepts of personality still further—though, again, he didn't mention counterparts per se. He started by commenting on my experience with Maumee once more. Then he continued:)

Now: a footnote to our [private] session of last night. Ruburt was correct: Lives <u>are</u> simultaneous. You can live more than one life at a time—in your terms now—but that is a loaded sentence. You are neurologically tuned in to one particular field of actuality that you recognize.[2] In your terms and from your viewpoint only, messages from other existences live within you as ghost images within the cells, for the cells recognize more than you do on a conscious level. That is, for a brief time, Joseph *(Rob)* was consciously able to perceive a portion of another existence.

<u>You could not be consciously aware of those other realities all of the time, and deal with the world that you know</u>. You have several time and space tracks in operation at once, then, but you acknowledge only certain neurological messages physically. Yet there is more to the body than you perceive of it, and this is difficult to explain to you . . . If you can think of a multidimensional body existing at one time in various realities, and appearing differently within each one while still being whole, then you can get some glimpse of what is involved.[3]

Now our friend Joseph here was able to handle another reality while still being involved in this one. *(To me:)* Neurologically, you crossed your messages. You were aware of ghost images that you usually do not recognize, and those were translated into ghost sense data. *(To the class;)* That is, he knew the black woman was not in the physical room with him in this space and time, running through his studio [where he had the experience]. But in other terms, she was indeed running in another environment that our friend was able to see, and to superimpose over the reality he knew, while keeping both intact.

(Here I asked Seth if the strong thrilling sensations I'd repeatedly felt at the time had anything to do with my perceptions of the "ghost images" of Maumee and her surroundings. Seth answered:)

Those were the result of the neurological changeover, and they are your particular symbol that this is occurring. Others will have symbols of their own.

But such pictures are there for any of you who want to view them. When you are ready to see them, you will. Many of you are not ready to meet those kinds of data . . . for a certain kind

of finesse is required—a balance that you are learning. And each
of you knows intuitively when you are open to such encounters.

There are, of course, future memories as well as past ones . . .
as Joseph often says, "When you think of reincarnation, you
do so in terms of <u>past</u> lives." You are afraid to consider future
lives because then you have to face the death that must be met
first, in your terms. And so you never think of future selves,
or how you might benefit from knowing them. . . .

*(The material in these recent excerpts rather prepared us for
Seth's introduction of counterparts, then, in Session 721. In ESP
class the next evening [on November 26], Seth began contending
with some of the questions that instantly arose as a result of his
new material. I'd just read aloud portions of the 721st session
when one longtime student, whom I'll call Florence, commented
that there "has to be a balance between each of us and our
counterparts." Speaking strongly and humorously, Seth immediately took over the discussion.*

(To Florence:) Far be it from me to disturb your ancient ideas
of yin and yang, or Jung, or good and evil, or of right and
wrong, or of good and bad vibrations! I was beginning a new
body of material, and so we have not finished with it by a long
shot! What I hope to say is that your world exists in different
terms than those you recognize, and that reincarnation is indeed
a myth and a story that stands for something else entirely.

Each of you takes part in your world—and in your time as you
understand it, and in your terms, all the creatures of the earth
participate in the century. You work out creative challenges and
possibilities. You are born into different races, into different
cultures, with different—but the same—desires . . . There are
many things that you are learning. And so, if you will forgive
me, my dear Florence, I will use you as an example.

For there is also a version of our Florence, a young man in
China, who does not weigh even 70 pounds, and who is 26 years
old. *(Florence is in her late 40's.)* He has starved for years. He
feels very vulnerable. It does not particularly help that young
man when our Florence piles on weight because <u>she</u> then feels
less vulnerable, and more protected from her world.

On the other hand, our young man sometimes dreams of being
overweight, and it is one of his most satisfying dreams. Now
those dreams are going to help him in his own manner, for he is

already working on some concepts involving the planting of fields that will benefit the people in his village.

In his particular village, the elders believe that there is some merit to being underweight. Our young man hates the Americans. He believes that this is an opulent, luxurious, and wicked society, and yet he yearns toward it with all his heart.

Now our Florence is working with her own ideas of good and evil, searching for what she <u>thinks</u> of as an aesthetic and moral code that she can rely upon. Her counterpart had that code, but found that he could <u>not</u> count upon it. Each is working on the same series of challenges. There are also two other counterparts. Between the four of them, the century is being covered. *(To Florence, smiling:)* I will tell you about that at another time. It is not <u>my</u> suspense story—it is your own![4]

(Florence: "What you said about my counterpart in China makes perfect sense to me."

(Then Seth came through with his aside, as he referred to a guest:) One small note to our astrologer-in-spirit over there. One tiny, wicked hint! Each of you has a birthday that you recognize— <u>one</u> birthday—but there are hidden variables, because of what I am saying here tonight, that do not apply in those charts because you have not thought of them.

Now in your terms only, these other counterparts are like latent patterns within your mind. Echoes. How many of you have actually thought of what the unconscious may be? Or, the voices that you hear within your mind or heart? Are they yours? To what counterparts do they belong? And yet each of you, in your own identity, has the right to do precisely as you wish, and to form your own reality. . . .

(And, later in the session:) I will give you an example. There is a member of the class—and *(with obvious amusement)* I will close my innocent eyes so that I do not give the secret away— but there is a class member who is indeed a fine Jesuit, handling problems of great weight, having to do with the nature of religion. There is a renegade priest who has been in this class, and who ran off to California; he likes to put the boot to theology and "do his own thing." There is also an extremely devout woman who lives in England. All of these counterparts are dealing with the nature of religion. They are experiencing versions of religion because it interests them.

[Each of] you will create the attributes of reality that interest

you and work with them in your own way. If you want to study
the nature of religion and do a good job of it, then you must be
among other things a skeptic and a believer, and an Indian and a
Jew, say. Otherwise you will not understand anything at all, and
have a very lopsided picture. And *(to a black student)* you
cannot know what it is like to be black in this culture—you may
not agree here—unless you are also white in it. . . . Now I
return you to yourselves and to your counterparts.

*("Well," I said to Jane after class, as we discussed the
Chinese-American situation cited by Seth, "I don't know about
counterpart relationships in other kinds of realities, but it's certainly obvious that at least some physical counterparts can hate
each other . . ." So the larger self, I thought, would be quite
capable of seeking experience through its parts in every way
imaginable. Although it might be difficult for us to understand,
let alone accept, the whole self or entity must regard all of its
counterparts as sublime facets of itself—no matter whether they
loved, suffered,[5] hated, or killed each other or "outsiders."
Within its great reaches it would transform its counterparts'
actions in ways that were, quite possibly, beyond our emotional
and intellectual grasp. At the same time, the self would learn and
be changed through the challenges and struggles of its human
portions.*

*(On more "practical" levels, we thought that behavior among
nations might be changed for the better if the idea of counterparts
were understood, or at least considered—if, for instance, many
of the individuals making up a country realized that they could
actually be acting against portions of themselves [or of their
whole selves] in the persons of the "enemy" country, and so
modified the virulence of their feelings. The nations of the world
would benefit greatly from even a small improvement in their
relationship with each other. And if an individual strongly dis-
liked a counterpart in another land, wouldn't this quality of
emotion be detrimentally reflected in the person doing the hating?*

*(So far we've been dealing with the idea of counterparts in our
own physical reality. By way of contrast, however, Seth stated
last month in the 713th session, after 10:32:)* Nothing exists
outside the psyche, however, that does not exist within it, and
there is no unknown world that does not have its psychological
or psychic counterpart. *(Before that, from Session 712:)* To some

extent or another, there are counterparts of all realities within your psyche.

(Continuing to trace such references back through the material, I'd like to direct the reader to several passages from the 683rd session for Volume 1 of "Unknown" Reality; in them Seth contends with variations on the counterpart theme as they're developed in certain other probable realities:

(1.) It is quite possible, for example, <u>for several selves to occupy a body</u>, and were this the norm it would be easily accepted. That implies another kind of multipersonhood, however, one actually allowing for the fulfillment of many abilities of various natures <u>usually</u> left unexpressed. It also implies a freedom and organization of consciousness that is unusual in your system of reality, and was not chosen there.

(2.) In some systems of physical existence, a multipersonhood is established, in which three or four "persons" emerge from the same inner self, each one utilizing to the best of its abilities those characteristics of its own. This presupposes a gestalt of awareness, however, in which each knows of the activities of the others, and participates; and you have a <u>different</u> version of mass consciousness. Do you see the correlation?

("Yes," I said.)

In the systems in which evolution of consciousness has worked in that fashion, all faculties of body and mind in one "lifetime" are beautifully utilized. Nor is there any ambiguity about identity. The individual would say, for example, "I am Joe, and Jane, and Jim, and Bob."[6] There are physical variations of a sexual nature, so that on all levels identity includes the male and female. Shadows of all such probabilities appear within your own system, as oddities. Anything apparent to whatever degree in your system is developed in another.

(Seth's material on counterparts did make us wonder about Jane's and his earlier uses of the word and its concepts. Checking backward through part sessions and Jane's poetry, I soon learned that her intuitive grasp of the term had always been truer than mine, for I'd carried the idea that "counterpart" implied a status of opposites rather than the complementary one it really does. Seth also used the term in its correct sense.[7]

(The entire poem, Dear Love, which Jane wrote for me in December 1973, can be found in Note 3 for the 713th session. I want to repeat the first verse of it for obvious reasons, although

all of the poem is an excellent creative exposition of counterpart ideas:

> *Dear love,*
> *what times unmanifest*
> *in our lives reside*
> *beneath our nights and days?*
> *What counterparts break*
> *within our smiles,*
> *what cracks appear in other skies*
> *as we talk and drink coffee*
> *in quiet domestic grace?*

(In Chapter 19 of Personal Reality, *I found this line of Seth's in the 667th session for May 30, 1973:)* For reason and emotion are natural counterparts.

(Ten sessions earlier, there's a particularly evocative reference to counterparts in the 657th session for April 18, 1973, in Chapter 15 of Personal Reality. *In retrospect that material seems to be a clear indication of the later development of the counterpart concept—and one passage could well refer to "Unknown" Reality* long before that project was ever thought of as far as Jane and I were concerned. Seth:)*

In a way that will be explained in another book for those interested in such matters, there is a kind of coincidence with all of these present points of power[8] that exist between you and your "reincarnational" selves. There are even biological connections in terms of cellular "memory."

. . . those selves are different counterparts of yourself in creaturehood, experiencing bodily reality; but at the same time your organism itself shuts out the simultaneous nature of experience.

(During that same month in 1973 Jane wrote Apprentice Gods, *a long poem that's included in Chapter 16 of* Adventures in Consciousness. *In the poem she probed for the origins of our personified gods, and referred to counterparts as follows:*

> *. . . for how like us these earth gods are,*
> *yet next to us, superstars,*
> *bigger than life counterparts,*
> *dramatizing us beyond degree*

*and running off with the show
as vicariously we watch
them play our parts.[9]*

*(Also consider these two still-earlier excerpts from the 520th
session for March 20, 1970, in Chapter 3 of* Seth Speaks:)

Quite literally, the "inner" self forms the body by magically
transforming thoughts and emotions into physical counterparts . . .

Now whenever you think emotionally of another person, you
send out a counterpart of yourself, beneath the intensity of
matter, but a definite form.

(And from a far older session, the 44th for April 15, 1964:)

. . . the so-called laws of your camouflage physical universe
do not apply to the inner universe . . . However, the laws of the
inner universe apply to <u>all</u> camouflage universes . . . Some of
these basic laws have counterparts known and accepted in various camouflage realities.

*(Appendix 12 contains lengthy quotations from the 44th ses-
sion, including the whole of the passage just cited.*

*(And what about the very first counterpart references in our
session? In Chapter 1 of* The Seth Material, *Jane described how
we began these sessions [on December 2, 1963] through our use
of the Ouija board. During the first three sessions the material
came from a Frank Withers—who, it developed in the 4th session, was one of the "personality fragments" making up the Seth
entity, or whole self. Just before Seth announced his presence to
us in that same session, Frank Withers spelled out a remark
through the board that meant little to Jane and me at the time:
"One whole entity may need several manifestations, even at
simultaneous so-called times."*

*(Though Frank Withers never used the word "counterpart,"
we see now that this can be a reference to the concept of
simultaneous reincarnations, to that of counterparts, or to both.*

*(Seth himself first used "counterpart" in the 6th session for
December 11, 1963. At the time—and for a long while afterward—
his employment of the word meant little, if anything, to Jane and
me. The newly begun sessions already contained a number of
unfamiliar terms and ideas: In the 4th session three days earlier,
for instance, Seth had just given us our entity names [Ruburt for
Jane, Joseph for me], and touched upon the psychic links connecting the three of us. Any subleties afforded by concepts like*

counterparts would have quite escaped us. For that matter, at the time we didn't know whether or not the sessions would continue. Nor were we particularly concerned about the issue.

(In the 6th session, however, I made quite an intuitive remark: I told Jane I had the notion that Ruburt had once been Joseph. It took me a while to recognize that this had simply been my way of groping toward the realization that Seth, Jane and I did have a strong psychic relationship. Though we'd started these sessions with the Ouija board, Jane had made such a rapid progression that she was already giving some material vocally. However, at the time we still used the board to obtain answers to most of our questions. After I made my statement about Ruburt and Joseph, Seth spelled out his reply through the board's pointer as it moved quickly beneath our fingertips:)

Part of same entity or counterpart.

(And so 11 years were to pass before Seth began his outright discussion of his very provocative concept of counterparts.)

NOTES: Appendix 10

1. For material on the Roman soldier, see the first notes for sessions 715–16; on Maumee and Nebene, see notes 1 and 9, respectively, in the 721st session.

I could list a few other past lives I'm supposed to have known, and so could Jane. Some of those we've picked up on our own. Over the years Seth has also come through with a modest number of reincarnational experiences involving the three of us, as well as others concerning any two of us. Examples are given in Appendix 7 in Volume 2 Part I. But Jane and I are more intrigued by passages in Appendix 7 like this one, from the 398th session for March 11, 1964: "Personalities are not static things. Entities are eternal. They are not as nicely nor as neatly packaged out, one to a body, as your psychologists believe."

A published relationship in which Seth, Jane, and I took part, one that's innocent of counterpart overtones, as far as our material indicates, happened in Denmark in the 1600's. In *Seth Speaks*, see Session 541 for Chapter 11.

2. I've directed the reader to them before—but in Volume 1 of *"Unknown" Reality* see Jane's information on neurological speeds in appendixes 4 and 5. As I wrote in Note 19 for Appendix 1 in Volume 2 Part I: "My personal opinion is that although many may find it difficult reading, Appendix 4 contains some of the most important material in Volume 1." Jane also referred to her ghostly "Saratoga experience" in that appendix: Both she and Seth dealt with it in sessions 685–86.

3. In the opening notes for the 718th session, I wrote that I'd just finished a series of diagrams for Jane's *Adventures*. In Diagram 1 for Chapter 10, I tried to show schematically the same idea Seth mentions here, but with the terminology Jane used in her own book. She wrote about a series of Aspect selves orbiting a nonphysical source self, then continued: "Imagine a multidimensional Ferris wheel, each separated section being an Aspect self. As our 'seat' approaches the ground level, we're the Aspect who intersects with the space-time continuum, and life starts. But this Ferris wheel moves in every possible direction, and its spokes are ever-moving waves of energy, connecting the Aspects with the center source. Each other position intersects with a different kind of reality in which it is, in turn, immersed."

4. Seth never did tell Florence any more about her other counterparts, though. Nor did she ask him to; she worked with the information he'd already given her, plus whatever she could divine for herself.

5. I thought of Seth's material on pain and suffering, as presented in Appendix 1 in Volume 2 Part I. See the excerpts from the 580th session for *Seth Speaks*, and the 634th session for *Personal Reality*.

6. Perhaps I should have briefly discussed it in Volume 1, but ever since Seth orginally gave his "Joe, Jane, Jim, and Bob" material (as I call it) in the 683rd session, I've wondered about possible connections between the probabilities described in that session and our own reality: How much of our species' distorted, intuitive knowledge of those probable realities may appear as myth and oddity in our camouflage universe? I'm thinking about androgyny, of course, which is the concept of both male and female in one, and/or of hermaphroditism, wherein a person or animal possesses the sexual organs of both the male and the female. Considering our personal lack of conscious knowledge about androgyny and such related concepts at the time, Jane and I think it most interesting that Seth came through with that particular material in the 683rd session.

A little investigation gave us glimpses into numerous instances in which blended masculine and feminine qualities are contained in the gods of our very ancient myths. The same principles of androgyny can be found in much of the literature of our own century. Whether scientific or not, myths may contain the deepest truths of all for our species, at least in conventional terms: Jane and I are intrigued to think that the sources for those verities could spring partly from other realities.

Much could be written here—volumes, easily. I'll simply add that in religious terms alone Christ can be seen as androgynous, in that he's obviously a symbol of the unification of opposites—whether of the conscious and the unconscious, the feminine and the masculine, this reality and others, the mystical and the "practical," and so forth. And a number of old disciplines thought that before the creation of Eve from his body, Adam, the first, original man, was really male and female.

All of which reminds me that to many viewers the "portraits" I paint are balanced equally between the masculine and feminine, regardless of whether the subject in any one of them is male *or* female. The paintings are of personalities I see mentally rather than physically; they do represent, I believe, my efforts to unify in any particular image my intuitive appreciation of the male/female qualities embodied within each of us.

7. See Note 10 for the 721st session.

8. A longer version of this material from the 657th session is presented in Note 3 for Session 683, in Volume 1; I wanted to tell readers a little about counterparts then—not only to get them interested in Volume 2 before it was published, but to show the direction in which Seth's material was headed.

That same 657th session contains Seth's extremely useful statement: "The Present Is the Point of Power." From it he proceeds to show how all that we are—whatever our individual belief systems may be—stems from the brilliant focus of our physical, mental, and spiritual abilities in "present" experience.

9. It's interesting to see how Jane's *Apprentice Gods* echoes and enlarges upon the following lines from another long, but quite youthful and dramatic poem that she wrote in 1949, when she was 19 years old:

> *Return o my brother, counterpart of heaven,*
> *For I am permitted to cry only through your voice . . .*

EPILOGUE

In the 82nd session, which was held on the evening of August 27, 1964, Seth said: "When man realizes that he, himself, creates his personal and universal environment in concrete terms, then he can begin to create a private and universal environment much superior to the [present] one, that is the result of haphazard and unenlightened constructions.

"<u>This</u> is our main message to the world, and this is the next line in man's conceptual development, which will make itself felt in all fields, and in psychiatry perhaps as much as any."

In one way or another all of Seth's books are elaborations of that basic message, stated nine months after his sessions with us began in December 1963. It should be obvious that the two volumes of *"Unknown" Reality* are further ramifications of that thesis, for here Seth shows us the usually invisible psychological dimensions that underlie the known world. He reveals the very structure upon which our free will rests: for if events were immutable or fated, no free will would be possible.

As far as we can see, Seth's reincarnational, counterpart, and probable selves, and his families of consciousness, suggest the varied, complicated structure of human personality—and hint of the invisible psychological thickness that fills out the physical event of the self in time.

The two volumes of *"Unknown" Reality* hardly tie truth up in neat packages, though, so that after completing them the reader can claim to know all of the answers. In fact, Seth's material always raises more questions to stimulate the intellect and intuitions, and these two books are no exception. In a sense, they *are* incomplete and complicated at times, with new terms, for the unknown reality they attempt to describe will, I fear, always elude us to some extent; and new terms are needed as old ones become stereotyped and worn.

Seth told us ahead of time, of course, that *"Unknown" Reality* would follow an intuitive and inner organization rather than a linear one, and that this writing method would itself arouse the creative, revelatory characteristics of the psyche. Material on any given subject may start, go on for a while, then either stop almost in mid-sentence or "evolve" into another topic. Yet underneath, the books ride securely upon rhythms that reflect the psyche's deep resources.

Now it seems that my own purposes in preparing these volumes were too gargantuan to ever accomplish more than partially. I wanted to show the ever-widening vital reactions that Seth's dictation of *"Unknown" Reality* had on our personal lives, and how those effects rippled outward. It's almost impossible to describe the creative frustration I sometimes felt—for no matter how fast I worked to record the sessions themselves, noted our day's activities, hunted down the references pertinent to a given discussion, I couldn't truly keep up: Reality kept splashing over the edges of my notes. New events kept happening, surfacing from usually hidden dimensions.

It seems clear now that Seth knew all along that this would happen. The creative explosions begun with these books still erupt, for *"Unknown" Reality* does seem to have a life of its own, one that defies definition, and that even now serves as a springboard for new psychic and creative experience. Talk about probable realities! This manuscript seems to possess dimensions that place it—and Jane and me—in many probabilities at once. As I type its pages for the final time, I'm back at our old Water Street apartments, and in our new "hill house" at once; I'm referring to 1975 sessions and recording Seth's dictation on his latest book as well. Sometimes I feel like saying: "One reality at a time, please."

In vital ways, Seth's material itself *is* timeless, yet its production, of course, is tied to the events of our lives. I hope my notes provide that "living story"—the narrative that gives the material its flesh in our time. The material itself can stand on its own, though, and we trust it will continue to do so when Jane and I are through with this particular joint physical adventure. Then Seth's work will fall back upon the timeless quality that always illuminated it.

In any case, I feel that the entire production, Seth's dictated works and my running commentaries and references, adds up to extra dimensions of creativity that can be sensed, if not described. When I get *that* feeling of psychologial multiplicity, I realize that the goal I had in mind was at least somewhat realized.

Then also, I remember what Seth said about being reckless in the pursuit of the ideal. (See the Introductory Notes.) I don't know that I was that daring, but I was persistent despite the hesitations and misgivings. So along with Seth's work, we tried to share our reality with the reader, and to provide a platform in time for knowledge that must basically straddle our ideas of time and reality alike.

Long before I finished my part of *"Unknown" Reality*, Seth and Jane had started their next book: *The Nature of the Psyche: Its Human Expression.* I recorded those sessions, of course, while keeping up with my own work. Jane finished her *Psychic Politics,* and began some new poetry and world-view material. She was taking calls from readers in all parts of the country, trying to keep up with the mail, participating in an occasional radio interview, and, for most of that time, conducting her classes. And oh, yes, both of us also did a lot of ordinary living, such as moving and getting settled in our new home and entertaining friends now and then. Yet none of those "outside" events were fully removed from *"Unknown" Reality.* They found their way into the pages, the sessions, somehow, even if only by *feel* or inference. For how could any one event not jostle all of the others in lives so closely bound?

Yet we think now that such extensive notes have served their purposes for Seth's material, at least for some time, so those books-in-the-works will carry minimum notes—as they do, say, in *Seth Speaks.* For one thing, as I write this Epilogue, Seth has finished *The Nature of the Psyche,* and has already begun still *another* book. *Psyche,* as Jane and I call it, contains some excellent new material, such as Seth's first discussions of sex—including lesbianism, homosexuality, and bisexuality—as well as other related subjects that we know, from our correspondence, to be of intense general concern. By using simple session notes only, we can get that next book to the public in a minimum of time, and it should be published shortly after this second volume of *"Unknown" Reality*—perhaps within just a few months.

Also, Jane has long since completed *The World View of Paul Cézanne: A Psychic Interpretation,* which was published in 1977; and she's finished *The Afterdeath Journal of an American Phi-*

losopher: The World View of William James—both books growing out of the world-view material given by Seth in *"Unknown" Reality*.

The luxurious creativity displayed by Seth's and Jane's work raises more questions about the abilities of the psyche than it seems we can ever hope to answer. Despite the different lights in which Seth may be regarded, despite the varying degrees of reality his existence may be granted by others, there can be no doubt of his individuality or productivity as it's displayed in his books.

And again, at latest count Jane was written three books (including *Psychic Politics*) since Seth began *"Unknown" Reality*—and worked on several others—so what is the relationship between the human psyche and such "other" sources of creativity and knowledge?

No one, whether that individual is a psychic, a mystic, a writer, a poet, or even if he or she combines all those qualities (as I think Jane does), can encompass all of the incredible differences within the human species. I believe that thick, sprawling works like *"Unknown" Reality* offer some important answers, but beyond that it's up to the multidimensional, multitudinous, over four billion *multinational* individuals on this planet to follow their own intuitions and seek answers in their personal ways. Lots of those people will never hear of the Seth material—nor, as Seth himself has said, will they ever *need* to—but then, Jane and I know that some *will*, and so we proffer what we can.

We have so much to learn about out inner and outer worlds that once an attempt is made to discuss those large issues, a host of questions arise. What I for one finally get down on paper, then, must be very incomplete when compared to what I *don't* write, or don't know. Jane and I, for instance, have never particularly cared for the term "ESP," or *extra*sensory perception (my emphasis), since to us it implies misleading conceptions about certain inner abilities. We hardly think those attributes are "extra" at all, although they're obviously more developed or consciously available in some individuals than in others—but then, so is a "gift" for music, or baseball or whatever. (I'll add here that Jane calls her class an ESP class for the obvious reason that the term has become so well known that most people understand something of its implied meaning.)

After making those points, however, I note with some amusement that I find it difficult indeed to believe that many millions of people must wait for a handful of their "superior" peers—philosophers, scientists, psychologists, parapsychologists—to tell them it's *all right* to believe in at least a few of the inner abilities that each of us possesses, to whatever degree. Obviously, numerous individuals simply refuse to wait for the official light of recognition to shine forth.

That wait could be a very long one. Who is to help initiate meaningful changes in our psychological and social orders? Surely Jane feels the necessity to turn aside from the selected dogmas of our time. For to her, and to me, our world's present definitions of personality are as limited as the conventional meaning implied by the term ESP. We hope that Jane's work can help expand such concepts.

We also think science is "objective" enough in its own terms of serial time and measurement, as it claims to be, but that eventually it must *choose* to look inward as thoroughly as it does outward. To us, much of the turmoil in the world results from our steadfast refusal to accept a major portion of our natural heritage. We project our inner knowledge "outward" in distorted fashion; thus on a global scale we thrash about with our problems of war, overpopulation, and dwindling natural resources, to name but a few.

According to Seth, each of us chose such a course at this time—but now, we think, a time of imperative change is necessary if we are to continue our progress as a species. A new blending of inner and outer consciousness—a new, more meaningful coalition of intellectual and intuitive abilities—will be the latest step in the process of "consciousness knowing itself," as Seth has described it.

I don't think our conventional social systems, including our scientific ones, are going to resolve our questions within Jane's and my personal lifetimes. I'm not putting down our cultures and science either, since they very accurately reflect the collective lives and conditions that we've chosen to create. But Jane and I *do* want to know more; we're sure that Seth can help us here.

Whatever or whoever Seth is, or whatever the nature of the Seth-Jane relationship, we long ago decided that we could learn from it. No need to dogmatically insist upon reincarnation as being a "fact," or upon the existence of Seth's counterparts or the families of consciousness. In the material as a whole there are bound to be significant clues as to the nature of the human animal: creative clues that can't help but enlighten us in many—and sometimes unexpected—ways. I deal with some of the material we've acquired about the Seth-Jane relationship in Appendix 18 for Session 711, in Section 4; but here I want to stress our overall interest in knowledge, whatever that knowledge may be, and wherever it may lead us.

As I've joked with Jane more than once: "If there's life after death, each of us in turn will find it out—including the nonbelievers. And if there isn't—well, no one will ever know *that*. Either way, there's absolutely nothing to worry about. . . ." So in the meantime the search can be fun, and intriguing—even a passion—but at the same time, without absolutism or any Messianic drive to change the world.

But if Seth-Jane are at all right, then consciousness is more than encompassing enough to embrace all that we are, and everything that each of us can even remotely conceive of doing or being. Try as we might, we'll not exhaust or annihilate consciousness: Whatever we accomplish as people will still leave room for—indeed, *demand*—further ramifications and development. And in the interim we can always look at nature with its innocent, spontaneous order to sustain us. We can at least observe, and enjoy, the behavior of other species with whom we share the world.

For in closing, I'd like to return to one of my favorite happenings: the migration of geese. I wrote the following notes in October 1975, some seven months after Jane and I had moved into our "new" house:

"The view of sky sweeping over our hill makes it much easier to see the great flights of geese heading south for the winter. Twice this week in the daytime, and once at night, large flocks have passed over. On each occasion I heard them while I was working inside the house, then rushed out into the yard. The geese seem to be more numerous on cloudy days and clear nights.

"One late-afternoon gaggle reached nearly from horizon to horizon, in three long and very noisy V-formations. And always, one bird led each V, with the two sides of the bird 'lettering' trailing back quite unevenly—wobbling, flexing, shifting. What free sociable claques, I thought. Amazing, the way their honking carried back to Jane and me as we stood in the driveway. We watched the geese fly toward the hills on the far side of the valley; we could still hear them even when they'd become practically invisible.''

In its way the nighttime visitation was even more mysterious, for that time I looked up at a starlit but moonless sky that didn't have a cloud in sight—and heard this multitudinous *sound* moving across it. The night was chilly. Jane was sleeping. All of the qualities of the birds' flight were heightened for me by its very invisibility, for while I actually saw no geese at all, that sound was everywhere. And what guided those creatures, I wondered—magnetic lines of force, genes, innate knowledge—or what? And I knew that no objective reasoning processes alone could explain their magnificent flight.

Somehow the twice-yearly, north-and-south migrations of the geese have become symbols for me of the known and unknown qualities of life—sublime and indecipherable at the same time, enduring yet fleeting, and almost outside of the range of human events. For me, those migrations have become portents of the seasons and of the earth itself as it swings around ''our'' sun in great rhythms. The one consciousness (mine) stands in its body on the ground and looks up at the strange variations of itself represented by the geese. And wonders. In their own ways, do the geese wonder also? What kind of hidden interchanges between species take place at such times? If the question could be answered, would all of reality in its unending mystery lie revealed before us?

Robert F. Butts
September 1978

INDEX

ABOUT THE AUTHOR

Born in 1929, JANE ROBERTS grew up in Saratoga
Springs, N.Y. where she attended Skidmore College.
Besides writing poetry, short stories, children's litera-
ture, novels, and metaphysics, her enormously popular
non-fiction includes: *Seth Speaks, The Seth Material,
The Nature of Personal Reality, Nature of the Psyche,*
and *Adventures in Consciousness*. Roberts died in 1984.
Her husband, Robert Butts, is an artist and resident of
Elmira, N.Y.

SETH
The Classic Channellings of SETH
by Jane Roberts

Seth is an immortal "being of intelligence" who channelled his insights through Jane Roberts. His revelations of secrets of life, death, the universe, and our unknown and untapped potentials are recorded verbatim in the classic "Seth books". As Roberts would fall into a trance, Seth's own voice would emerge; these channellings from Seth provide powerful insights from the beyond that are blueprints for those who want to expand their own universe and potential.

☐ **THE SETH MATERIAL**
Meet Seth. In the first compelling SETH volume, Seth makes his presence known in startling ways. He induces out-of-body experiences, is "tested" by a psychologist, and reveals secrets of reincarnation, the nature of God, physical reality and dreams. (27948-3/$4.95)

☐ **SETH SPEAKS**
Seth reveals more about himself and his incredible knowledge, including: what to expect immediately after death; how to glimpse into past lives, ways to contact the dead. He also gives new revelations about what really happened on Calvary, the three lost civilizations before Atlantis, and more. (25592-4/$4.95)

☐ **THE NATURE OF PERSONAL REALITY**
Seth dictates answers for those who want to apply his ideas to daily life. He discussed "the soul in flesh", the birth of conscience, the nature of the body and creativity, expressions of soul outside the flesh, among other transforming concepts. (24845-6/$4.95)

☐ **ADVENTURES IN CONSCIOUSNESS**
With a consciousness dramatically changed by Seth, Jane Roberts reveals how Seth opened doors to past lives, mental telepathy and other realities. He introduced probable selves and "The Source Self", "The Focus Identity" Aspects and even Apprentice Gods. All to expand our understanding of the psyche and help open one up to new levels of awareness. (27871-1/$4.95)

☐ **THE NATURE OF THE PSYCHE: Its Human Expression**
Seth discusses, for the first time, human sexuality. He reveals: a startling new concept of self, the real origin of dreams, and how we choose our physical death. Includes simple psychic exercises you can do. (27830-4/$4.95)

And, for the first time in a low-priced mass market edition:

The Edgar Cayce story is one of the most compelling in inspirational literature. Over the course of forty years, "The Sleeping Prophet" would close his eyes, enter an altered state of consciousness, and then speak to the very heart and spirit of mankind on subjects such as health, healing, dreams, meditation, and reincarnation. His more than 14,000 readings are preserved at the Association for Research and Enlightenment.